Modern Collector's Dolls

COVER DOLL:

Monica Studio's
Hard Plastic
"Marion"

MODERN COLLECTOR'S DOLLS

SECOND SERIES
Modern Collector's Dolls

by
Patricia R. Smith

EDITORS,
Who are recognized authorities in their fields:

Joan Ashabraner
Sibyl DeWein
Jeanne Niswonger
Karen Penner
Jane Thomas
Dorothy Westbrook

Other books by author

The Armand Marseille Dolls
Modern Collector's Dolls (Vol. 1)

COLLECTOR BOOKS

Published by Collector Books
Box 3009
Paducah, Kentucky, 42001

Distributed by

Crown Publishers, Inc.

419 Park Ave. South
New York, New York 10016

ACKNOWLEDGMENTS

Once again my special thanks must go to my husband, Dwight, for his interest and photography and to the following for their special friendship and help: Mary Partridge, Ellie Haynes, Bessie Carson, Jean Grossman, Sibyl DeWein, Joan Ashabraner, Jane Thomas, Jeannie Niswonger, The Treasure Trove and Mona Anderson, County Tyrone, Ireland. And the following for the loan of their dolls: Jayne Allen, Patricia Allin, Sue Allin, Yvonne Baird, Barbara Belding, Peggy Boudreau, Alice Capps, Alma Carmichael, Pearl Claspy, Grace Cowlick, Margaret Esler, Irene Gann, Edith Goldsworthy, Margaret Groninger, Sharon Hazel, Verena Holzley, Wanda James, Virginia Jones, Lucille Kimsey, Roberta Lago, Ruth Lane, Carrie Perkins, Mrs. Joe Pine, Kay Shipp, Connie Snapp, Joyce Stafford, Kathy Walters, Margaret Weeks, Dorothy Westbrook, Leslie White and Lita Wilson.

My very special thanks go to Bob and Kathy Walters, who saved me several weeks work by tackling the Index for this volume.

Dolls on loan have been acknowledged with the pictures: All other dolls belong to the author. All photographs, unless credited, are the work of Dwight Smith.

The Maish Collection was photographed by Ron A. Hensel, sports car racer and photographer, who has been both editor and photographer for a Sports Car Club of America publication. Mr. Hensel is currently working on a photo book of children entitled "The Real People."

About the Author
PATRICIA R. SMITH

SCHOOLS: Page School for Girls, Los Angeles, California
St. Mary's, Santa Barbara, California
Nevada State, Nevada
St. Theresa, Kansas City, Missouri

DEGREES: Pedogogy
Adult Psychology
Child Psychology
Dogmatic Theology
Apologetics
Literary Methods

OTHER: "Famous Artists" Course, studying art layout and design. A commissioned
artist, who specializes in "faces" and religious art.
Studied with "Famous Writers School" in Connecticut on fiction aspects.

WORK: Has worked in Occupational Therapy Departments in Psychiatric Wards.
As Assistant Advertising Director for large catalog order firm. Member of
Ad Club. Worked as substitute teacher in local school system.

PUBLISHED: Articles and short stories on such varied subjects as: "Teen-age Dating",
"How to Sculpture A Face", "Comparative Religions", "The Art Of Being A
Wife", "Safety Afloat", "That Life-Jacket May Save You", "What It Is All
About (USCGAUX)", "The Day That Tim Drowned", "What Is Religion?",
"The Ins and Outs of Ceramics", "You Can Paint".

HOBBIES: Archery, Boating, Sewing, Collecting dolls.

ORGANIZATIONS: National Field Archers Ass'n, U.S. Coast Guard Auxiliary, Council of
Catholic Women, Lake of the Ozarks Yachting Assn'n. Independence Gay
Ninety's Doll Club. National Federation of Doll Clubs.

DEDICATION

This second volume of Modern Collector's Dolls is dedicated to all who love and appreciate the world of dolls and especially to our friends, Ralph and Jay Minter. Also to my favorite 11 year old collector, Leslie White.

Contents

Alexander--30" "Mimi" 1961. Shown in Tyrolean
outfit. Jointed in 12 places. $50.00.

Modern Collector's Dolls

This book is designed to be a companion to Volume 1 of Modern Collector's Dolls and the index from Volume 1 will be included, with revised prices for those dolls.

85% of the dolls, in this volume, are originally dressed, but please be reminded that there are several "originals" for many dolls!! The doll companies, in so many cases, have issued the same doll in several different outfits.

New or Revised Information to Volume 1: Modern Collector's Dolls

The following page numbers refer to Volume 1.

Page 11: The largest Dionne Quint is a 24" baby doll.

Page 12: Under 1941: Should read "Jeanie," not Jennie Walker.

Page 19: Scarlett is "Southern Girl" of 1942.

Page 20: 17" "Kathy" is wearing a "Cissy" dress. (1958). Maggie Mixup was made in 1960 rather than 1952. Mouth is a special one and used on the "Little Lady Cosmetic" dolls and some Internationals.

Page 23: 11" Marme is a 1960 or 1961 model.

Page 25: Marybel has brown eyes. Kelly has blue eyes, bangs slightly curled and short, to ear lobe, with curls all around base. Pollyanna has blue eyes, braids and freckles. Country Cousin has blue eyes, braids but no freckles. Lonely Doll has long curl ponytail from back crown of head. Also, this year, the Elise was of this same mold.

Page 27: Laurie came out in 1967.

Page 39: "New Born Baby" also sold as "Toodles Travels" with carbed, mattress. No. 1603.

Page 44: Arranbee "Little Angel" was first doll to say "Papa" 1939-40.

Page 49: Littlest Angel is actually "Li'l Imp" with a hair cut.

Page 140: "Little Miss Betty" was also "Peggy Petite" 1952-55.

Page 156: Sparkle Plenty was also sold as Baby Blondy in 1947.

Page 157: Baby Coos was designed by Bernard Lipfert and patterned after his grand daughter.

Page 159: Saucy Walkers were endorsed by Piper Laurie.

Page 160: Blessed Event and Kiss Me are the same doll.

Page 165: Miss Ideal was also called Terry Twist.

Page 168: Pebbles and Bam Bam were creations of Bernard Lipfert.

Page 172: Tabatha was also sold as a "Thumbelina" 1967.

Page 177: Patti Playful with short red/orange hair was sold as Patti Partridge.

Page 226: "Angel" was made by Field Enterprises. 1956.

Page 227: "Stunning" is also 1960 "Sweet Judy" by Deluxe Premium Corp.

Page 295: Doll shown as Ginny is a Wee Imp.

General New Information

In 1964 the Hans Newdecker Co. of Winchester, Ind., put Maggie Head and Kane's pixies and clowns into production (vinyl); marked "H&K." They also produced a porcelain series of Famous Inventors dolls including Ben Franklin, Thomas Edison, George Washington Carver, Henry Ford, McCormick, Orville and Wilbur Wright, Eli Whitney and Alexander Graham Bell. Also children's play dolls advertised under the name "Kane's Rebels," made in porcelain in sizes 5" to 14," these in 1963.

In 1943 Montgomery Ward asked Effanbee to make a colored Ann Shirley. They made a black bride doll and Ward's advertised it to be used as a centerpiece for weddings.

The 1935 Alexander "Little Colonel" dolls had blonde mohair wigs, sleep eyes and all but the 13" had open mouth/teeth. Also the "Little Lady Cosmetic" dolls were the 8" "Wendy" with smile mouth. They came in a shadow box with a set of cosmetics. She wears spats, pantaloons, blue dress and pinafore of polka-dot with pink trim. The 1974 discontinued Alexanders are: Maggie, Sound of Music, Baby Jane, Portrait Elise and all Portrettes. New are, Miss USA (8") and Baby Precious.

Remco, in Feb. 1974, has gone out of business. The Miner Industries has acquired the "Sweet April" doll and accessories.

Kewpie molds and related items have been sold by Strombecker to the AMSCO Division of Milton Bradley.

George Borfeldt issued a plastic and marked Bi Lo, in 1950 and it was sold through the FOA Swartz Co.

Eegee's Saucy Walker type is called "Susan Stroller" 1953.

Ideal's first Negro ethnic doll was in 1951.

Nancy Ann Storybook made a doll called "Demure Miss" in hard plastic. (17").

The following are marks (numbers) that are known to be used by different doll manufacturers:

3...Roberta Doll Co.

③..Uneeda

170...Horsman Doll Co.

210...Arranbee Doll Co.

750...Sayco

Ⓟ..Rosemary Doll Co. bought by Arranbee Doll Co. and then purchased by Vogue, who is now owned by Tonka Corp.

Ⓧ..Attributed to Madame Alexander.

Made in USA...Arranbee, Ideal, Horsman, Irwin and Imperial Crown.

Price Guide

The prices in this book are the retail prices of the dolls, if bought from a dealer. Prices change by demand and supply, but doll prices are fairly stable and only once in awhile do prices "shoot up" and generally this is due to a stimulated interest in a particular doll.

When I am asked "What is the value of my doll?" I always take two things into consideration. Number one is, how much sentimental value is placed on this particular doll, was it a childhood doll, a family heirloom? If so, this tends to impress the owner that the doll may be far more valuable than it really is and the truth of price may be upsetting. The second is condition.

The condition of the doll is uppermost in pricing! An all original and in excellent condition doll will bring top prices, where one that is damaged or without original clothes will bring less. The cost of doll repair has soared and it is wise to judge the damage and estimate the cost of repair before you buy or sell a damaged doll.

An "all original" means original clothes and original wig/hair. This type of doll is what the prices in this book are based on. The prices shown are top dollar prices for excellent and original dolls. If your doll is less than original, discount, from the prices shown, to allow for condition.

Another factor in pricing is size. For example, a 14" Princess Elizabeth will bring less money than a 21" Princess Elizabeth, a 7½" Dionne Quint will be worth less than a 14" Dionne Quint.

No one knows your collection better than yourself and in the end you must ask yourself "Is the doll important enough, to me, to pay the asking price?" If so, you will buy it. If not, you will pass it by.

Revised prices for Volume 1 are located in the index section of this book.

Additional Care And Repair Hints

To remove stains from vinyl: Rub butter into the stain and put doll in the sunlight for a couple of days. Rigid vinyl has to be in the sunlight for about a month.

This from Lita Wilson: "Spots on vinyl: Cover the spot with mercurochrome, let dry, take enough cotton to cover spot made by mercurochrome and dip it in clorox. Wring out and put on spot, being careful to keep it from getting on hair or in eyes. Sometimes you have to turn the doll face down. Leave the cotton on until dry. It will flake off and if the spot isn't out...do it again. Most stains can be removed this way."

And from Bessie Carson: "Fantastic is good on hard plastic but for safety, always rinse. Usually anything packaged in plastic containers won't harm plastic. For vinyl and stubborn spots on hard plastic use Boraxo hand soap, the powdered kind."

Adele Gioscia says "With rubber and early vinyl that is jointed, remove the arms and legs carefully and stuff with kapok or cotton to keep from collapsing. Stuff head also. Sprinkle with baby powder. Keep doll dressed or covered with a cloth. Do not store rubber or early vinyl in plastic or sunlight." And "To clean composition: Use Johnson & Johnson Kleen & Shine and after composition is clean use Johnson's furniture paste wax to help from further crazing and it will make the doll sparkle."

The prices shown are for dolls that are all original and in excellent condition.

The A&H Doll Manufacturing Co. of Long Island City, New York was active from 1947 through 1969. In 1948 this company put out the "Marcie" doll, modeled from a child. The A&H dolls were beautifully dressed and dolls and clothes were designed by artist and doll manufacturer: Amram Haddad.

A&H Doll Co.--7" "Lady Hamilton" Hard plastic, sleep eyes, glued on mohair wig. 1948. Mint. orig. $3.00. (Maish Collection)

A&H Doll Co.--8½" "Dainty Dolly" All hard plastic with light brown mohair. Sleep blue eyes. Walker, head turns. Marks: none. $5.00.

4

A&H Doll Co.--7½" "Musical Sweetheart" All hard plastic with glued on brown hair. Blue sleep eyes. Stands on music box and revolves. Marks: A Marcie Doll, on stand. $3.00.

A&H Doll Co.--8" "Lady Lettie" All hard plastic with glued on brown hair. Blue sleep eyes. Molded on shoes. Marks: This is a Marcie Doll. 1951. $2.00.

In 1953 the A&H Doll Co. put a series of 12 dolls on the market called "Dolls of Destiny." Shown is the Empress Eugenie. All are 10½". The others are: Mary Todd Lincoln, Queen Victoria, Priscilla Alden, Molly Pitcher, Empress Josephine, Queen Elizabeth I, Marie Antoinette, Elizabeth Woodville Grey, Betsy Ross, Queen Isabella and Martha Washington. All included a storybook telling of the personality.

A&H Doll Co.--10½" "Empress Eugenie" (1826-1920) Hard plastic walker, head turns. Molded shoes and socks. Stapled on wig. Side curls stapled on separately. Blue sleep eyes. Removable clothes. One of the "Doll of Destiny" line. Marks: Pat's Pend., on back. Tag: A Doll of Destiny/Empress Eugenie/1826/1920. Box; A&H Doll Co. 1953. $18.00.

Dolls by
MADAME ALEXANDER

"The Most Beautiful Dolls in the World"

Edited by

JANE THOMAS

OLD TOWN DOLL AND TOY EMPORIUM
2611 San Diego Avenue
San Diego, Calif. 92110

"To all of your readers with kindest regards from, all us Janes! (East to West) Grandma Jane, Barbara Jane, Baby Janie, Jane Withers, "Baby Jane" (Juanita Quigley), "Big" Janie (Standing), "Little" Janie (ballerina) and Jane Thomas.

Bobby Q and Susie Q from comic strip. $65.00 each.

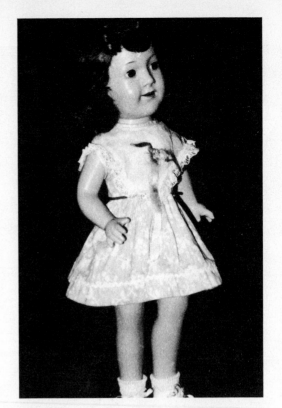

Alexander--7" "China Round the World Series" All composition. One piece head and body. Glued on black wig. Painted blue eyes. Painted on socks and shoes. Original clothes. Marks: Mme/ Alexander, on back. ca. 1936. $22.00.

Alexander--17" "Jane Withers" All composition with glued on brown wig. Sleep green eyes. Open mouth with four teeth. Marks: 17, on back. 1936. $75.00.

Child Star: Jane Withers.

Alexander--10" "Little Shaver" Mask face with stockinette wired posable arms. Auburn floss hair. Painted features. Original. Marks: Little Shaver/Madame Alexander, on tag. Courtesy of Peggy Boudreau. 1937. $60.00.

Alexander--14" "Scarlett O'Hara" All composition. Black mohair glued on wig. Blue sleep eyes. All original yellow organdy dress, slip and pantaloons. Green shoes. Marks: Mme Alexander on head. 1942. $65.00.

Alexander--14" "Ginger Rogers" All composition body same as Scarlett O'Hara, Sonja Henie, etc. Green sleep eyes. Blonde page boy wig. Orig. pale green taffeta dress, plaid long full petticoat, blue velvet bows. Green slippers. 1940's. $85.00 (Maish Collection)

Alexander--14" "Wave" All composition with glued on dark blonde wig. Blue sleep eyes. Original clothes. Marks: Mme Alexander, on head. Tag: W.A.V.E./Madame Alexander. ca. 1944. $55.00.

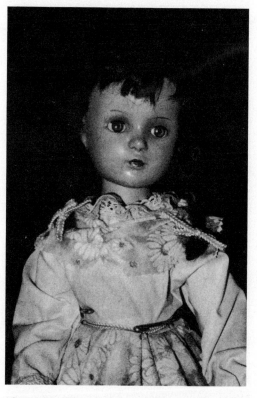

Alexander--21" "Margaret O'Brien" All composition with dark auburn glued on wig. Blue/green sleep eyes. Marks: Alexander, on head and back. 1946. $75.00.

9

Alexander--9" "Scotch" All composition with glued on blonde hair. Painted blue eyes. Waist not jointed. Marks: Wendy Ann/Mme Alexander/New York, on back. Scotch/Madame Alexander, on tag. ca. 1938. $22.00. (Courtesy Virginia Jones)

Alexander--9" "Norwegian" All composition with glued on blonde hair. Painted blue eyes. Waist not jointed. Marks: Wendy Ann/Mme Alexander/New York, on back. Norwegian/Madame Alexander, on tag. ca. 1938. $22.00. (Courtesy Virginia Jones)

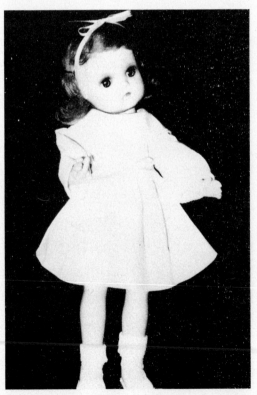

Alexander--9" "Swiss" All composition with glued on blonde hair. Painted blue eyes. Marks: Mme Alexander/New York, on back. Swiss/N.Y. USA, on tag. Waist not jointed. ca. 1938. $22.00. (Courtesy Virginia Jones)

Alexander--14" "Jeannie Walker" All composition with legs attached to wood. The first of its kind, in the U.S.A. Glued on brown wig. Brown sleep eyes. Bent right arm. Marks: Alexander/Pat. No. 2171281. 1939. $45.00.

10

Alexander--14" "Bride" All composition with blonde wig. Blue sleep eyes. Eyeshadow. Original. Marks: Mme. Alexander, on head. Tag: Madame Alexander. ca. 1946. $50.00.

Alexander--17" "Babs, The Iceskating Girl" All hard plastic with glued on blonde floss-like hair. Blue sleep eyes. Original. Marks: Alexander, on head. Tag: Madame Alexander, etc. 1949. 45.00.

Alexander--14½" "Alice In Wonderland" All hard plastic with glued on blonde wig. Blue sleep eyes/lashes. Original clothes. Marks: Alex., on head. Tag: Alice In Wonderland/by Madame Alexander. ca. 1949. $35.00.

Alexander--14" "Nina Ballerina" All hard plastic with glued on blonde wig. Blue sleep eyes. Unjointed ankles. Original clothes. Marks: Alex. on head. Tag: Nina Ballerina/By Madame Alexander. 1949. $40.00.

11

Alexander--14½" "Fairy Queen" All compostion. Brown sleep eyes. All original (minus wand) 1947.

Alexander--9" One piece latex body, arms and legs. Vinyl head. Glued blonde wig over molded hair. painted features. Original clothes except hat. Marks: Alexander, on head. Tag: Madame Alexander. ca. 1950. $18.00.

Alexander--14" "Prince Charming" & "Cinderella" Marks: Madame Alexander/New York USA, on Prince's tag. Cinderella/Madame Alexander, on tag. 1950. $55.00 each. (Courtesy Carrie Perkins)

Alexander--18" "Violet" Marks: Alexander, on head. Madame Alexander, on tag. Jointed at elbows and knees and "walking doll." 1951. $35.00. (Courtesy Carrie Perkins)

Alexander--14" "Alice In Wonderland" All hard plastic with glued on blonde wig. Blue sleep eyes. Original. Marks: none. Tag: Madame Alexander/All Rights, Etc. 1951. $30.00.

Alexander--18" "Sonja Henie" Hard plastic body, arms and legs. Early vinyl head. Glued on blonde wig. Blue sleep eyes. Open/closed mouth. Light cheek dimples. Original clothes. Marks: Alexander, on head. Tag: Madame Alexander. 1951. $45.00.

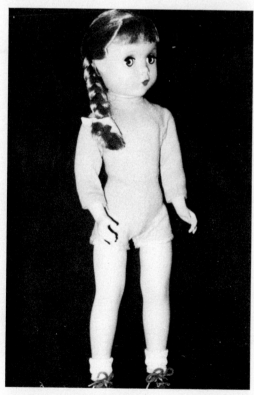

Alexander--18" "Kathy" All hard plastic. Glued on ash blonde wig. Large blue sleep eyes. Original bodysuit. Rollers missing from shoe skates. Marks: Madame Alexander, on tag. 1951. $38.00.

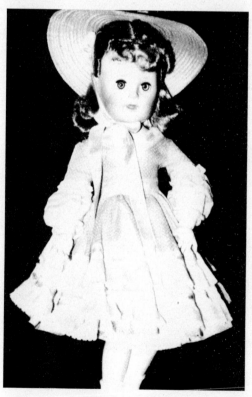

Alexander--17" "Madeline" All hard plastic with vinyl head. Glued on ash blonde hair. Blue sleep eyes. Ball-jointed elbows, wrists, knees. Original. Marks: Alexander, on head. Dress tag gone. Shown in booklet "Madame Alexander Fashions for Madeline" 1952. $35.00.

13

Alexander--"McGuffey Ana" 1955. $35.00.

Alexander--15" "Cynthia" Marks: Cynthia/ Madame Alexander, on tag. 1952. $50.00. (Courtesy Roberta Lago)

Alexander--16" "Rosebud" One piece stuffed vinyl body and legs. Vinyl arms and head. Rooted yellow blonde hair. Blue sleep eyes/ lashes. Open/closed mouth. Marks: Alexander, on head. 1953. $18.00.

Alexander--18" "Active Miss" All hard plastic with ball jointed elbows and knees. Jointed wrists. Glued on blonde wig. Deep blue sleep eyes that have a "liquid" look and whites are tinted pale blue. Walker, head turns. Original clothes. Marks: Tag: Madame Alexander. Alexander, on head. 1954. Same doll as "Sweet Violet." $35.00.

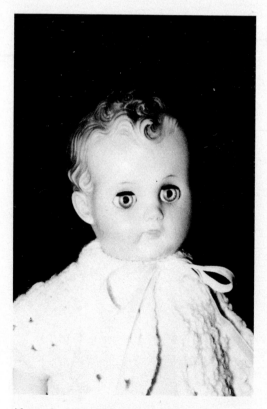

Alexander--13" "Christening Baby" All vinyl with one piece stuffed body and legs. Molded brown hair. Blue sleep eyes. Open/closed mouth. Marks: Alexander, on head. 1954. $20.00. (Courtesy Margaret Weeks)

15

Alexander--18" "Binnie Walker" Hard plastic with vinyl over-sleeved arms. Jointed elbows and knees. Glued on blonde wig. Blue sleep eyes. Original clothes. Marks: Alexander, on head. Tag: Binnie Walker/Madame Alexander. 1955. $30.00.

Alexander--8" "Jo of the Little Women" All hard plastic with jointed knees. Marks: Alex. on back. Alexander-Kins/Jo, on tag. 1955. $30.00. (Courtesy Kay Shipp)

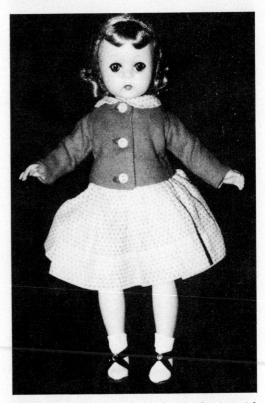

Alexander--8" "Queen" All hard plastic with jointed knees. Marks: Alex. on back. Alexander-Kins/By Madame Alexander, on tag. 1956. $35.00. (Courtesy Kay Shipp)

Alexander--12" "Lissy" All hard plastic with jointed elbows and knees. Medium heel feet. Rooted brown hair. Blue sleep eyes. Marks: Lissy/By Madame Alexander, on tag. 1956. $28.00. (Courtesy Kay Shipp)

Alexander--8" "Groom" Marks: Alex., on back. 1956. $30.00. (Courtesy Kay Shipp)

Alexander--20" "Cissy as Queen" Hard plastic with vinyl over sleeved arms. Jointed elbow. Ash blonde wig. Blue sleep eyes. High heels. Original. Marks: Alexander, on head. Tag: Cissy/Madame Alexander. 1957. $95.00.

Alexander--12" "Lissy" Marks: Lissy/By Madame Alexander, on tag. 1957. $28.00. (Courtesy Kay Shipp)

Alexander--8" "Billy" & "Wendy Ann" Marks: Alex., on back. Alexander-Kins/By Madame Alexander, on tags. ca. 1957. $35.00 & $25.00. (Courtesy Kay Shipp)

17

Alexander--16½" "Elise Bride" Hard plastic body and head. Jointed knees and ankles. Vinyl over sleeved arms. Jointed elbows. Original clothes. Marks: Mme/Alexander, on back. Alexander, on head. 1958. $35.00. (Courtesy Allins Collection)

Alexander--10" Cisette in an Original Dress. $18.00.

Alexander--10" "Cissette" Pink and lace dress. High heel gold shoes. Tag: Cissette/Madame Alexander. 1959. $18.00.

Alexander--10" "Sleeping Beauty" All hard plastic with glued on blonde wig. Blue sleep eyes. Not jointed at knees. Marks: Mme/Alexander, on back. Madame Alexander/Presents Walt Disney's Sleeping Beauty, on tag. 1959. $25.00. (Courtesy Virginia Jones)

Alexander--8" "Aunt Agatha" All hard plastic with jointed knees. Marks: Alex., on back. Alexander-Kins/By Madame Alexander, on tag. 1957. $35.00. (Courtesy Kay Shipp)

Alexander--18" "Renoir" Hard plastic body and legs. Jointed knees. Vinyl arms and head. Jointed elbows. Glued on brown wig. Blue sleep eyes. Marks: Mme/Alexander/1958 (backward 1928), on head. Tag: Elise/Madame Alexander. $30.00.

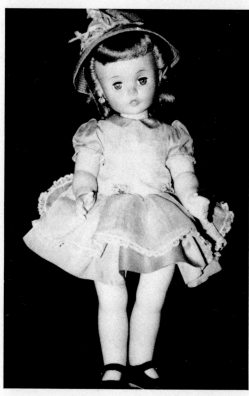

Alexander--16" "Kelly" All rigid vinyl with rooted blonde hair. Blue sleep eyes. Pierced ears. Jointed waist. Original. Marks: Madame Alexander (In Circle) 19, upside down 2,8, Mme/1958/Alexander, in circle on back. $25.00. (Courtesy Margaret Weeks)

Alexander--10" "Cissette" White dress with red flowers. Gold shoes. Tag: Cissette/By Madame Alexander. 1958. $18.00.

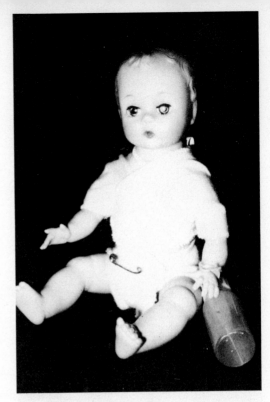

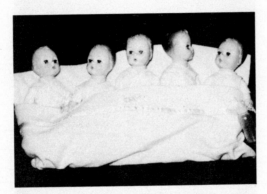

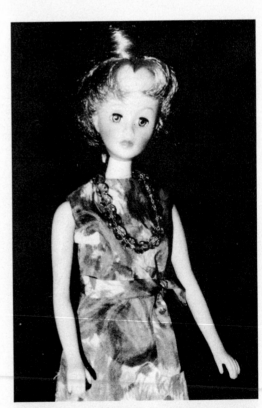

Alexander--7" "Quintuplets" Vinyl bodies with hard plastic head. Molded light brown hair. Blue sleep eyes. Open mouth/nursers. All original. Tags: Mfg. of the Original Quintuplets/By Madame Alexander (Referred to as the "Fisher Quints.") 1964. $15.00 each. Set of 5--$95.00. (Courtesy Virginia Jones)

Alexander 7" "Quints" 1964.

Alexander--12" "Janie" Plastic body and legs. Vinyl arms and head. Rooted blonde hair. Blue sleep eyes. Posable head. Original dress. Marks: Alexander/1964, on head. $18.00.

Alexander--12" "Brenda Starr" Hard plastic body and legs. Outside jointed hips. Jointed knees which will turn in complete circle for very posable legs. Very tiny feet. Vinyl arms and head. Rooted red-orange hair with one lock of long hair on top. Blue sleep eyes. Original clothes. Marks: Alexander/1964, on head. Alexander, on back. Tag: Brenda Starr/By Madame Alexander. 1964. $22.00.

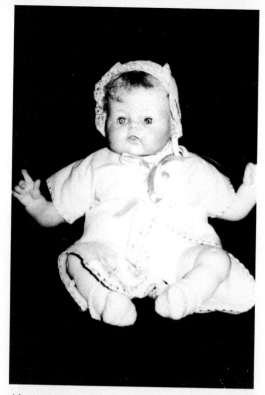

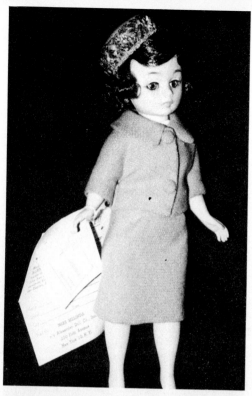

Alexander--14" "Kitten" Cloth body. Vinyl arms, legs and head. Rooted white hair. Small blue sleep eyes/molded lashes. Open/closed mouth. Both feet wrinkled on the bottom. All toes curled under on left foot. Marks: Alexander 1961, on head. Tag: Kitten/By Madame Alexander. 1962. $9.00.

Alexander--10" "Jacqueline" All hard plastic with glued on brown wig. Blue sleep eyes, blue eye shadow. Jointed knees. Original clothes. Marks: Mme/Alexander, on back. 1962. $28.00.

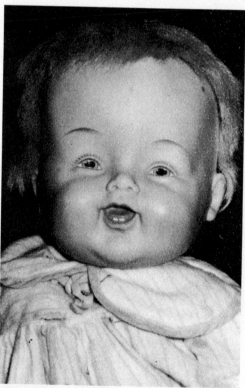

Alexander--10" "Cissette Ballerina" All hard plastic with glued on blonde wig. Blue sleep eyes. High heel feet. Unjointed ankles. Original clothes. Marks: Mme/Alexander, on back. Tag: Cissette/By Madame Alexander. 1962. $22.00.

Alexander--25" "Lively Huggums" Stuffed cloth body, legs and upper arms. Gauntlet vinyl hands. Vinyl head with rooted blonde hair. Painted blue eyes. Open/closed mouth with molded tongue and two painted lower teeth. Mechanism makes head and body move. Knob winder on back. Marks: Alexander Doll Co Inc, on head. Tag: Lively Huggums/By Madame Alexander. 1963. $15.00.

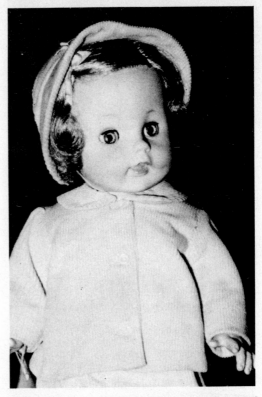

Alexander--10" "Cissette Ballerina" All hard plastic with glued on brown wig. Blue sleep eyes. High heel feet. Jointed knees. Pierced ears. Original clothes. Marks: Mme/Alexander, on head. Tag: Cissette/By Madame Alexander. ca. 1960. $22.00.

Alexander--14" "Caroline" All vinyl with rooted blonde hair. Blue sleep eyes. Open/closed mouth. Original. Marks: Alexander/1961, on head. Alex. 1959/13, on back. Caroline/Madame Alexander, on tag. $65. (Courtesy Margaret Weeks)

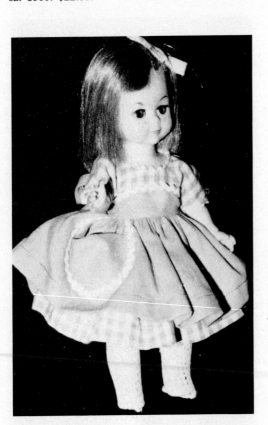

Alexander--8" "Maggie Mixup" Blue checkered dress with solid blue apron. Tag: Alexander-Kins/By Madame Alexander. 1961. $35.00.

Alexander--8" "French" All hard plastic. Jointed knees. Walker head turns. Glued on brown wig. Blue sleep eyes. Marks: Alex., on back. Tag: French/By Madame Alexander. 1961. $15.00.

Alexander--21" "Sleeping Beauty" Hard plastic body, legs and head. Vinyl, unjointed arms. Glued yellow/blonde hair. Blue sleep eyes. High heels. Original clothes. Marks: Alexander, on head. Tag: Madame Alexander/Presents/Walt Disney's/Authentic/Sleeping Beauty. 1959. $115.00.

Alexander--21" "Sleeping Beauty" 1959.

Alexander--16" "Pollyanna" All rigid vinyl with softer vinyl head. Rooted blonde hair. Blue sleep eyes. Jointed waist. Marks: Mme/Alexander, in circle/1958, on head. Pollyanna/By Madame Alexander, on tag. 1960. The 5 in the date is reversed. $25.00. (Courtesy Virginia Jones)

Rag--17" "Funny" All cloth. Tag: Madame Alexander. Dress Tag: Funny/Madame Alexander. 1960's. $10.00.

Alexander--8" "Wendy" Red polka-dot dress. Tag: Alexander-Kin. $15.00.

Alexander--8" "Wendy" Pink dress and over apron of pink. Tag: Alexander-Kins/By Madame Alexander. ca. 1964. $15.00.

Alexander--12" "Janie" Plastic body and legs. Vinyl arms and head. Blue sleep eyes. Marks: Alexander/1963, on head. 1965. $18.00.

Alexander--8" "Peruvian Boy" All hard plastic with brown hair. Blue sleep eyes. Marks: Alex., on back. Peruvian Boy/By Madame Alexander, on tag. Jointed knees. 1965. $35.00. (Courtesy Virginia Jones)

18" "Aimee" See Hasbro section for full description.

18" "Aimee" in her Victorian dress. Made by Hasbro. See Hasbro section for full description.

"Aimee" This is how her clothes are packaged. This outfit is called "Red Velvet." Made by Hasbro.

25

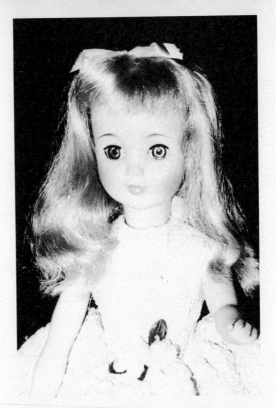

Alexander--8" "Red Riding Hood" All hard plastic. Knees not jointed. Original. Marks: Alex., on back. 1965. $10.00.

Alexander--17" "Polly" Plastic body. Vinyl arms, legs and head. Rooted blonde hair. Blue sleep eyes. Marks: Alexander Doll Co. Inc./1965, on head. Polly/By Madame Alexander, on tag. $22.00.

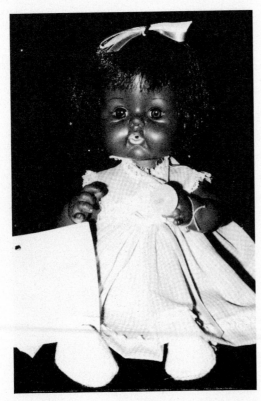

14" "Baby Ellen" All vinyl with rooted dark brown hair. Brown sleep eyes. Marks: Alexander/1965, on head. Madame Alexander, on tag. 1965. $16.00. (Courtesy Kay Shipp)

Alexander--11" "Gretel" Plastic body and legs. Vinyl arms and head. Rooted blonde hair. Blue sleep eyes/lashes. Palms down. Posable head. Original "Sound of Music" clothes. Marks: Alexander/1964, on head. Tag: Gretel/From The Sound of Music/Madame Alexander. 1965. $25.00.

Alexander--17" "Maggie" Plastic and vinyl. Rooted brown hair. Blue sleep eyes/long lashes. Original. Marks: Alexander/1966, on head. Maggie/Madame Alexander, on tag. Discontinued: 1973. $25.00.

Alexander--8" "African" All dark toned hard plastic. Black caricul type hair. Brown sleep eyes. Jointed knees. Marks: Alex., on back. African/By Madame Alexander, on tag. 1966. $35.00. (Courtesy Virginia Jones)

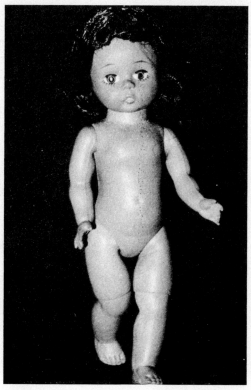

Alexander--8" "Hawaiian" 1966, 67, 68 & 69. $35.00.

Alexander--8" Bride from "Americana Series" All hard plastic with glued on brown wig. Blue sleep eyes/molded lashes. Original dress. Marks: Alex., on back. Tag: Madame Alexander. 1966. $35.00.

27

Furga's "Emma". (Courtesy Virginia Jones)

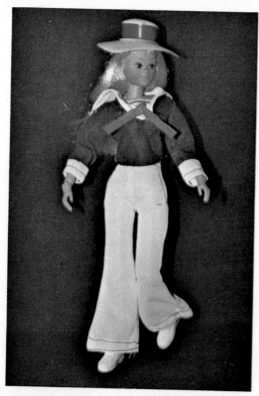

"Dinah-Mite" in the Sport Set Sailor Suit. Made by Mego. Corp.

"Dinah-Mite" shown in her Sports Set: Scuba gear. By Mego. Corp.

"Dinah-Mite in the Sport Set Motor Cycle outfit. Made by Mego. Corp.

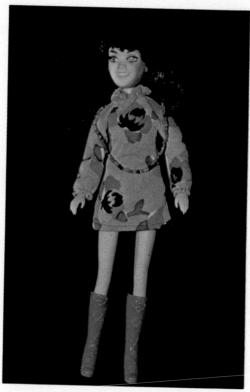

9" "Music" Refer to Hasbro section for full description.

Alexander--8" "Thailand" All brown hard plastic. Jointed knees. Original. Marks: Alex., on back. 1966. $15.00.

Alexander--8" "Scarlett" All hard plastic with glued on brown wig. Green sleep eyes. Jointed knees. Original clothes. Marks: Tag: Scarlett/ By Madame Alexander. 1966. $18.00.

Alexander--14" "Gidgit" Plastic body and legs. Vinyl arms and head. Rooted black hair. Blue sleep eyes. Marks: Alexander, on head. 1966. $18.00.

Alexander--20" "Coco" Plastic body and legs. Ball jointed, very posable waist. Unjointed hips. right leg molded in a bent position. Vinyl arms and head. Rooted dark blonde hair. Brown sleep eyes. Blue eyeshadow. Black eyeliner. Original clothes. Marks: Alexander/1966, on head. 1966. $120.00.

Alexander--21" "Scarlett" Hard plastic body and legs. Jointed knees. Vinyl arms and head. Blue sleep eyes. Blue eyelids and blue eyeshadow. High heels. Original clothes. Marks: Alexander/ 1961, on head. Tag: Madame Alexander. 1967. $95.00.

Alexander--14" "Disneyland Snow White" This costume is made only for Disneyland and Dis-neyWorld. The colors are Red, blue, gold and white. These were started about 1967. Marks: Madame Alexander, on tag. A Doll/Madame Alexander, on wrist tag. (Courtesy Roberta Lago) $22.00.

Alexander--21" "Agatha" Marks: Alexander/ 1961, on head. Agatha/Madame Alexander, on tag. 1967. $95.00. (Courtesy of Roberta Lago)

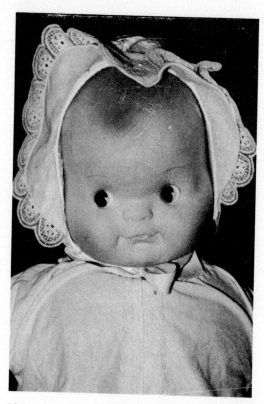

Alexander--22" "Pumpkin" Cloth and vinyl. Molded, painted hair. Painted eyes to side. Marks: Alexander, on head. 1967. $16.00.

"Dawn's Model Agency Models" Refer to Deluxe Topper (Reading) for full descriptions.

"Denise" of Dawn's Model Agency.

14" "Gumdrop" and 8" "Babykin" #1428. Marketed in 1966. Original. Marks: Gumdrop: 1962/Effanbee, on head. Babykin: Effanbee 1964, on head. (Courtesy Virginia Jones)

18" "Susie Sunshine" Marks: Effanbee 1964. This is shown in the Effanbee 1964 catalog as #1941. See catalog picture, in Effanbee section.

Alexander--Left to Right
14" "Granny" 1966. Courtesy Roberta Lago.
$35.00.
8" "McGuffey Ana" in 1964 & "American Girl" in
1963. Roberta Lago. $35.00
14" "Sheri Lewis" 1959. Roberta Lago. $50.00.
15" "Snow White"1952. Roberta Lago. $25.00.

Alexander--Left to Right
14" "Mary Martin" ca. 1950. Carrie Perkins.
$50.00.
18" "Madaline" 1953. Roberta Lago. $35.00.
18" "Alice In Wonderland" 1951. Roberta Lago.
$28.00.
16½" "Elise Ballerina" 1959. Roberta Lago.
$32.00.

Alexander--Left to Right
11" "Agatha" 1968. Roberta Lago. $25.00.
21" "Scarlett" 1966. Roberta Lago. $95.00.
21" "Renoir" 1967. Roberta Lago. $95.00.

Alexander--Left to Right
8" "Amish Boy & Girl" 1966. Roberta Lago.
$35.00 each.
8" "Spanish Boy (1964) & Spanish Girl (1961)
Roberta Lago. $35.00 & $15.00.
12" "Suzy" (1970), $15.00 "Janie" (1964), $18.00
& "Rosy" (1969), $15.00. Roberta Lago.

Madame Alexander's Easter Dolls** of the 1968 season were made especially for the West Coast, at the request of the Madame Alexander Salesman. The dress is yellow and also the hat. They came in 8" & 14". Only 300 of these matching outfits were made. $45.00.

14" "Cinderella" Courtesy Roberta Lago. $22.00.
14" "Easter Girl"** Courtesy Roberta Lago. $45.00.
8" "Scarlett" Courtesy Roberta Lago. $18.00.
8" "Alice In Wonderland" Courtesy Carrie Perkins. $18.00.
Peter Pan, Wendy, Michael & Tinker Bell. Courtesy Roberta Lago. $95.00 set.
12" "Renoir Child" Courtesy Roberta Lago.

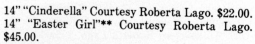

11" "Portrettes" Clockwise: Godey, Scarlett, Scarlett, Renoir, Melanie, Renoir, Godey, Gibson Girl. All courtesy Roberta Lago. $25.00 each.

Alexander--8" "Cowgirl & Cowboy" Marks: Alex., on back. Cowgirl/By Madame Alexander, on tag. Cowboy/By Madame Alexander, on tag. 1968. $35.00 each. (Courtesy Kay Shipp)

Alexander--11" "Southern Belle" All hard plastic with jointed knees. Glued on blonde wig. Blue sleep eyes. Blue eyelids. Original clothes. Marks: Mme/Alexander, on back. Tag: Southern Belle/By Madame Alexander. 1968. $25.00.

Alexander--21" "Lady Hamilton" 1968. $95.00.

Alexander--8" "Japan" All dark toned hard plastic. Brown hair. Brown sleep eyes. Different face, with a smile. Jointed knees. Marks: Alex., on back. Japan/By Madame Alexander, on tag. 1968. $18.00. (Courtesy Virginia Jones)

37

Alexander--8" "Rumania" All hard plastic with jointed knees. Brown wig pulled back into long wig. Brown sleep eyes. Original clothes. Marks: Alex., on back. Tag: Rumania/By Madame Alexander. 1968. $10.00.

Alexander--8" "Finland" All hard plastic with glued on blonde wig. Blue sleep eyes/molded lashes. Jointed knees. Original clothes. Marks: Alex., on back. Tag: Finland/By Madame Alexander. 1968. $10.00. (Courtesy Leslie White)

11" "Godey" All hard plastic with jointed knees. Glued on red wig. Blue sleep eyes. Original clothes. Marks: Mme/Alexander, on back. Tag: Godey/By Madame Alexander. 1969. $25.00.

Alexander--14" "Jenny Lind & Her Listening Cat" Marks: Jenny Lind/By Madame Alexander. 1969. $30.00. (Courtesy Kay Shipp)

14" "Wendy" Plastic body and legs. Vinyl arms and head with rooted blonde hair. Blue sleep eyes. Original clothes. Marks: Alexander 1965, on head. Tag: Wendy/Madame Alexander. Wrist tag: Walt Disney/Wendy. 1969. $20.00.

Alexander--14" "Peter Pan" Plastic body and legs. Vinyl arms and head. Blue sleep eyes. Rooted blonde hair. Original clothes. Marks: Alexander 1965, on head. Tag: Peter Pan/By Madame Alexander. Wrist Tag: Walt Disney/Peter Pan. 1969. $20.00.

Alexander--14" "Jinny Lind" Plastic body and legs. Vinyl arms and head. Rooted yellow blonde hair. Blue sleep eyes. Original clothes. Tag: Jenny Lind/By Madame Alexander. 1970. $20.00.

Alexander--14" "Heidi" Plastic body and legs. Vinyl arms and head. Rooted blonde hair. Blue sleep eyes. Original clothes. Marks: Tag: Heidi/Madame Alexander. 1970. $20.00.

39

Alexander--21" "Renoir" Hard plastic body and legs. Jointed knees. Vinyl arms and head. Rooted black hair. Blue sleep eyes. Original clothes. Marks: Alexander, 1961, on head. 1970. $95.00.

Alexander--12" "Lucinda" Plastic body and legs. Vinyl arms and head. Rooted long blonde hair. Blue sleep eyes. Marks: Alexander/1964, on head. Lucinda/By Madame Alexander, on tag. 1970. $22.00. (Courtesy Virginia Jones)

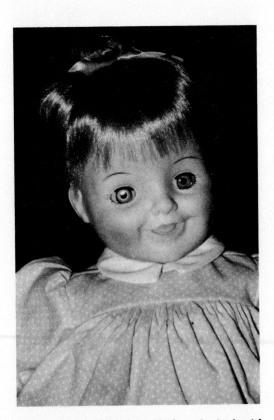

Alexander--11" "Southern Belle" All hard plastic with glued on black hair. Brown sleep eyes. Blue eyelids. Jointed knees. High heel feet. Original clothes. Marks: Mme. Alexander, on back. Tag: Southern Belle/By Madame Alexander. 1971. $18.00.

Alexander--20" "Smiley" Cloth and vinyl with rooted blonde hair. Blue sleep eyes. No teeth. Has molded fingernails. Marks: Alexander/1970 on head. Tag: Smiley/By Madame Alexander. Original clothes. 1971. $12.00.

40

Alexander--14" "Renoir, Portrait Child" Plastic body and legs. Vinyl arms and head. Rooted blonde hip length hair. Blue sleep eyes/lashes. Original clothes. Marks: Alexander/1965, on head. 1972. $22.00.

Alexander--14" "Janie" Cloth and vinyl. Rooted blonde hair. Blue sleep eyes. Original clothes. Marks: Alexander/1972, on head. 1972. $25.00.

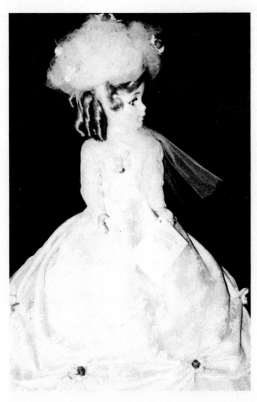

Alexander--14" "Lucinda" Plastic and vinyl with rooted long light brown hair. Blue sleep eyes. Original. Marks: Alexander/1965, on head. Tag: Lucinda/Madame Alexander. 1973. $15.00.

Alexander--21" "Gainsboro" Hard plastic body and legs. Jointed knees. Vinyl arms and head. Rooted strawberry blonde hair in sausage curls. Original clothes. Marks: Alexander/1961, on head. 1973 issue. $95.00.

41

American Character--16" "Sally" Cloth body with cryer. Straight composition legs. Composition swivel head on compo. shoulderplate. Dark blonde, glued on human hair wig. Bright green sleep eyes/lashes. Original dress. Marks: Petite/Sally. 1935. $35.00.

American Character--28" "Debutante Walker" All composition with glued on mohair. Blue sleep eyes. Open mouth/four teeth. Cryer box center of stomach. Walker. Eyeshadow. Original. Marks: Am. Char., High up on head. 1939. $50.00 See below for picture of body.

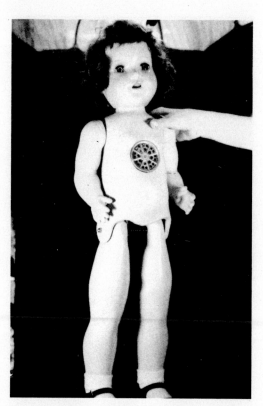

American Character--28" "Debutante Walker" All composition. Unusual "walking" mechanism spring. Cryer in tummy. A very heavy doll. Auburn mohair glued on wig. Gray blue sleep eyes. Left hand: all fingers separated up from first joint. Right hand: all molded together. Four teeth, felt tongue. Two-stroke eyebrows. Original clothes. $50.00 (Maish Collection)

American Character--26" "Jimmy-John" Cloth body. Early vinyl arms, legs and head. Molded hair. Large blue sleep eyes. Marks: Amer. Char. on head. 1954. Character in movie "Easy Way" with Cary Grant. $30.00.

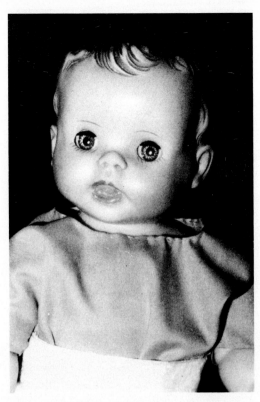

American Character--13" "Ricky Jr." One piece stuffed vinyl body and legs. Early vinyl arms and head. Blue sleep eyes. Open/closed mouth. A wire inside body will bend so legs will bend. Marks: Amer. Char. Doll., on head. 1955. $12.00.

American Character--21" "Ricky Jr." All vinyl with molded hair. Blue sleep eyes. Open mouth/ nurser. Marks: Amer. Char. Doll, on neck. 1956. $25.00 (Courtesy Wanda James)

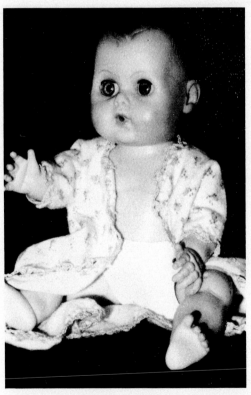

American Character--20" "Sweet Sue" Dressed as "Sunday Best." Pale blue dress. 1956. $30.00.

American Character--10½" "Tiny Toodles" All vinyl with molded, painted hair. Blue sleep eyes. Open mouth/nurser. Separate large toes. Marks: American Character Doll Co. 1956, on head. $12.00.

43

American Character--20" "Groom" Sweet Sue dressed as groom (pants are not original.) Lambs wool red glued on wig. Hard plastic with vinyl arms jointed at elbows. Walker, head turns. Marks: A.C., on head. $30.00.

American Character--Betsy McCall in party dress, style #8205. 1958. $17.00.

44

American Character--7½" "Whimette" Plastic body and legs. Vinyl arms and head. Rooted bright red hair. Painted olive green eyes. Marks: Amer. Char. Inc./1963/Hong Kong, on head. $4.00.

American Character--17" "New Tiny Tears" All vinyl with rooted blonde hair. Blue sleep eyes. Open mouth/nurser. Marks: American Doll & Toy Corp., on head. This doll was introduced as the "New" Tiny Tears and it was not successful. 1961-64. $8.00.

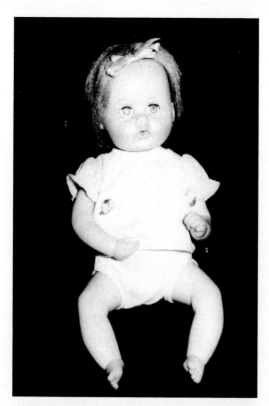

American Character--8½" "Teeny Weeny Tiny Tears" All vinyl. Rooted blonde hair. Blue sleep eyes. Open mouth/nurser. No tear ducts. Marks: 1964/AM. Char. Doll, on head. Original clothes. $4.00. (Courtesy Vickie Johnston Collection)

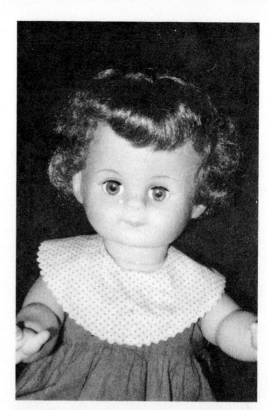

American Character--19" "Sally Says" Plastic and vinyl with rooted blonde hair. Blue sleep eyes. Battery operated talker. Same face as the Alden's 1966 "Walking Suzy Steps" with straight hair/big walking feet. Marks: American Doll & Toy Corp./1964, on head. Sold through FOA Swartz in 1965. Says 11 phrases. $9.00.

American Character--9½" "Cricket" Tressy's little sister. Plastic and vinyl with rooted ash blonde hair. Hair "grows" by pressing stomach button, to shorten, put metal key into back and turn. Painted blue eyes. Bendable legs. (not snapping knees) Marks: American Character/ 1964. Original basic doll. $10.00.

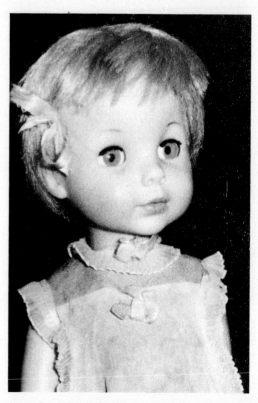

American Character--17" "Margaret-Rose" Plastic body and legs. Vinyl arms and head. Rooted blonde hair. Blue sleep eyes/lashes. Marks: Amer. Char./1966. $6.00.

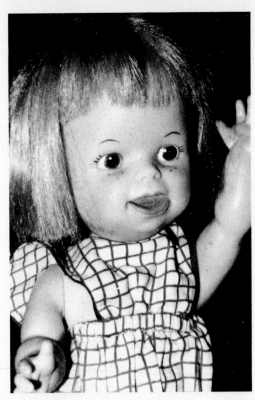

American Character--13" "Freckles" Plastic body and legs. Vinyl arms and head. Rooted blonde hair. Painted brown eyes. Freckles. Walker. Face changes by moving left arm up or down. Marks: Amer. Char. Inc./1966. $7.00.

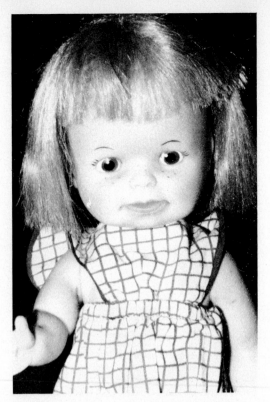

American Character--13" "Freckles" other face.

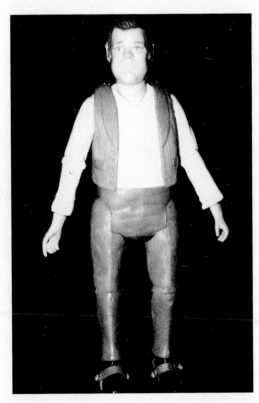

American Character--8" "Hoss Cartwright" All hard vinyl with molded on clothes. Molded hair and painted features. Marks: HL & HR on upper and lower arms. 1/HL and 3/HR, on legs. Unable to read marks on head. 1966. $28.00. (Courtesy Alice Capps)

American Character--8" "Ben Cartwright" All solid vinyl. Molded gray hair. Painted features. Jointed elbows, wrists, knees. Feet turn. Molded on basic clothes. Marks: A Large "C"/ American Character, center of back. 1966. $25.00.

46

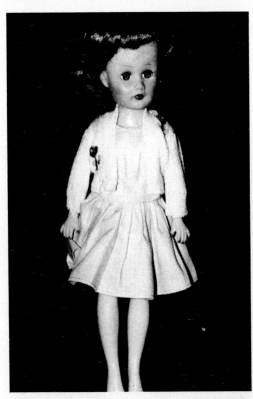

American Character--17" "Sweet Sue" Shown in original ski outfit. 1955. $30.00. (Courtesy Mary Partridge)

American Character--10½" "Toni" all excellent quality vinyl. 1955. An original dress. Marks: American Character, in a circle on back. $22.00.

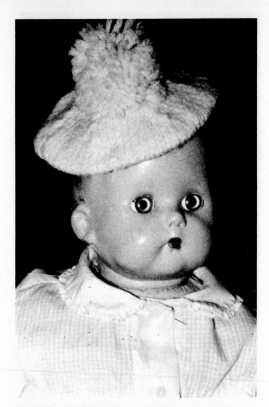

Arranbee--21" "So Big" Cloth body with composition arms, legs and head. Blue sleep eyes. Marks: R&B, on head. 1936. $28.00.

Arranbee--17" "Baby Donna" Hard plastic head with molded hair. Cloth body. Latex arms and legs. Marks: R&B, on head. 1949. $12.00.

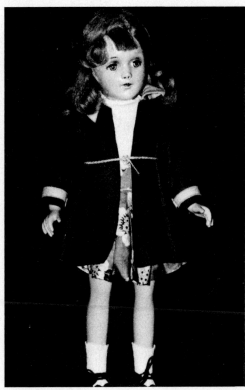

Arranbee--17" "Gloria Jean" 1940. To help promote her new movie "A Little Bit of Heaven." Eyes are special on this doll. A very vivid blue. Clothes are not original. $65.00. (Courtesy Mary Partridge)

Arranbee--15" "Susan" All stuffed vinyl with glued on brown wig. Blue sleep eyes. Toddler legs. Marks: Arranbee, on head. $30.00. 1952. (Courtesy Irene Gann)

"Lacy Lace Tea Party Kiddle." Refer to Mattel
Section.

Arranbee--17" "Nanette" In original ball gown and fur cape. 1953. $35.00.

Arranbee--14" "Nanette" Original skating dress and shoe skates. 1953. $35.00.

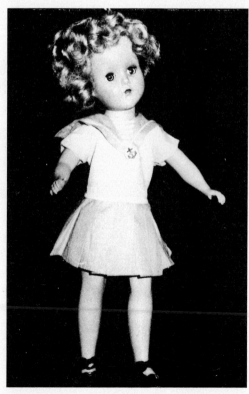

Arranbee--14" "Nanette" All hard plastic with glued on blonde wig. Blue sleep eyes. Marks: R&B, on head. 1955. $35.00.

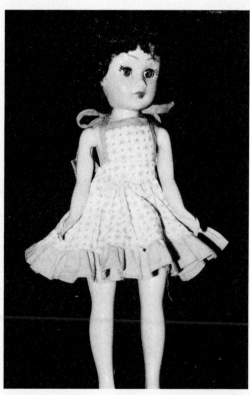

Arranbee--10" "Miss Cody" Hard plastic with vinyl head. Rooted brown hair. Three eyelash lines. Blue sleep eyes/molded lashes. High heel feet. Nail polish. Walker, head turns. Marks: ℗ on head. ca. 1950's $6.00.

Azrak--8" "Count Dracula" 8" "Frankenstein" Green skin tones. Fully jointed. Marks: Universal City/Studios Inc 1973/Azrak-Hamway Int'l Inc, on back. Hong Kong, on head. Mf'd for SS Kresge Co., on box. $3.00 each.

Azrak--8" "Wolfman" and 8" "The Mummy, A Super Monster" Plastic and vinyl with yellow skin tones. Jointed elbow, waist, knees and ankles. Marks: Universal City/Studios Inc 1973/ Azrak-Hamway Int'l Inc./Made in Hong Kong, on back. Hong Kong, on head. Mf'd for SS Kresge Co., on box. $3.00 each.

Baby Berry--13" "Lil Abner" One piece vinyl body, legs and arms. Vinyl head with molded hair. Painted features. Marks: Baby Berry Doll/ 1957, on head. (Courtesy Virginia Jones.)

51

"Todd's" Twin to "Tutti." One in jacket is #3556 Sundae Treat outfit. Marketed in 1966. One in cap is #3590, marketed in 1967. Marks: 1965/ Mattel Inc./Japan/4, on back. (Courtesy Sibyl DeWein)

16" "Kim" Refer to Shindana section for full description.

13" "Nancy" (Black) "Kim" (White) by Shindana.
Refer to Shindana section for full description.

"Truly Scrumptious" from Chitty, Chitty Bang, Bang. Refer to Mattel section for full description.

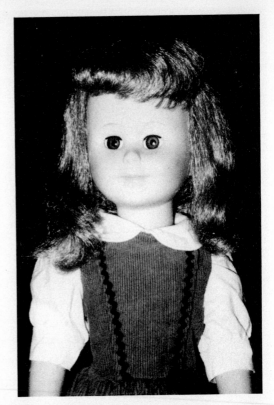

Uneeda--11½" "Betsy McCall" Plastic and vinyl with rooted light red hair. Small brown sleep eyes. Posable head. Original. Marks: none. Made by Uneeda Doll Co. $15.00.

Uneeda--22" "Betsy McCall" Plastic and vinyl. Jointed waist, wrist and ankles. Brown sleep eyes. Original clothes. Marks: none. $22.00. (Courtesy Margaret Weeks)

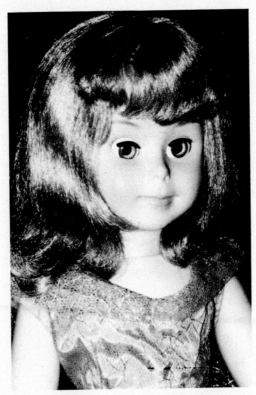

54

Uneeda--29" "Betsy McCall" Plastic and vinyl. Jointed waist and legs high near hip joint. Jointed ankles, wrist. Rooted blonde hair. Blue sleep eyes. Marks: McCall/1961/Corp. in circle. $30.00.

Uneeda--36" "Betsy McCall" Plastic and vinyl. Blue sleep eyes. Original dress. Marks: McCall Corp/1959, on head. Companion boy doll is "Sandy McCall." $45.00. (Courtesy Margaret Weeks)

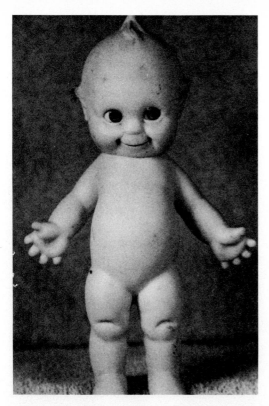

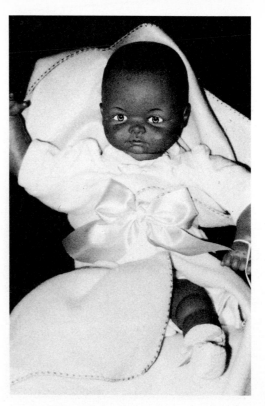

Cameo--7½" "Kewpie Doll" All rubber. Glass set in eyes. Squeaker in back. Marks: C on head. Cameo on back and Kewpie on the foot. Rose O'Neil on the other. $30.00. (Maish Collection)

Cameo--19" "Miss Peep" All vinyl. Inset brown eyes. Original. Marks: Cameo, head. Cameo Doll Products/Strombecker Corp., on tag. 1973. $20.00.

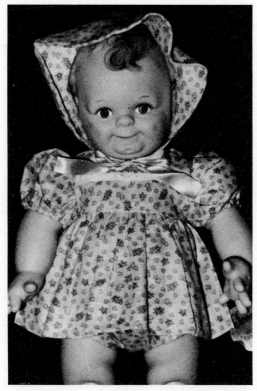

Cameo--14" "Scootles" All vinyl. Used original Cameo mold and at end of production, mold was destroyed. Marks: JK 1964/1973 LTD/Cameo/R7234, on head. Cameo, on back. Maxine's Limited Edition, on box. This is #852. $35.00.

Cameo--10" 'Kewpie Doll Beanbag" Cloth filled. Vinyl head and hands. Marks: Cameo/Hong Kong, on head. Tag: Kewpie/By Cameo, also: Cameo Doll/Division of Strombecker Corp. $4.00.

"The Sunshine Family" refer to the Mattel section for full description.

Marks: 1966 Mattel Inc. Clockwise (start 1:00). Lou #3537, Lola, Rose #3536, Lilac, Lorna #3535, Larky #3539. And one not shown is #3541 Lois Locket. (Colored)

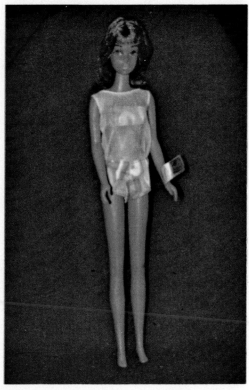

Mattel's "Black Francie." #1100 (Courtesy Margaret Biggers)

"Stacey" in Trail Blazers #1846. 1967.

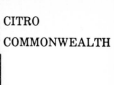

Commonwealth--10" "Carol" All vinyl with jointed waist. Rooted brown hair. Large blue sleep eyes. High heels. Painted toe and finger nails. Marks: W1, on head. 1957. $6.00.

Citro--25" "Polly Pond's Beauty Doll" One piece vinyl. Wire through legs so posable. High heels. Stuffed vinyl head. Saran hair. Blue sleep eyes. Pierced. Original. Came with Pond's face cream, etc. Sold for $21.95 in 1956. Marks: 4505, high on center crown. 1325-1/Made in USA, on neck flange. Tag: Polly Pond's Beauty Doll, Dressed in Daytime Ensemble. Citro Mfg. Co. $18.00.

Ginger is an unmarked doll. First registered in March 1955 by the Cosmopolitan Doll&Toy Co. Later Gingers with vinyl heads are marked Ginger, but the first dolls were all hard plastic, walkers with sleep eyes and big round eyes. The torso was similar to Ginny but the toes are smaller. Ginger was made in three sizes. 7½", 8½" and Baby Ginger.

Cosmopolitan--7½" "Ginger" Hard plastic body, arms and legs. Vinyl head with rooted medium blonde hair. Blue sleep eyes/molded lashes. Closed mouth. Marks: Ginger on head. 1956. Dressed as "December" of the "Ginger Dress of the Month Club." $5.00.

Cosmopolitan--8½" "Miss Ginger" All vinyl with rooted ash blonde hair. Blue sleep eyes/lashes. Closed mouth. 2nd and 3rd fingers molded together. High heel feet. Marks: Little Miss Ginger on back. 1956. $7.00.

Cosmopolitan--7½" "Ginger" All hard plastic with glued on wig. Blue sleep eyes/molded lashes. Walker, head turns. Original. Marks: none. Tag: Fashions For Ginger/Cosmopolitan Doll & Toy Corp. $5.00. (Courtesy Of Edna Hamlett)

Cosmopolitan--7½" "Cowgirl Ginger" Original cowgirl outfit. "Ginger" on shirt. "Deputy Mouseketter" and picture of Mickey Mouse on badge. Tag: Fashions for Ginger/Cosmopolitan Doll & Toy Corp. 1954. $5.00.

Gingers. Both vinyl head with hard plastic bodies. Dress is #111 of Playtime Series. Coat was sold under Separate Coats. #881. 1955. $5.00.

Cosmopolitan--Both are 8" high. Hard plastic all jointed body with vinyl heads. Characteristics: Very abundant rooted hair and rather poorly set sleep eyes. Marks: Ginger on head. Dress label reads: Fashions for Ginger by Cosmopolitan Doll & Toy Corp. Richmond Hill N.Y. trade mark. 1955. $5.00 each. (Maish Collection)

Cragstan--4½" "Trike Tike" Pin jointed hips and knees of plastic. Molded/painted on shoes and socks. Rooted brown hair. Painted blue eyes. Original. Marks: none. A Kiddle copy. $2.00.

59

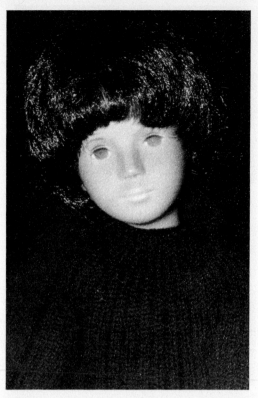

16" "Sasha" All rigid vinyl. Strung. Rooted white hair. Dark skin tones. Painted features. Marks: none. 1965. Created by Sasha Morgonthall. $18.00.

Creative Playthings--17" "Gregor" All dark toned rigid vinyl. Rooted dark brown hair. Painted brown eyes. Doll is strung. Posable head. Original. Marks: Wrist Tag: Made in/ Serie/England in circle, other side: Sasha. 1973. $18.00. (Courtesy Lita Wilson)

Deluxe Toys--29" "Sweet Rosemary" One piece unjointed body, arms and legs of stuffed vinyl. Vinyl head with rooted ash blonde hair. Blue sleep eyes/lashes. Sold through grocery stores 1957 to 1959. High heel feet. Marks: 251/AE, on head. 17, on back. Made by Deluxe Toys, division of Deluxe Reading, now out of business. Original clothes. $12.00.

Deluxe Reading--8" "Penny Brite" Shown in an original outfit. Marks: Deluxe Reading Corp/ 1963, on head. Deluxe Reading Corp/Elizabeth NJ/Pat. Pending, on back. $5.00. (Outfit courtesy Bessie Carson)

Hasbro--7" "Swinger" of the GoGo's. All vinyl with glued on yellow wig. Painted features. Marks: none. Original clothes. 1966. $4.00.

Deluxe Topper--7" "Hot Canary" of the Go Go's. All vinyl with glued on blonde wig. Painted features. Open/closed mouth, painted teeth. Original clothes. 1966. $4.00. (Courtesy Margaret Essler)

61

Topper--6½" "Yeah, Yeah" and "Slick Chick" of the Go Go's. All original and includes an all vinyl black poodle. $4.00 each.

Topper--6" "Fancy Feet" and 6½" "Kevin" "Double Dance Party" Rigid knees. Unjointed waist. Original. Marks: h22 and 11C. Base is battery operated. 1971. $9.00.

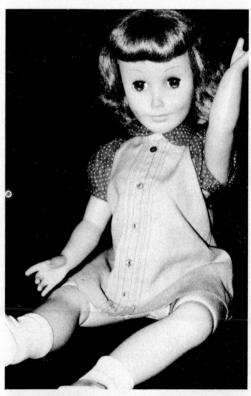

Deluxe Reading--22" Closed mouth version of "Susie Homemaker" Plastic and vinyl. Rooted blonde hair. Blue sleep eyes. Light cheek dimples. Marks: Deluxe Reading Corp/1964/2, on head. 1966. Also marked with 1964/4 and also 1964/30. $5.00.

Topper--6" "Dawn" Snapping knees. Jointed waist. Rooted blonde hair. Painted blue eyes/lashes, blue eyeshadow. Original. Marks: 343/S11A. 1970. $4.00.

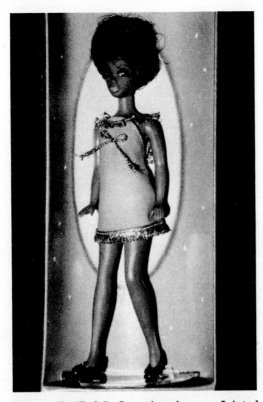

Topper--6" "Dale" Snapping knees. Jointed waist. Rooted black hair. Painted brown eyes to the left. Original. Marks: 4/H86, on head. $6.00.

Topper--6½" "Van" Snapping knees. Molded black hair. Painted brown eyes straight ahead. Original. Marks: none. $6.00.

Topper--6" "Angie" Snapping knees. Jointed waist. Rooted black hair. Painted brown eyes to the left/lashes. Marks: 51/D10. $5.00.

Topper--6" "Glori" Snapping knees. Jointed waist. Rooted red hair. Painted green eyes/lashes, straight ahead. Original. Marks: 154/S11, on head. 1970. $5.00.

63

Topper--6½" "Gary" Snapping knees. Molded black hair. Painted blue eyes to the left. Marks: none. Original. $5.00.

Topper--6" "Longlocks" Snapping knees. Jointed waist. Rooted long hair. Painted blue eyes to the right/lashes. Original. Marks: 92/H-17. $6.00.

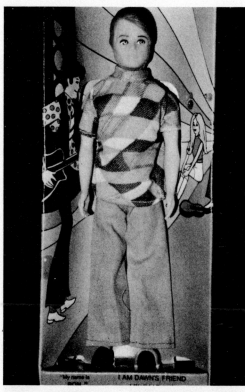

Topper--6½" "Ron" Snapping knees. Molded blonde hair. Painted blue eyes to the left. Marks: none. Original. $5.00.

Topper--6" "Dancing Dawn" Snapping knees. Jointed waist. Rooted blonde hair. Blue eyes to the left/lashes. Original. Marks: 543/H11a. $4.00.

Topper--6½" "Dancing Gary" Snapping knees. Jointed waist. Molded brown hair. Painted blue eyes to the left. Original. Marks: 1970/Topper Corp. $5.00.

Topper--6" "Dancing Dale" Snapping knees. Jointed waist. Rooted black hair. Painted brown eyes to the left. Original. Marks: 4/H 72, on head. $6.00.

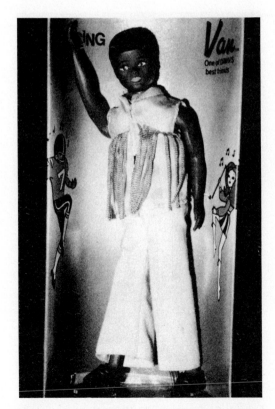

Topper--6½" "Dancing Van" Snapping knees. Jointed waist. Molded black hair. Painted brown eyes straight ahead. Original. Marks: none. $6.00.

Topper--6" "Dancing Longlocks" Snapping knees. Jointed waist. Rooted blonde hair. Painted blue eyes to the right. Original. Marks: H-17, on head. $6.00.

65

Topper--6" "Dancing Angie" Snapping knees. Jointed waist. Rooted black hair. Painted brown eyes to the left. Original. Marks. A8/10. $5.00.

Topper--6" "Dancing Glori" Snapping knees. Jointed waist. Rooted red hair (bangs) Painted green eyes to left/lashes. Marks: 2/H-11. Original. $5.00.

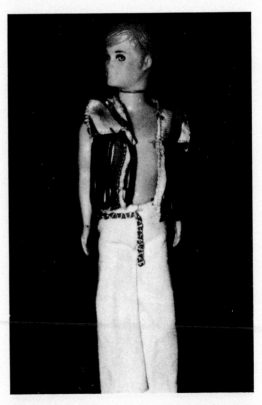

Deluxe Topper--6" "Dancing Ron" Dawn's boy-friend. Plastic body with vinyl arms, legs and head. Molded blonde hair. Painted blue eyes. Snapping knees. Marks: 1970/Topper Corp./Hong Kong. $5.00.

Topper--6½" "Kevin" Molded blonde hair. Painted blue eyes. Knees do not bend. Walker, head turns. Holes in bottom of feet for stand. Marks: 1970/Topper Corp/Hong Kong, lower back. $5.00.

Topper--6" "Denise" Snapping knees. Jointed waist. Rooted dark blonde hair. Painted blue eyes/lashes, straight ahead. Original. Marks: 11C, on head. 1970/Topper Corp/ Hong Kong, back. $8.00.

Topper--6" "Melanie" Snapping knees. Jointed waist. Rooted black hair. Painted brown eyes/lashes, to the right. Original. Marks: Al1A, on head. 1970. $8.00.

Topper--6" "Dinah" Snapping knees. Jointed waist. Rooted blonde hair. Painted blue eyes/lashes, straight ahead. Original. Marks: K-10, on head. 1970/Topper Corp/Hong Kong, on back. $8.00.

Topper--6" "Daphne" Jointed waist. Snapping knees. Rooted red hair. Painted green eyes/lashes, straight ahead. Original. Marks: H11A, on head. 1970/Topper Corp/Hong Kong, on back. $8.00.

Topper--6" "Connie Majorette" Snapping knees. Jointed waist. Rooted dark blonde hair. Painted blue eyes, to the right. Right arm jointed above elbow. Original. Marks: 311/K10, on head. $8.00.

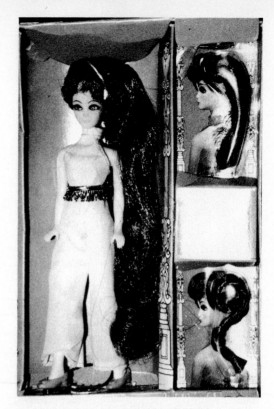

Topper--6" "Longlocks-Head to Toe" Snapping knees. Jointed waist. Rooted brown hair. Painted blue eyes, to the right. Original. Marks: M-17, on head. $5.00.

Topper--6" "Dawn-Head To Toe" Snapping knees. Jointed waist. Rooted blonde. Painted blue eyes/lashes, to the left. Original. Marks: H-11A, on head. 1970. $5.00.

Topper--6" "Maureen" Snapping knees. Jointed waist. Rooted brown hair. Painted brown eyes/lashes, straight ahead. Original. Marks: H11C, on head. 1970/Topper Corp/Hong Kong, on back. $8.00.

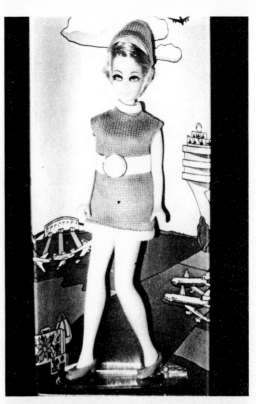

Topper--6" "Dancing Jessica" Snapping knees. Jointed waist. Rooted blonde hair. Painted blue eyes to the right/lashes. Original. Marks: H-7/ 110. $5.00.

Topper--6" "Jessica" Snapping knees. Jointed waist. Rooted blonde. Painted blue eyes/lashes, to the right. Marks: 11C. Original. 1970. $5.00.

Topper--6" "Kip Majorette" Snapping knees. Jointed waist. Rooted black hair. Painted brown eyes to the left. Right arms jointed above elbow. Marks: 11-7, on head. Original. $8.00.

Topper--6" "Dawn Majorette" Snapping knees. Jointed waist. Rooted blonde. Painted blue eyes, to the left. Right arm jointed above elbow. Marks: 878/K11A, on head. Original. $8.00.

69

Doll Artist--Bonnet head made by Lucille Kimsey. $45.00.

Doll Artist--Beautiful Parian head made by Lucille Kimsey. $45.00.

Doll Artist--Lovely Parian by Lucille Kimsey. $45.00.

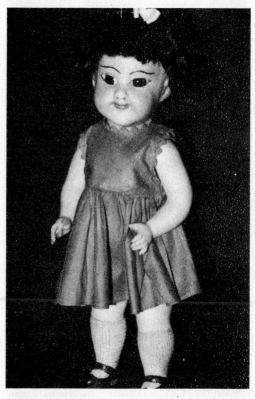

Doll Artist--10" "Grand-Daughter" By Ruth E. Fisher. All bisque with glued on human hair wig. Set brown eyes. Molded on shoes and socks. Marks: R.E.F., on head and back. 1939. $90.00.

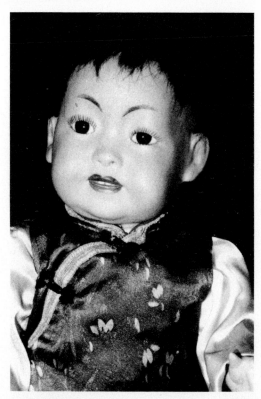

Doll Artist--14" Oriental. All bisque with olive skin tones. Open dome with set brown glass eyes. Open mouth/two teeth. Dressed by artist. Marks: Made in Germany/243/JDK/REP. By/ Ruth E. Fisher, on head. REP. By/Ruth E. Fisher, on back. 1939. $150.00.

Doll Artist--14" Oriental. All bisque with olive skin tones. Open dome. Brown glass eyes. Open mouth/two teeth. Dressed by artist. Marks: Made in/Germany/243/JDK/REP.By/Ruth E. Fisher, on head. REP/By Ruth E. Fisher, on back. 1939. $150.00.

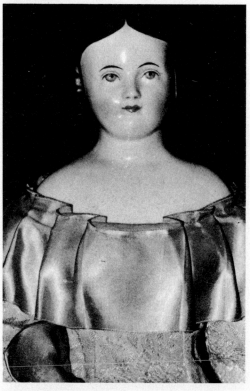

Doll Artist--16" "Parthenia" Ticking cloth body. Parian bisque head with blonde ornate hair and ribbons. Pierced ears. Original clothes include corset. Created before WWII by Emma Clear. Marks: Clear, with '46 between the C and L. $185.00.

Doll Artist--25" "Young Victoria" By Emma Clear. Cloth and china. Pink luster. Painted china high button shoes. 12 sausage curls. Corset with Humpty Dumpty Doll Hospital label. Created before WWII. This made in 1945. Marks: Clear, with '45 between the C and L. Original clothes. $265.00.

Doll Artist--6" "Primm Family" Doll house dolls. By Joyce Stafford. 1971. 12 sets sold and various singles.

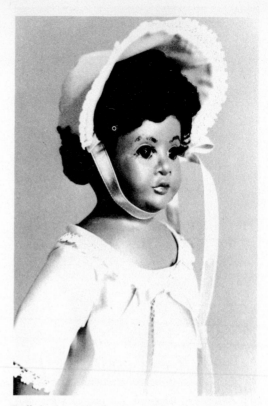

Doll Artist--13" "Buttercup" by Joyce Stafford. 1972. Limited edition. 12 sold.

Doll Artist--12" "Grace" By Joyce Stafford. 1972. Limited edition. 12 made and sold.

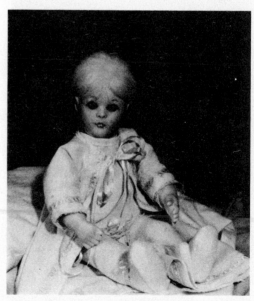

Doll Artist--13" "Birdie" By Joyce Stafford. 1973. Still for sale. So far 20 have been made.

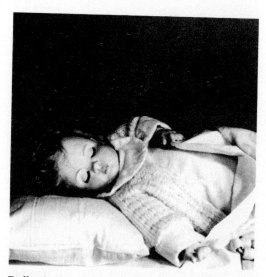

Doll Artist--13" "Sleepy Baby" by Joyce Stafford. 1968. Only one made. Artist collection. All early dolls were limited to 10-12. Now are sold for 1 year and then Joyce designs and makes new ones.

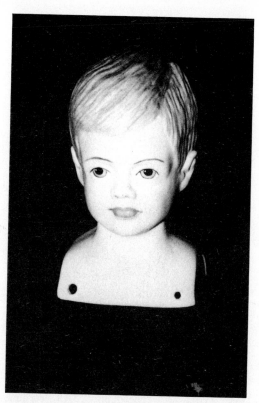

Doll Artist--1973 U.F.D.C. Convention head. Marks: Ken-Tuck 1973/Janet E. Masteller 1972. $22.00.

Doll Artist--9½" All bisque with open crown. Brown eyes. Open/closed mouth. Molded on shoes and socks. Marks: JOIS. 1973. Made by Joy Eason, Montrol, La. $60.00.

Doll Artist--7½" "Bru" All bisque with brown plastic eyes. Glued on brown dynel wig. Molded, painted shoes and socks. Marks: Lydia Hill. 1971. $60.00.

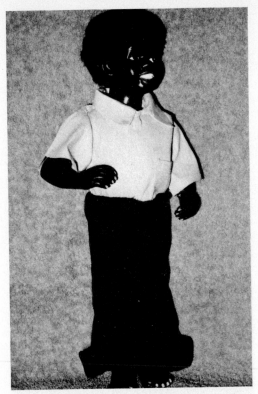

Doll Artist--13" "Nicodemus" All ceramic bisque. Stained. Fur wig. Marks: Nicodemus/ Maggie Head/1966, on head. Maggi Head, on body. $30.00.

Doll Artist--13" "Nicodemus Girl" All ceramic bisque. Stained. Fur wig. Marks: Nicodemus/ Maggi Head/1966, on head. Maggi Head, on body. $30.00.

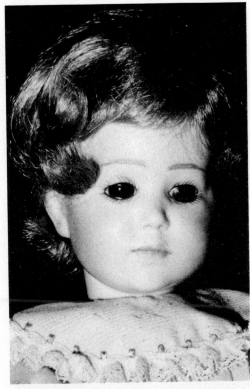

Doll Artist--Reproduction pouty by Rene McKinley. $75.00. (Courtesy Margaret Essler)

Doll Artist--10" "Bru Jne" by Ida May Staples. Kid/bisque. Swivel shoulder head. Open crown. Glass eyes. Marks: IMS/BRU Jne. 1972. $65.00. (Courtesy Margaret Essler)

Handmade--2" White mice in Boutique. Lady Mouse is trying on hats. A saleslady Mouse in a black dress with pearls is assisting, while a third mouse peeks from dressing room. Created by an Old Town Artist, Chicago 1967. Original price $40.00. (Maise Collection)

Handmade--Country Mice. 5" paper mache mice playing checkers in country store setting. Miniatures include pot belly stove, flour barrel, orange crate, cans of food, etc. $40.00. (Created by Donna Maish, 1970)

Doll Artist--17" "Bonnie Bru" by Gladys Draper. Socket on bisque shoulderplate. Bisque lower arms and legs. Dressed by artist. Marks: G Draper/Bonnie Bru. 1973. $85.00.

Doll Artist--37" "Cinderella" and 39" "Prince Charming" by doll artist Barbara Belding.

Doll Artist--28" "Sleeping Beauty" by Barbara Belding.

Doll Artist--48" "Snow White" and 32" to 36" "Dwarfs" by Barbara Belding.

Doll Artist--12" Apple Head Dolls (Middle, Sam Ervin, is 15½") by Barbara Belding.

Rag Doll--14" "Freckles" All handmade by "Marilynn." Embroidered features, yarn hair. All removable clothing. 1972. $7.00. (Maish Collection)

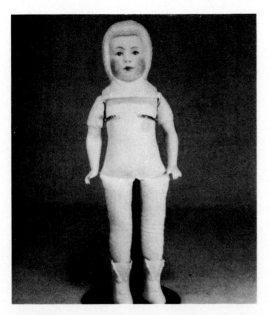

Doll Artist--Top: 12-13" "Snow Baby" Heubach mold with original, applied "snow." Painted eyes. By Judi Kahn. $35.00 includes hand and golashes/gold buckle.

Doll Artist--Left: 12-13" "By-Lo" Glass eyes. $25.00, head only. By Judi Kahn.

Doll Artist--Right: 12-13" "American Schoolboy" Glass eyes. By Judi Kahn. $35.00 with arms, legs a choice of eye color.

Doll Artist--16" "Tete Jumeau" By Judi Kahn, kit includes French arms, legs. $45.00.

Doll Artist--16" "Circle Dot Bru" By Judi Kahn. Kit, $45.00.

Doll Artist--Top: 16" "Negro Bru" By Judi Kahn. Kit. $55.00.

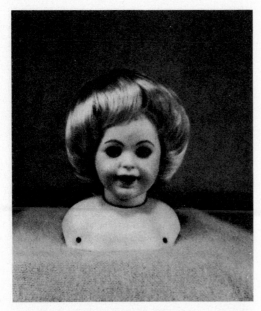

Doll Artist--Left: S.F.B.J. 236. By Judi Kahn. Kit. $45.00.

Doll Artist--Right: 16" S.F.B.J. 252, "Pouty" By Judi Kahn. Kit. $45.00.

Doll Artist--16" "Bru Jne" By Judi Kahn. Kit. $45.00.

Doll Artist--12" "Willie & Millie" K Star R 123. Kits. $35.00 each. By Judi Kahn.

Doll Artist--Two faced fashion. Sleep and awake. Kit comes with French hands to elbow, legs. By Judi Kahn. Kit. $40.00.

Doll Artist--Judi Kahn's Fashion asleep.

Doll Artist--Marked "165" Googly. By Judi Kahn. Kit. $45.00.

Doll Artist--"165" cut down to smaller size. By Judi Kahn. Kit $35.00.

Doll Artist--13" "Gancho" (Hungarian) original by Gertrude Florian. 1958. $150.00.

Doll Artist--15½" "Empress Carlotta" original by Polly Mann. Marked head and body. $150.00.

Dritz-Traum Co.--13" "Peggy McCall" All composition. Put out in sewing kit with three McCall
patterns, plus all composition dressmaker form.
Marks: Peggy's Dressmaker Form. Dritz-Traum
$22.00.

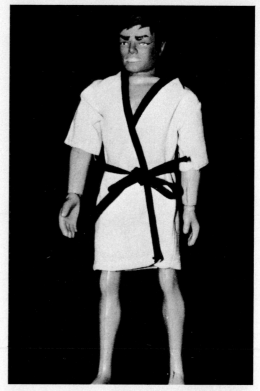

Durham--11½" "Marge" All flat vinyl. Pin jointed arms, legs and head. Molded, painted hair, ribbons and features. Marks: picture of world, D No. 1500/Durham Industries Inc./Made in Taiwan. 1970. $1.00.

Durham--9" "Kung Fu" Plastic and vinyl. Pull right arm forward, press top button and arm "chops." Pull right leg back, press bottom button and leg will kick. Marks: GI Hong Kong, on head. Mfg'ed in Hong Kong for SS Kresge Co, on box. Made by Durham Co. Kung Fu is a TV program and played by David Carradine. $3.00.

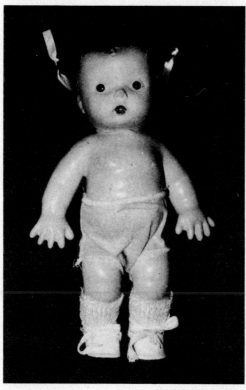

Eastern Rubber--8½" "Patty Pigtails" One piece latex body, arms and legs. Early vinyl head. Two brown yarn pigtails. Painted blue eyes. Freckles. Original. Marks: none. Box: Patty Pigtails/#400/The Eastern Rubber Specialty Co. 1952. $4.00.

Educational Crafts Co--13" "Junior Miss" All composition with molded high heel "wedgie" feet. Put out with three Butterick patterns. Marks: none. $22.00.

Eegee--14" "Lizabeth" All composition with glued on ash blonde hair. Blue sleep eyes. Eyeshadow. Open mouth with four teeth. Original clothes. Marks: none. Box: Lizabeth/By/Eegee. 1939. $35.00.

Eegee--19" "Miss Charming" All composition. All jointed. Green tin sleep eyes. Blonde mohair wig. Original. An excellent "Shirley" copy. Marks: E.G. 1936. $35.00. (Maish Collection)

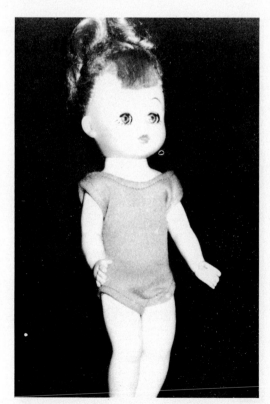

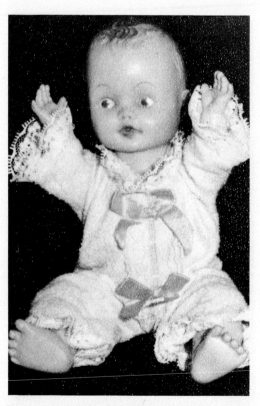

Eegee--8½" "Janie" also sold as "Sherry" One piece vinyl stuffed body. Vinyl head with rooted blonde hair. Blue sleep eyes. Marks: Eegee, on head. Eegee, on body. 1956. $4.00.

Eegee--10½" "Play Pen Pal" All vinyl one piece body, arms and head. Jointed hips. Molded hair and painted features. Open mouth/nurser. Marks: Eegee, on head. 1956. $3.00.

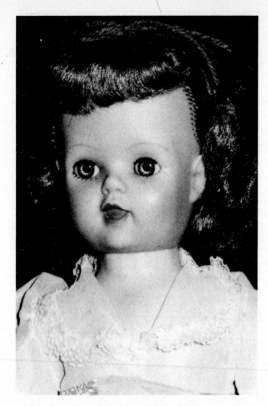

Eegee--20" "Miss Flexie" One piece stuffed vinyl body, arms and legs. Vinyl head with rooted red/brown hair. Blue sleep eyes/lashes. Open/closed mouth. Marks: Eegee, on head. Eegee/20, on back. Original dress. 1956. $5.00.

Eegee--10½" "Chubby Schoolgirl" Hard plastic body. Jointed knees. Stuffed vinyl head. Blue sleep eyes. Walker. Original clothes. Marks: Eegee, on head. 1957. $5.00.

Eegee--14" "Miss Debby" All one piece vinyl. Vinyl head with rooted long blonde hair. Large blue sleep eyes. Marks: 1½-H/Eegee, on head. Eegee/15H, on back. 1958. $6.00.

Eegee-17" "Miss Sunbeam" Plastic body and legs. Vinyl arms and head with rooted yellow hair. Blue sleep eyes. Open/closed mouth with molded, painted teeth. Dimples. Original dress. Marks: Eegee, on head. Miss Sunbeam, on apron. $10.00. (Courtesy Virginia Jones)

Eegee--9¼" "Kid Sister" All plastic with vinyl head. Rooted ash blonde hair. Painted features. Freckles. Marks: Eegee Co./38, on head. $3.00.

Eegee--12" "Shelly" All plastic with vinyl head. Rooted blonde hair with grow feature. Painted blue eyes. Pull ring in back for hair. Original. Marks: Eegee, on head. 1964. $4.00. (Courtesy Sharon Hazel)

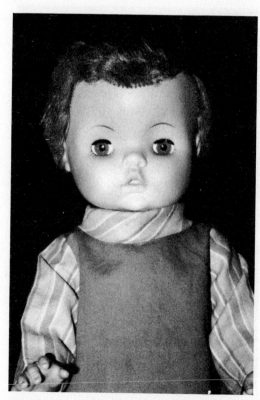

Eegee--19½" "Terri Talks" Plastic body and legs. Vinyl arms and head. Rooted blonde hair. Blue sleep eyes. Battery operated walker. Marks: 19U/Eegee Co/3. 1965. $6.00.

Eegee--14" "Playpen Baby" Plastic body and legs. Vinyl arms and head. Rooted blonde hair. Blue sleep eyes. Nurser with hole in roof of mouth. Marks: 13/14AA/Eegee Co. 1968. $3.00.

85

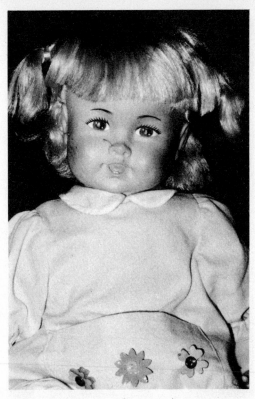

Eegee--23" "Babette" Cloth and vinyl. Rooted white hair. Painted features. Two painted lower teeth. Original clothes. Marks: Tag: Goldberger Doll Mfg. Co. Eegee, on head. 1969. $6.00.

Eegee--22" "Georgette" Cloth body with vinyl arms, legs and head. Rooted orange hair. Green sleep eyes/lashes. Freckles. Marks: 17 RNG/Eegee Co, on head. Tag: Goldberger Doll Mfg. Co. Inc. Original clothes. 1971. $6.00.

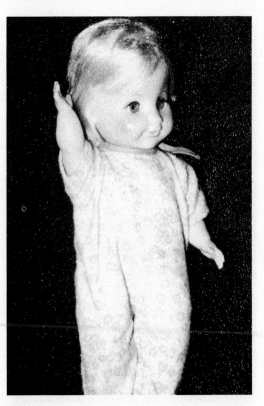

Eegee--11" Cloth body, bean bag type. Vinyl hands and head. Blonde rooted hair. Painted, side glancing eyes. Open/closed mouth. Dimples Music box, key wind in back. She wiggles as music plays. Marks: 14 BD/Eegee Co, on head. Tag: Body made in Hong Kong/Assembled & Stuffed in USA. Original clothes. $3.00.

Eegee--10½" "Mary Kay" Plastic body and legs. Vinyl arms and head. Rooted blonde hair. Blue sleep eyes. Open mouth/nurser. Original clothes. Premium for two box tops from Kelloggs. Marks: 10T/Eegee Co, on head. 1971. $3.00. (Courtesy Leslie White)

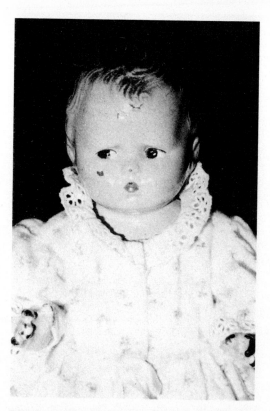

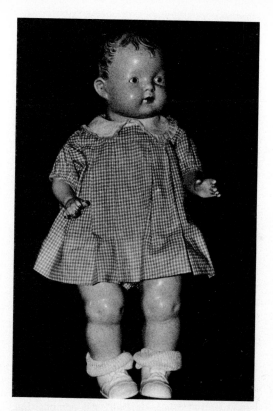

Effanbee--12" "Grumpy" Composition head/shoulderplate with full composition arms and legs. Cloth body. Straight legs. Marks: Effanbee/Dolls/Walk, Talk, Sleep, on shoulderplate. Made 1912 through 1939. $42.00.

Effanbee--17" "Baby Evelyn" Cloth and composition. Molded brown painted hair. Painted blue eyes. Fat toddler legs. Original. Cryer center back. Marks: Effanbee/Baby Evelyn. $45.00.

Effanbee--17" "Ice Queen" Called the "Open mouth Ann Shirley." Composition arms, legs and head. Hard rubber arms. Glued human hair wig. Brown sleep eyes. Open mouth/four teeth. Only made for few months as teeth would not stay in. Marks: Effanbee/Anne Shirley, on back. Designed by DeeWee Cochran. 1937. $85.00.

Effanbee--18" All composition with open mouth/4 teeth. Brown sleep eyes. Young girl's breasts. Marks: Effanbee/USA, on back. $60.00. (Courtesy Mary Partridge)

Effanbee--12" "Portrait Doll" All composition. All jointed. Blue sleep eyes. Painted rosebud mouth. Auburn mohair wig. Marks: none. 1940. $35.00. (Maish Collection)

Effanbee--18" "Little Lady" Dressed as bride. Marks: Effanbee, on head. Effanbee/USA, on back. This doll was advertised as a Bridal center piece for weddings. 1943. $45.00.

Effanbee--14" "Little Lady" Dressed as majorette. Original clothes. This is one model that was used by FOA Swartz as the Magnetic hand doll. Marks: Effanbee/Anne Shirley, on back. 1940. $45.00.

Effanbee--21" "Honey" Composition body, head and legs. Hard rubber arms. Glued on human hair wig. Blue flirty sleep eyes. Rosy cheeks. Feathered brows. Very pale fingernail polish. Original clothes, minus hat. Marks: Effanbee, head and body. 1948. $45.00.

Effanbee--8" All composition, all jointed. Painted features. Chubby character-type face. Marks: Effanbee, on back. 1940's. $35.00. (Maish Collection)

Effanbee--27" "Formal Honey" All composition with glued on yellow wig. Blue sleep eyes. Original clothes. Marks: Effanbee, on head. Tag: I am Honey An Effanbee Durable Doll. 1949. $85.00.

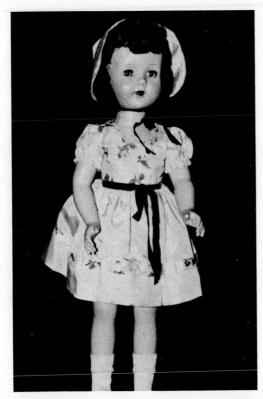

Effanbee--19" "Honey Walker" All hard plastic. An original outfit. Marks: Effanbee, on head and back. $30.00. (Courtesy Mary Partridge)

Effanbee--19" "Honey Walker" All hard plastic. Original Ball Gown. Marks: Effanbee, on back. $30.00. (Courtesy Mary Partridge)

Effanbee--19" "Honey Ballerina" All hard plastic. Jointed knees and ankles. Original. Marks: Effanbee, on head. (Original sticker price is $13.95). $35.00. (Courtesy Mary Partridge)

Effanbee--14" "Honeywalker" Dressed in an original dress. 1953. Marks: Effanbee, on head and back. 1953. $18.00.

Effanbee--10" "Happy Boy" All vinyl with molded hair. Closed painted eyes. Freckles. Open/closed mouth with molded upper tooth. Marks: 1960/Effanbee, on head. Effanbee, on back. $6.00.

Effanbee--21" "My Fair Baby" All vinyl rooted blonde hair. Blue sleep eyes. Open mouth/nurser. Cryer. Marks: Effanbee/1960, on head. $16.00.

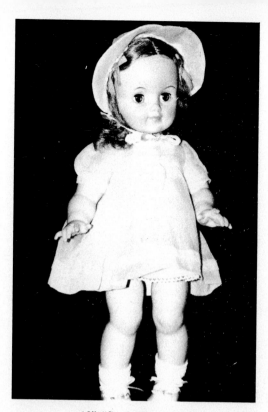

18" "Susie Sunshine" Original clothes.

18" "Susie Sunshine"

Effanbee--The circled face is the "other" Susie Sunshine and her picture is in the color section in the center of this book. Marketed in 1966. $20.00.

18" "Susie Sunshine" Original Clothes.

18" "Susie Sunshine" Original clothes.

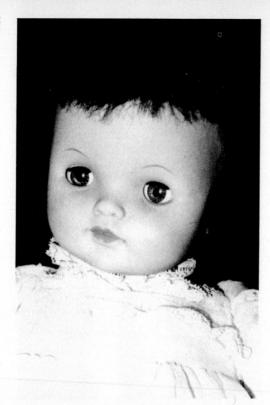

Effanbee--18" "Sugar Plum" Cloth and vinyl. Rooted brown hair. Blue sleep eyes. Original dress. Marks: Effanbee/1964. $7.00.

Effanbee--18" "Twinkie" Cloth and vinyl with rooted white hair. Blue sleep eyes. Cryer. Marks: Effanbee/1965/9500L, on head. $5.00.

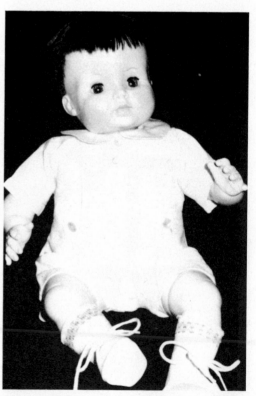

92

Effanbee--12" "My Fair Baby" All vinyl with molded hair. Blue sleep eyes/lashes. Open mouth/nurser. Short toddler legs. Also sold same year with the Dy Dee type hands. Marks: 13/Effanbee/1968, on head. Effanbee/1968, on body. $4.00.

Effanbee--16" "Sugar Plum" Cloth body with vinyl arms, legs and head. Rooted dark brown hair. Blue sleep eyes/lashes. Marks: 14/Effanbee/1969/1949, on head. Original clothes. $5.00.

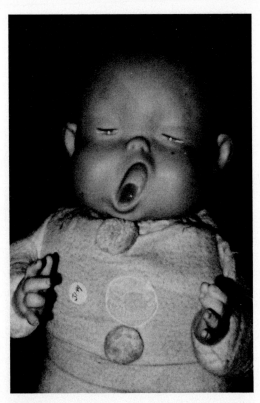

Ellanee Doll Co--15" "Yawning John" All cloth with vinyl arms and head. Blue painted eyes. Marks: L-E, on head. By Ellanee Doll Co. 1971. $15.00. (Courtesy Jayn Allen)

Fisher Price--14" "Baby Ann" Cloth and vinyl with rooted blonde hair. Painted brown eyes. Original. Marks: 60/188460/1973/Fisher Price Toys, on head. Fisher Price Toys/204., on tag. $9.00.

Fisher Price--14" "Audrey" Cloth and vinyl with rooted red hair. Painted blue eyes. Freckles. Original. Marks: 168240/1973/Fisher Price Toys, on head. Tag: Fisher Price Toys/203. $9.00.

Fisher Price--14" "Natalie" Cloth and vinyl with rooted dark blonde hair. Painted brown eyes. Original. Marks: 168320/1973/Fisher Price Toys, on head. Tag: Fisher Price Toys/202. $9.00.

93

Fisher Price--14" "Jenny" Cloth and vinyl with rooted brown hair. Painted blue eyes. Freckles. Original. Marks: 168380/1973/Fisher Price Toys, on head. Tag: Fisher Price Toys/201. $9.00.

Fisher Price--14" "Mary" Cloth and vinyl with rooted blonde hair. Painted blue eyes. Original. Marks: 168420/1973/Fisher Price Toys, on head. Tag: Fisher Price Toys/200. $9.00.

Fisher Price--14" "Elizabeth" Cloth and vinyl with rooted black hair. Painted brown eyes. Marks: 18/168630/1973/Fisher Price Toys, on head. Tag: Fisher Price Toys/205. Original. $9.00.

94

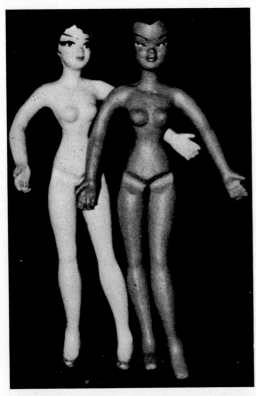

Flagg Dolls--7" "Flagg Dancing Dolls" All vinyl. Posable. White doll called "Rhumba" and wore a Rhumba dress with turbin. Black doll is Haitian with long dress and head piece. Most Flagg Dolls had rooted dynel hair. ca. late 1950's. $6.00 each.

Fleishchaker--17" All stuffed lastic plastic. Flanged joints. Hand embedded hair. Blue sleep eyes. Open/closed mouth. Wide spread legs. Marks: Copyright 1951 Lastic Plastic, on head. Lastic Plastic/1951, on back. Made by Fleischaker Novelty Co. $15.00. (Courtesy Dorothy Westbrook)

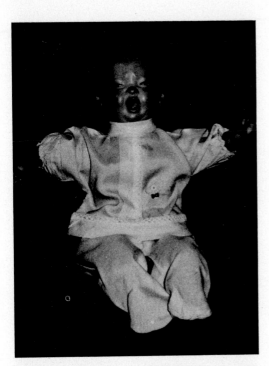

16" "Bi Bye" Cloth body. Early vinyl arms, legs and head. Lightly molded brown hair. Blue painted eyes. Marks: Lastic Plastic-'49, on neck flange. This is a trademark of Fleischaker Novelty Co. Venice, Calif. This is on a tag with original doll. Other side: Bi Bye Baby/One Week Old/I Have Come To Play/Cuddle Me and/Hold Me Close/Love Me Everyday. $12.00. Information courtesy Ada Harper, Dallas, Texas.

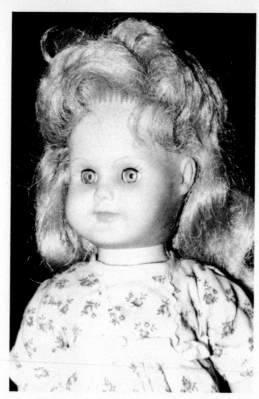

Canada--12½" "Louise" Plastic and vinyl. Rooted blonde hair. Blue sleep eyes/molded lashes. Marks: Regal Toy/Made in Canada. 1962. $5.00.

Canada--10" "Love Me, Indian" Plastic body and legs. Vinyl arms and head. Rooted black hair. Painted features. Marks: Regal/Made in Canada, on head. Regal/Canada, on back. Original clothes. 1964. $4.00.

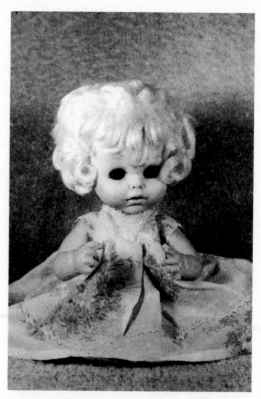

Canada--7" "Nova Scotia Tartan Advertising Doll" All hard plastic. Glued on brown wig. Blue sleep eyes. Original clothes. Marks: Reliable/Made in Canada, on back. 1958. $2.00.

Reliable--14" "Mary, Baby" All plastic, all jointed. Blue eyes, heavy lashes, yellow lips and platinum rooted wig. Redressed. 1969. $3.00. (Maish Collection)

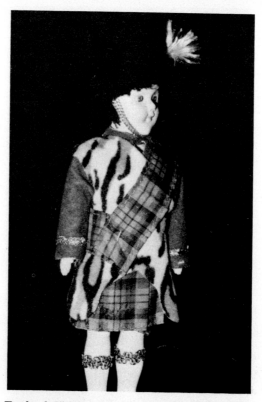

England--8" "New Zealand Native" All hard plastic. Jointed shoulders and hips. Black button sleep eyes with indented pupils. Hand painted face. Molded hair. Original. Marks: Rosebud, on lower back. 1955. $6.00.

England--7" "Royal Scot" All hard plastic with blue sleep side glancing eyes. Molded on shoes. Original. Marks: Rosebud, on back. 1956. $4.00.

England--9½" "Scot Lad" Composition swivel head. Felt body. Stitched fingers. Painted features. Mohair wig. Marks: Old Cottage Doll-Eng. Design Center-London. $25.00. (Maish Collection)

England--6" "Highland Lass" All hard plastic. Jointed arms. Sleep eyes. Glued on mohair wig. Taffeta and felt costume. Velvet hat. Marks: Roddy Made in Eng. 1946. $6.00. (Maish Collection)

97

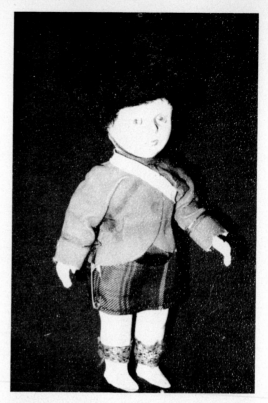

England--6" "Husar Guard" All hard plastic. Jointed arms only. Molded on shoes and socks. Original. Marks: Rosebud, on shoulders. 1961. $4.00.

England--6" "Palace Guard" All plastic with glued on plastic hat. Blue sleep eyes. Painted on shoes and socks. Marks: Rosebud. 1958. $4.00.

England--16" "Jeannie" All vinyl with rooted white hair. Blue sleep eyes. Nurser. Ball jointed arms and legs. Marks: 1964/Politoy/¾ Eye, on head. Politoy/Made in England/16G, on back. $5.00.

England--3" "Mice Dolls" All felt. Marks: Dressed Mice, hand made and designed by E M Brickdale, Herts, England. 1965. $10.00 each. (Maish Collection)

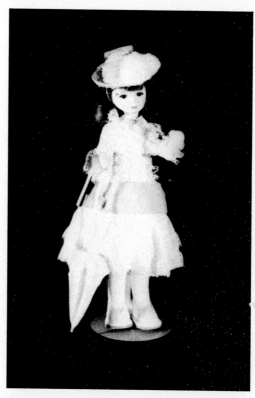

England--9" "Victorian Girl" Composition swivel head, all felt body, stitched fingers. Painted features. Mohair wig. Marks: Old Cottage Doll-England. Selected for the Design Center-London. 1968. $25.00. (Maish Collection)

England--9" "Victorian Girl" Composition swivel head. All felt body. Painted features. Mohair wig. Marks: Old Cottage England. Selected for the Design Center London. 1968. $25.00. (Maish Collection)

England--9" "Scots Lass" Composition swivel head. All felt body. Painted features. Mohair wig. Marks: Old Cottage Doll-England. Selected for the Design Center London. 1968. $25.00. (Maish Collection)

England--9" "Grandma" Composition swivel head, all felt body, stitched fingers. Painted features. Mohair wig. Marks: Old Cottage Doll-Eng. Selected for The Design Center London. 1968. $25.00. (Maish Collection)

99

England--9½" "Pearly King," 7" "Pearly Girl"
Composition swivel head. All felt body. Painted
features. Mohair wig. Marks: Old Cottage Doll
England Design Center London. 1970. $25.00.
(Maish Collection)

England--9½" "London Bobby" Composition
swivel head. All felt body. Painted features.
Mohair wig. Marks: Old Cottage Doll England
Design Center London. 1970. $25.00.

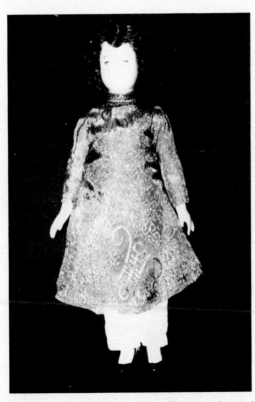

France--8½" "India" All celluloid. Jointed
shoulders and hips. Painted features, socks and
shoes. Glued on hair. Marks: France 6/SNF, in
diamond/21, on back. 1939. $12.00.

France--13" "Marina" Plastic and vinyl. Open/
closed mouth. Original. Marks: Clodrey/20126-
921, on head. Clodrey/Polyflex/Made in France,
on back. 1964. $7.00. (Courtesy Lita Wilson)

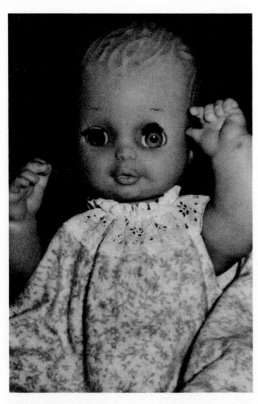

France--11" "Poupee Lee" Plastic and vinyl. Blue sleep eyes. Open mouth/nurser. Marks: none. By Clodey of France. 1970. $6.00.

Foreign--13" "Claudine" 1971, "Michael" 1972, "Elizabeth" 1973. Plastic and vinyl. Rooted dark brown hair. Blue sleep eyes. Marks: Clodrey/ 20126921, on head. $6.00. (Courtesy Kathy Walters)

Foreign--17" "Claudine" All plastic (early) with glued on brown human hair wig. Flirty blue sleep eyes. Marks: Made in France/GE GE/ 115, on back. Ge Ge, on head. Made by G. Giroud & Cie, Montrebson, France. 1956. $20.00.

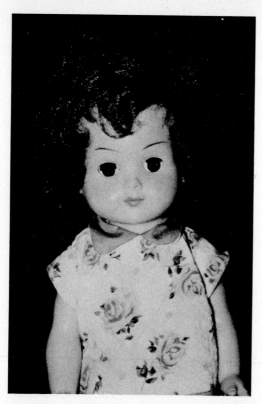

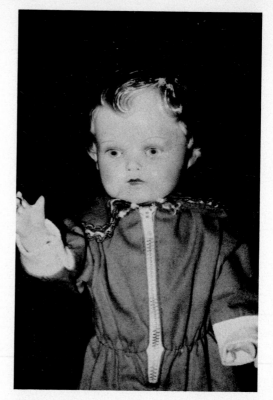

Germany--13" "Leeka" All vinyl with rooted black hair. Sleep brown eyes. Blue eyeshadow. Original. Edmund Knock Co. Coburg, Germany. Marks: EK/36/62, on head. NR-1, on back. 1961. $5.00. (Courtesy Margaret Weeks)

Germany--13" "My Playmate" All celluloid with molded brown hair. Painted blue eyes. Red dots corners of eyes. Painted nostrils. Jointed shoulders and hips. Doll is strung. Marks: J.K/ Koge, in triangle, on back. 1937. $20.00. (Courtesy Margaret Weeks)

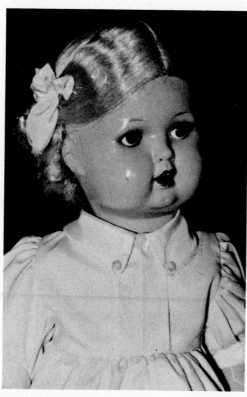

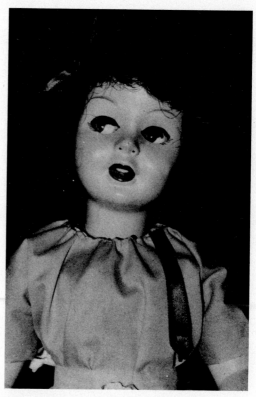

Germany--19" "Greta" All hard plastic with glued on blonde wig. Blue sleep eyes. Open mouth/two teeth. Cryer. Marks: Diamant/45/ 48, on head. Diamant, on back. 1954. Doll has open crown made by Schneider and Hartwig of Coburg, Germany. $17.00.

Germany--19" "Lousita" All early plastic over paper mache. Glued on brown hair. Blue flirty eyes. Open/closed mouth with two painted upper teeth. Feathered brows. Cryer. Marks: 3 M's/52, on back. 3 M's, on head. 1956. Made by Maar-Sohn. $15.00.

102

Germany--10½" All rubber. Head and body in one piece. Jointed arms. Molded hair. Painted features, shoes and socks. Original dress cotton and felt. Marks: Made in Western Germany on back #04522 on foot. About 20 years old. $12.00. (Maish Collection)

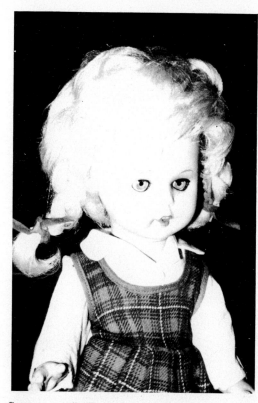

Germany--11" "Bettina Lee" Plastic body and legs. Vinyl arms and head with rooted white hair. Blue sleep eyes. Two molded upper teeth. 1964. Original. Marks: 3 M's/30/10, on head. 1900/30/Made in/Germany, on back. A Trademark of Maar & Sohn Co. $8.00. (Courtesy Margaret Weeks)

Germany--19" "Lisa-Bella" Plastic and vinyl. Blue sleep eyes. Pull string talker. "Hello, my name is Lisa-Bella", etc. Original. Marks: 4F1II/ES, on back. 45, on arms. Made by Emasco. Maar & Sohn Co. $22.00.

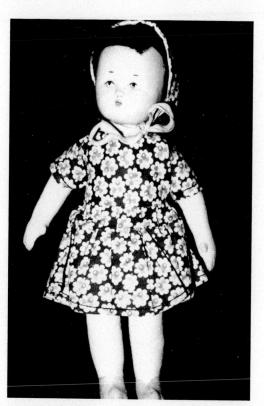

Germany--8" "Oleagh" Cloth body with stitched fingers. Celluloid head with painted blue eyes. Glued on brown hair. Original. Marks: Turtle, on head. Tag: Oleagh. By Rheinische Gummi & Celluloid Fabric. $4.00.

103

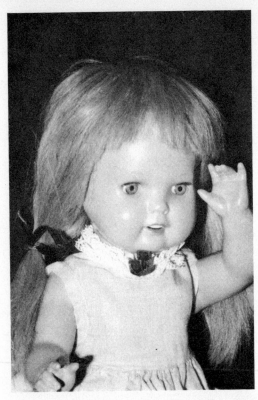

Germany--15" "Isabell" All rigid strung plastic. Glued on blonde human wig over molded hair. Blue sleep eyes, tin lids. Open mouth with painted teeth. By Rheinische Gummi & Celluloid Fabric, Mannheim, Neckarau. Marks: Turtle/35, on head. 40, on back, arms and legs. 1957. $12.00.

Germany--17" "Terria" Plastic and vinyl. Ball jointed knees, elbows. Jointed wrists. Rooted blonde hair. Blue sleep eyes. Marks: Turtle, in diamond, head and body with 44, in square: Schildkrot AG/Vorm. Rheinische Gummi/Und Celluloidfabric 1970, plus: Made in Germany/ Patents Pending. $9.00.

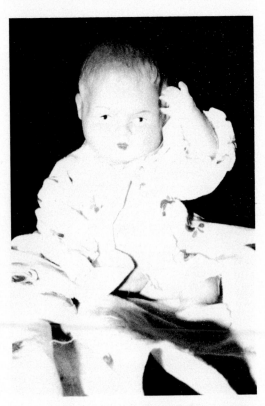

Germany--3" "Doll House Grandmother" All plastic with painted on shoes and socks. Molded hair and painted features. Marks: ED/3/8/Germany, on back. 1960. $3.00.

Germany--6" "Pette" Plastic and vinyl. Molded hair. Painted features. Marks: 18/Germany, on back. 1969. $3.00.

Germany--11½" "Gretta" All light weight, dark toned plastic with glued on black hair. Blue sleep eyes/lashes. Posable head. Marks: none. $4.00.

Hawaii--9" "Leialoha" (Beloved Child) Plastic body with vinyl arms, legs and head. Rooted black hair. Brown sleep eyes. Original. Made for Lanakila Crafts, Inc. Marks: Made In/Hong Kong, on back. 1973. $5.00.

Hong Kong--7" All plastic. Arms swing away from body. Molded hair with hole for ribbon. Blue sleep eyes. Legs hinged to be walker. Molded on shoes and socks. Marks: Made In/ Hong Kong, on back. ca. 1960's. $2.00.

Hong Kong--11½" "Mariclaire" by J.C. Penny Co. Plastic body with jointed waist. Vinyl arms, legs and head. Legs are wide spread. Rooted yellow hair. Painted blue eyes/lashes. Very turned up nose. Marks: 155, high on head. Made in Hong Kong, on back. $4.00.

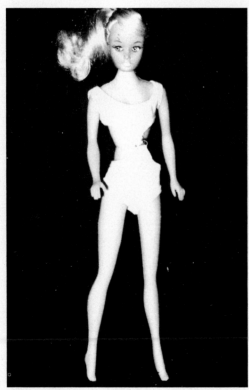

Hong Kong--11½" "Waikki Girl" Plastic and vinyl and has suntan skin tones. Jointed waist. Painted blue eyes. Marks: Made in/Hong Kong. $5.00.

Hong Kong--5½" Vinyl head. Painted eyes. Jointed arms and legs. Rooted wig. Marks: Hong Kong #7006. All original. 1964. $4.00. (Maish Collection)

Hong Kong--7" "Pixie" All vinyl. Jointed arms and legs. Painted features. Rooted brown hair. One of "Pixie" dolls sold by Sears and Wards. 1965. $5.00. (Maish Collection)

Hong Kong--13" "Tiny Traveler" Plastic body and legs. Vinyl arms and head. Rooted brown hair. Painted blue eyes. Jointed waist. Marks: Made in Hong Kong. Original clothes. 1968. $3.00.

Hong Kong--6" "Betty" of Twins, Betty & Bob. Plastic and vinyl with rooted blonde hair. Painted features. Original dress. Marks: Hong Kong, high on head. 1970. $1.00.

Hong Kong--6" "Baby Bright Eyes" Plastic and vinyl with rooted brown hair. Painted blue eyes. Open/closed mouth. Original. Posable head. Marks: D/King/Hong Kong, on head. Made In/ Hong Kong, on back. 1971. $2.00.

107

Hong Kong--12" "Captain Amos" Plastic and vinyl with one row of rooted white hair far back on head. Rooted beard. Painted blue eyes. Original. Marks: Made in/Hong Kong. 1971. $8.00.

Hong Kong--7½" "Simple Simon" Plastic and vinyl with rooted yellow hair. Painted blue eyes. Original. Marks: Made in Hong Kong, on back. Box: Dis't by/F.W. Woolworth Co. 1972. $3.00.

Hong Kong--7½" "Hans Brinker" Plastic and vinyl with rooted yellow hair. Painted blue eyes. Original. Marks: Made In/Hong Kong, on back. Box: Dis't by F.W. Woolworth Co. 1972. $3.00.

Hong Kong--8" "Heidi" (Switzerland) & "Tomoko" (Japan) Plastic and vinyl. Rooted hair. Painted eyes. Both original. Marks: Hong Kong/on head. Made In/Hong Kong, on backs. Package: Imperial Toy Corp. 1973. $3.00 each. (Courtesy Leslie White)

Hong Kong--8½" "Taffy" Plastic and vinyl. Rooted yellow hair. Painted blue eyes. Open/closed mouth. Original. Marks: Hong Kong, on back. Tag: Made Exclusively for Herman Pecker & Co. Inc./New York NY. 1973. $3.00.

Hong Kong--11½" "Texaco Cheerleader" Plastic and vinyl with rooted yellow blonde hair. Painted blue eyes. Palms down. Tiny high heel feet. Original. Sold as premium with oil change at Texaco stations. 1973. Marks: 56/Hong Kong, on head. Hong Kong, on back. $5.00.

Hong Kong--5" "Picture Pretty Jan" Plastic and vinyl with rooted white hair. Painted blue eyes. Open mouth/nurser. Original. Marks: PC, in square/Hong Kong, on back. 1973. $3.00. (Courtesy Margaret Essler)

Hong Kong--6½" "Balloon Blower" All vinyl with molded blonde hair, molded clothes. Painted features. Freckles. Blows up balloon. Lever on top of hat releases air. Marks: Hong Kong, on head. Made in/Hong Kong, on feet. 1973. $2.00. (Courtesy Leslie White)

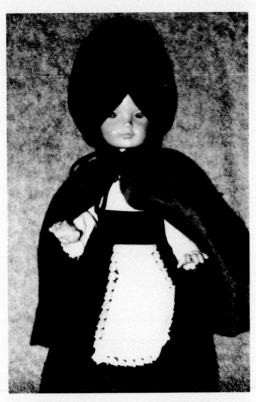

Ireland--8" All plastic with tiny blue sleep eyes. Black floss hair. Painted on shoes and socks. Original. Marks: Clown, in oval/Made in/Republic/Of Ireland/Celtic Toys, on back. 1970. $7.00.

Ireland--8" All plastic with tiny blue sleep eyes. Black floss hair. Painted on shoes and socks. Marks: Clown, in oval/Made in/Republic/Of Ireland/Celtic Toy, on back. 1970. Original. $7.00.

Ireland--8" All plastic with tiny blue sleep eyes. Black floss hair. Painted shoes and socks. Original. Marks: Clown, in oval/Made in/Republic/Of Ireland/Celtic Toys, on back. 1970. $7.00.

Ireland--14" "Crolly Doll" All vinyl with blue sleep eyes. Marks: Crolly Doll/Made in the Republic/of Ireland, on back. Original. 1972. $8.00.

110

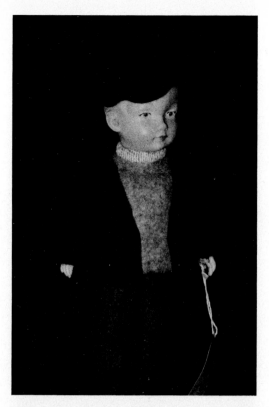

Ireland--11" "Shawn" Plastic and vinyl with molded hair. Inset stationary eyes. Original. Marks: Crolly Doll/Made in the Republic/Of Ireland, on back. Box: Made By/Gaeltarra Eireann. 1972. $8.00.

Ireland--13½" "Erin, and Irish Sovenir Doll" Plastic body and legs. Vinyl head and arms. Rooted dark brown hair. Blue sleep eyes. All original. Tag: One of the Traditional Dolls by/ Shannon Industries Ltd/Made in The Republic of Ireland. 1972. $7.00.

Ireland--8" "Timothy" White plastic one piece body and legs. Pink plastic arms and head. Molded hair. Tiny blue sleep eyes. Original. Marks: Clown, in oval/Made in/Republic/Of Ireland/Celtic/Toys, on back. 1970. $8.00.

Ireland--8" "Leprachaun" White one piece body and legs. Pink plastic arms and head. Chin split for beard. Painted features. Removable clothes. Original. Marks: Clown, in oval/Made in/Re-public/Of Ireland/Celtic Toys. 1973. $9.00.

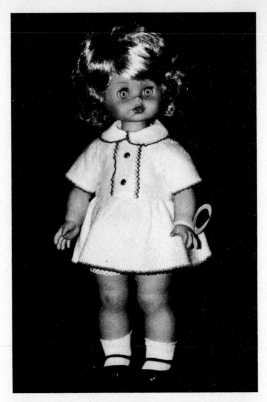

Italy--14" "Bed Doll" All plastic with glued on dark brown wig. Blue sleep eyes. Original. Marks: Franca, on head. Made in Italy by Bom Bole Franca Co. 1959. $6.00.

Foreign--21" "Daniela" Plastic and vinyl. Blue sleep eyes. Rooted blonde hair. Battery operated. Sings and talks with a slight accent. Marks: 2/F, in circle. Box: Daniela/Bombole/Franca/Made in Italy. Original. 1971. $22.00.

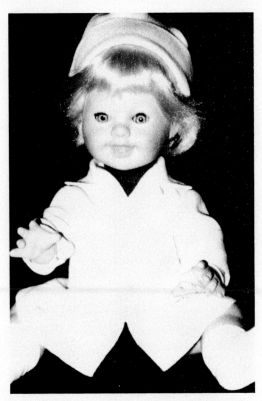

112

Foreign--9" "Bibi" All vinyl. Light brown sleep eyes. Original. Marks: Franca, on head. Made by Effe, Italy/Bombole/Franca. $7.00.

Italy--14" "Smiling Baby" (Called Smiling Tot, 1966) Plastic and vinyl with rooted white hair. Blue sleep eyes. Two molded lower teeth. Marks: 1964/IC, in square/Made In Italy, on back. 1964. Face designed by Bonomi. Made by Italocremona. Original. $10.00. (Courtesy Kathy Walters)

Italy--15" "Mara Beth" All painted plastic over mache. Open dome with mache cover. Glued on dark blonde wig. Amber sleep eyes. Cryer. Marks: Furga/Italy/37, on head. 1953. Original. $22.00. (Courtesy Lita Wilson)

Italy--14" "Arabella" All plastic with glued on brown mohair. Blue sleep eyes. Marks: Furga/Italy, on head. Made in/Italy/Furga, on back. 1954. Original. $22.00.

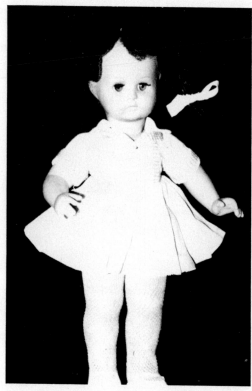

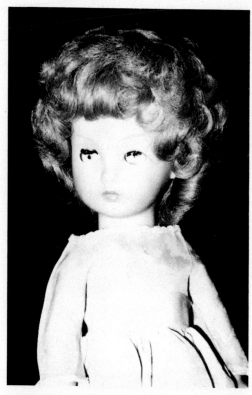

Italy--15" "Nina" All early hard plastic. Open crown with rocker blue sleep eyes. Original dress. Marks: 37, on neck. Tag: Furga/Made in Italy. Imported by American Character in 1957. $22.00.

Italy--16" "Rosella" Plastic body and legs. Vinyl arms and head with rooted blonde hair. Very pale blue eyes. Marks: Made in Italy, on head. 1963 Furga. $8.00. (Courtesy Margaret Weeks)

113

Italy--17" "Sylvie" All vinyl with rooted white hair. Blue stationary eyes. Marks: Furga, Italy, on head. Furga, on back. 1965. Also "Simona" in 1968. $8.00.

Italy--15" "Mariana & Modestino" All vinyl. Rooted silver white hair. Blue sleep eyes. Marks: Furga Italy, on head and back. Both original. Girl is almost identical to marked Jolly Toy (1966) "Cutie." $10.00 each.

Italy--13" "Mary Ella" Plastic and vinyl with rooted knee length hair. Blue sleep eyes. Dimple in right cheek. Original dress. Marks: Furga Italy, on head. Furga/Made in Italy, on back. 1968. $8.00.

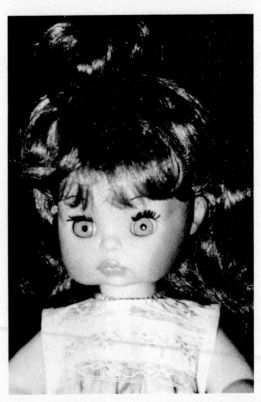

Italy--15" "Claudina" Plastic and vinyl. Rooted blonde hair. Blue sleep eyes. Marks: Furga Italy, on head. 1970. $6.00.

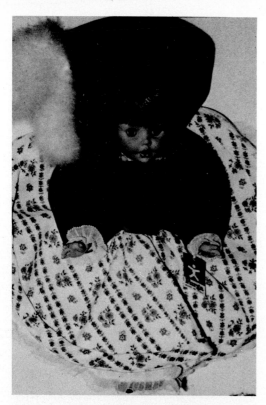

Italy--13" "Clementina" All vinyl with rooted red hair. Pale amber sleep eyes. Original. Marks: Furga Italy, on head. 1972. $30.00.

Italy--19" "Tenderella" Cloth body, upper legs and arms. Vinyl arms and lower legs. Vinyl head with rooted brown hair. Blue sleep eyes. Original. Marks: Furga Italy, on head. L. Furga/ Made in Italy, dress tag. 1973. $15.00.

Italy--5½" "Tilly" Plastic and vinyl. Rooted brown hair. Blue sleep eyes. Original. 1972-3. Marks: 10401/Furga/Italy. $4.00.

Italy--14" "Fiammetta" Plastic and vinyl with rooted orange/red hair. Blue sleep eyes. Freckles. Original. Marks: Furga/7107, on head. Tag: L. Furga/Made in Italy. 1973. $30.00.

115

Italy--20" "Adrain Bambino" All plastic with molded hair. Blue sleep eyes. Baby legs. Open/closed mouth with molded tongue. Original. Sold through WT Grant Co. Marks: picture of stork carrying baby/Made in Italy, on back. 1972. Made by Galba. $5.00.

Italy--21" "Mia Nina" All plastic with molded hair. Blue sleep eyes. Straight legs. Sold through WT Grant Co. Marks: picture of stork carrying baby/Made in Italy. Original clothes. 1972. Made by Galba. $5.00.

Italy--8" "Petro" All plastic with molded hair. Blue sleep eyes. Original. Marks: Picture of Stork/Made in Italy. 1968. Made by Galba. $3.00.

Italy--16" "Bettina" Plastic and vinyl with rooted dark brown hair. Blue sleep eyes. Blue eyeshadow. Young teen figure. Doll is strung. Same body and hands as Shasta dolls. Marks: Sebino, on head. 1968. Made by Tecnogiocattoli. $12.00. (Courtesy Lita Wilson)

116

Italy--17" "Juli" Plastic and vinyl with rooted white hair. Blue sleep eyes. Original. Marks: Girl with braids holding up an M, in oval/Italy, with Migliorati, in a square, on head. Migliorati/ Made in Italy, on back. $9.00. (Courtesy Lita Wilson)

Italy--5½" "Melita" All plastic with glued on black hair. Blue sleep eyes. Beautiful hands. Original. Marks MQ, in diamond with picture of tree. 1967. $4.00.

Italy--11" "Happy Andrina" All vinyl with rooted ash blonde hair. Blue side glancing sleep eyes/lashes. Freckles. Open/closed mouth. Four molded, painted teeth. Dimples. Marks: Ratti/ Made in Italy, on head. Ratti, over picture of two rats sitting up/30/Made in Italy, on back. 1964. Original. $12.00.

Italy--7" "Dutch Boy" & 5½" "Denmark Girl" Both are all hard plastic. All jointed. Glued on wigs. Well made clothes. Marks: "MQ in triangle made in Italy" on back. Label on girl's apron reads Sams & Danmark. $5-$6 each. (Maish Collection)

117

Japan--6" "Shirley Temple" All bisque. Molded hair and painted features. Marks: Japan. ca. 1930's. $25.00. (Courtesy Lucille McKimsy)

Japan--7" "Carnival Lady" All celluloid. Marks: W, in circle/Japan. 1930's. $5.00.

Japan--7" "Suzie May" Tin with celluloid arms and head. Painted googly eyes. Key wind. Three rollers on bottom. As doll moves arms swing and head turns. Original. Marks: ▲/Made in Japan. 1935. $5.00.

Japan--4" "Fat Character Toddler" Original dotted swiss dress. Marks: Japan on back. 1940. $10.00. (Maish Collection)

118

Japan--3½" Molded blue hair ribbon, pink roses on ear. Ribbed socks. Blue shoes. Wired on arms. Impressed made in Occ. Japan. ca. 1940's. $10.00. (Maish Collection)

Japan--5½" All bisque. Wired on arms and legs. Molded and painted hairbow, shoes and socks. Original dress. Marks: Japan, 1940. One of the last of the old time bisques to come from Japan. $15.00. (Maish Collection)

Japan--6" Bisque head, composition body, arms and legs. Squeaker box in tummy. These are the same classic design as the others but are of a later date, perhaps about 1945. $15.00 each. (Maish Collection)

Japan--3" Porcelain Kokeshi Doll, 5" Clay Kokeshi Doll, 7" Wooden Secret Horse decorated with applied paper and cloth. ca. 1950. $5.00-$10.00 each. (Maish Collection)

119

Japan--4" China Afro man and woman. Pierced ears with earrings. "Snow" Coralene hair and trim. 1958. $7.50 pair. (Maish Collection)

Japan--12" "McDare" Plastic body and legs. Vinyl arms and head. Molded brown hair. Brown painted eyes. Marks: G, on head. K56, under left arm. K53, under right arm. McDare/ A.C. Gilbert Co./Japan, on tag. 1965. $5.00.

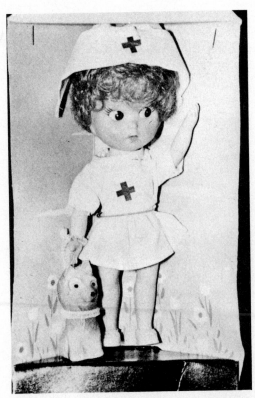

Japan--5½" "My Candy" All plastic. Marks: East West Corp/1966/Japan. Box: My Candy/By Collette/East West Corp. Set had: Dachshund, Terrier, Spitz, Collie, Poodle and Bulldog. Doll came dressed in slacks, dress, Bride, Flowertime, Nurse and leotard, each had a different dog. $3.00. (Courtesy Mary Partridge)

Japan--9½" "Musical Revolving Mimi" Silk over cotton and wire. Jointed neck. Posable arms. Glued on reddish mohair. Large painted blue eyes. Detachable lid music box. Marks: Jaymar Musical Revolving Doll. Original clothes. 1966. $4.00.

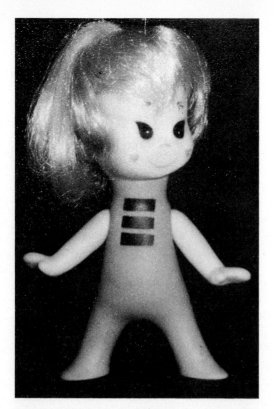

Japan--4½" "Mini, the Martian" All one piece blue vinyl. Painted features. Rooted blonde hair. Marks: J. Swedlin Inc. 1967/Made in Japan, on head and body. Set of six: Prof. Pook, Marti, Mini, Bonnie, Meri & Teenie. Outfits sold separately. $3.00.

Japan--15" "Diana" Silk over cotton and wire, body, arms, legs and head. Glued on silver hair. Large painted blue eyes. Jointed neck. Marks: Jaymar. Original clothes. 1967. $7.00.

Japan--8" "Bimby" Soft plastic body, arms and legs. Vinyl head with rooted blonde hair. Inset stationary blue eyes. Arms and legs are strung. Marks: none. Original clothes. 1967. $2.00.

Japan--11" "Baby Princess" Plastic and vinyl. Molded on socks with attached tin shoes/rollers. Key wind. Rooted blonde hair. Painted features. Marks: Made in/Japan, bottom on foot. Japan, on head. Kanto Toys, in circle/Made in Japan, on back. 1968. $7.00.

121

Japan--8" "Twin Dandy" All vinyl with rooted orange hair. Side glancing painted green eyes. Left eye black. Marks: Japan, bottom of right foot. Original clothes. 1968. $3.00.

Japan--8" "Twin Tandy" All vinyl with rooted orange hair. Painted green eyes that are crossed. Marks: Japan--bottom of right foot. Original clothes. 1968. $3.00.

 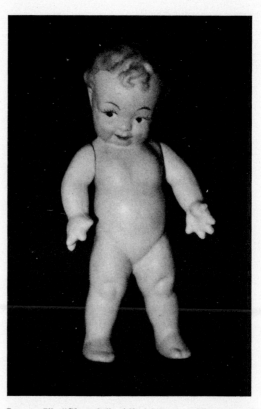

Japan--6" "Popo" All vinyl with rooted white hair. Painted blue eyes and eyeshadow. Vinyl wings. Marks: 169/Kamar Inc./Japan, on head. Tag: My Name is Popo/I Am Made of Love. 1969. $2.00.

Japan--5" "Skeetle" All bisque with jointed shoulders. Marks: none. Paper tag: Copyright/ Shackman/Made in Japan. Box: Skeetle. 1972. $7.00.

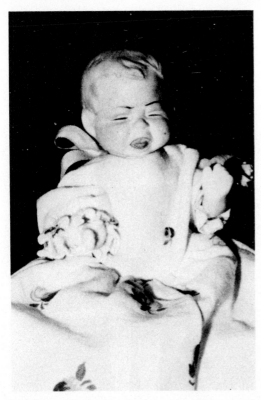

Japan--4½" "Crying Baby" All bisque with molded yellow hair. Painted features. Marks: Copyright/Shackman/Made in Japan, on paper sticker. 1973. $5.00.

Japan--9" "Baby Paula" Plastic body, arms and legs. Vinyl three sided head. Painted features. Plastic knob on top of head makes head turn. Marks: a double circle/Made in/Hong Kong on back. Original top. 1971. $2.00.

Japan--9" "Baby Paula" Showing her unhappy face.

Japan--9" "Baby Paula" Shows her face, asleep.

Japan--9" "Fascination" Vinyl arms and head. Glued on brown hair. Painted blue eyes. Music box in base. Large plastic wind up knob in lower base. As music plays, doll moves in circle. Original. Marks: Japan, on bottom. 1973. $7.00.

Japan--9" "Mannikin Doll" Wood body jointed at shoulders, hips, knees and elbows. Wood hands. Bisque head with molded hair, ribbon and flowers. Head tilted forward. Marks: none. Box: Copyright/Shackman/Made in Japan. 1964 to date. $5.00.

Mexico--9½" "Luisa" All paper mache. String jointed arms and legs. Folk art dolls are colorfully painted shocking pink, fuschia, and peacock blue. One has a ponytail. They were bought in 1964 but I would suppose are still being made. Marks: Made in Mexico. Paid $5.00 each. (Maish Collection)

124

Peru--9" Composition head, legs and arms. Cloth filled body. Painted features. Yarn braids and painted hair. From Lima, Peru. 1969. $22.00. (Maish Collection)

Peru--8" Peruvian man and woman. Composition head, hands and legs. Cloth body. Yarn hair. Authentic costumes of the region. Bought in 1969. $22.00 each. (Maish Collection)

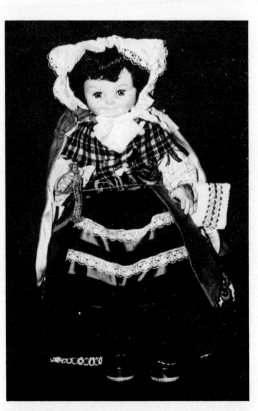

Wales--6" All hard plastic. Jointed arms. Blue sleep eyes. Molded hair. Highlander. Silk taffeta and velvet costume. Hand dressed. Marks: Rogark Made in Wales U.K. 1960. $8.00. (Maish Collection)

Wales--15" "Welsh" All vinyl with sleep eyes. Dimples. Skirt of Brethyn Cartren (Homespun Tweed). Velvet apron, lined with red silk. Paisley pattern back skirt. Red cape, Vigella lined with silk and hood. Lace stockings. Wooden clogs with horse shoe design on bottom. Made in Wales. 1973. $42.00.

125

Fortune Toys--8" "Pam" All hard plastic with glued on blonde saran wig. Blue sleep eyes/ molded lashes. Molded on shoes. Knees not jointed. Walker, head turns. 1955. $8.00.

Fortune Toys--8" "Pam" Early Pam. Not a walker. Molded on shoes. Orginal clothes. Dressed as Little Bo Peep. $8.00.

Fortune Toys--7½" "Pam" All hard plastic. Glued on pale green dynel wig. Turning head walker. Dressed in pale green satin and net ballet outfit. Molded on shoes. 1956. $8.00. (Maish Collection)

Fun World--7" "Sparky" Lavender hair. Marks: Made in/Hong Kong/Fun World Inc/1973. $2.00.

126

Fun World--8" "Flop Tot, The Floppy Moppet" "Bean" stuffed cloth body, arms and legs. Vinyl head, jointed on vinyl neck peg. Molded orange hair. Painted features. Marks: Tag: Floppy Moppet/Fun World. 1972. $1.00.

Fun World--7" "Kitty Coed" Plastic and vinyl with rooted white hair. Painted features. Jointed waist. Original. Marks: Made In/Hong Kong/Fun World/Inc. A Christmas gift from my favorite 10 year old, Leslie White. 1973. $4.00.

Fun World--7" "Sparky Clown" Plastic and vinyl with rooted orange hair. Painted features. Original. Marks: Made in/Hong Kong/Fun World Inc. 1973. $2.00.

Fun World--7" "Sparky" Brown hair. Marks: Made In/Hong Kong/Fun World Inc./1973. $2.00.

Ganda--7½" "Poland" All hard plastic with glued on blonde wig. Large blue sleep eyes/molded lashes. Doll is strung. Original clothes. Marks: 1973 Ganda Toys Ltd/Made in Hong Kong, on back. Dress tag: Foreign Friends/No. 108 Mexico. Base: Made in Hong Kong/Ganda Toys Ltd/Pat. Pend. $3.00.

Ganda--7½" "Mexico" All hard plastic with glued on brown wig. Large brown sleep eyes/molded lashes. Doll is strung. Original clothes. Marks: 1973 Ganda Toys Ltd/Made in Hong Kong, on back. Dress tag: Foreign Friends/No. 106 Mexico. Base: Made in Hong Kong/Ganda Toys Ltd/Pat. Pend. $3.00.

Gem--11" "My Baby" All composition with brown celluloid over tin sleep eyes. Painted lashes below only. Open/closed mouth. Marks: Gem, on head. 1935. $30.00.

Gilbert--11½" "Honeywest" Plastic and vinyl with rooted blonde hair. Painted features. Original. Marks: K99, on head. Made by Gilbert Toys 1965. $10.00.

128

Hasbro--12" "G.I. Joe-Marine." 1965. $5.00 with outfit.

Hasbro--12" "G.I. Joe-Soldier" 1965. $5.00 with outfit.

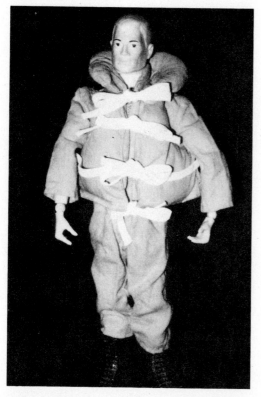

Hasbro--12" "G.I. Joe-Airforce" 1966. $5.00 with outfit.

Hasbro--12" "G.I. Joe-Navy" 1966. $5.00 with outfit.

Hasbro--12" "G.I. Joe Astronaut" 1966. $5.00 with outfit.

Hasbro--G.I. Joe" in snow outfit. 1966. $5.00.

Hasbro--4" "Monkee" All vinyl. Rooted hair. Painted features. Original. Marks: 1967/Hasbro/Hong Kong. $4.00.

Hasbro--4¼" "Dolly Darling" Rooted red hair. Painted green eyes. 1965. $2.00. (Courtesy Mary Partridge)

Hasbro--5" "Jamie" date for Dolly Darling. Marks: 1965/Hasbro/Japan. $3.00. (Courtesy Margaret Weeks)

Hasbro--4¼" "Dolly Darling-Friday" Plastic and vinyl. Molded blonde hair and ribbon. Painted brown eyes. Molded on shoes. Marks: 1965/ Hasbro/Japan, on back. Tag: Dolly Darling/ Hasbro. Also called "Let's Bowl" $2.00.

Hasbro--4¼" "Dolly Darling-Sunday" Rooted yellow hair over molded and painted yellow hair. 1965. $2.00.

Hasbro--4¼" "Dolly Darling-Wednesday" Rooted blonde hair. Painted blue eyes. Outfit also called "Fancy Pants" 1965. $2.00. (Courtesy Mary Partridge)

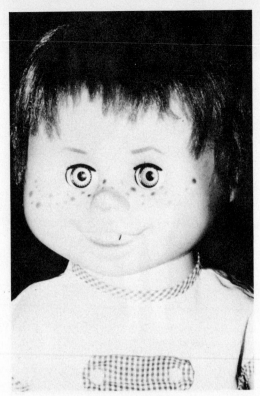

Hasbro--21" "That Kid" Plastic and vinyl with rooted red hair. Blue sleep eyes. Freckles. Two molded upper teeth. Battery operated. Reposition arm, head and he says different things. Built in sling shot in hip pocket, pull and he talks. Marks: Hasbro/1967, on head. Patent Pending/1967 Hasbro, on back. $18.00.

Hasbro--3" "Daisy Darling" All vinyl. Plastic flowers. Orange hair. Brown eyes. Pin. Marks: 1968/Hasbro/Hong Kong. $2.00.

Hasbro--4¼" "Dolly Darling-Saturday Date" Rooted brown hair. Painted brown eyes. 1968. $2.00.

Hasbro--4¼" "Dolly Darling-Sunday" with molded hair. 1968. $2.00. (Courtesy Mary Partridge)

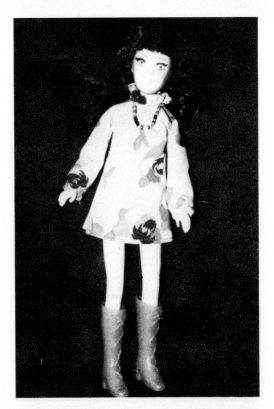

Hasbro--2" "Lily Darling" Of the Flower Darlings. 1968. Included in this set of pins were: Violet, Daphne, Dahlia, Daisy and Rose. $2.00.

Hasbro--9" "Music" One of the World of Love Series. Plastic and vinyl with rooted dark brown hair. Painted blue eyes/lashes. Bendable (snapping) knees. Jointed waist. Smiling mouth. Original. Marks: Made in/Hong Kong/Hasbro/US Pat. Pend, on back. 1971. $9.00. (Courtesy Lisa and Tanya Cowlick)

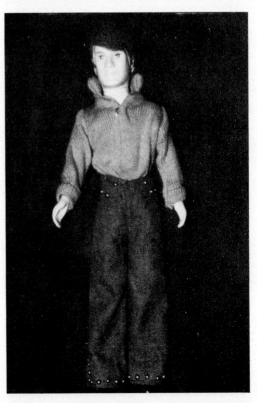

Hasbro--9" "Peace" of the World of Love Group. All vinyl with rooted black hair. Painted brown eyes/lashes. Jointed waist. Original clothes. 1971. Marks: 6/Hong Kong/Hasbro/US Patented, low on back. Tag: The World of/Love by Hasbro/Made in Hong Kong.

Hasbro--9" "Adam" Plastic and vinyl with molded hair. Painted features. Jointed waist and snapping knees. Original. Marks: Hasbro/US Pat Pend/Made in/Hong Kong. 1971. $6.00.

133

Hasbro--9" "Flower" In additional outfit. 1971. $5.00. (Courtesy Grace Cowlick)

Hasbro--9" "Peace" In extra outfit. 1971. $5.00. (Courtesy Grace Cowlick)

Hasbro--9" "Soul" In original different outfit. 1971. $5.00. (Courtesy Grace Cowlick)

Hasbro--9" "Love" In nickers outfit. 1971. $5.00. (Courtesy Grace Cowlick)

Hasbro--9" "Love" In purchased additional outfit. 1971. $5.00. (Courtesy Grace Cowlick)

Hasbro--10" "Leggy Sue" Plastic and vinyl with rooted black hair. Painted brown eyes. Very long legs. Original clothes. One of set of four: Kate, Nan, Sue, Jill. Marks: 1972/Hasbro/Hong Kong, on hip. $4.00.

Hasbro--10" "Leggy Nan" Brown hair. Original clothes. 1972. $4.00.

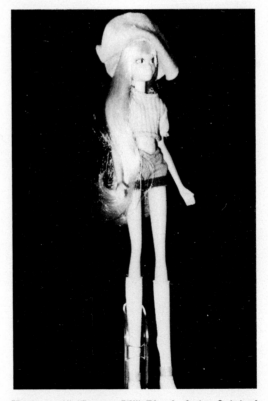

Hasbro--10" "Leggy Jill" Blonde hair. Original clothes. 1972. $4.00.

Hasbro--10" "Leggy Kate" Orange hair. Painted green eyes. Original. 1972. $4.00.

Hasbro--18" "Sweet Cookie" Plastic and vinyl with rooted white hair. Painted blue eyes. Freckles. Painted teeth. Jointed waist, elbows. Original. Marks: Hasbro, Inc/Pat. Pend. 1972, on head. Hasbro/Made in USA, on back. $5.00.

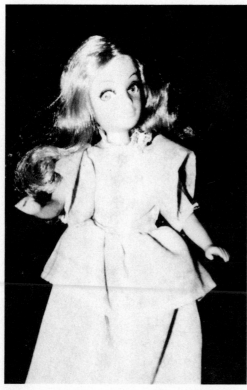

136

Hasbro--9" "Bonnie Breck" Plastic and vinyl. Rooted blonde hair. Large painted blue eyes. Jointed waist. Snapping knees. Med. high heel feet. Original. Marks: Made In/Hong Kong, on back. Tag: Beautiful/Bonnie Breck/Made in Hong Kong. 1972. $6.00. (Courtesy Sharon Hazel)

Hasbro--18" "Aimee" Plastic and vinyl with jointed waist. Brown sleep eyes. Came with extra 6 "designer original" jewelry and hair changes. Marks: Hasbro Inc. 1972. $12.00.

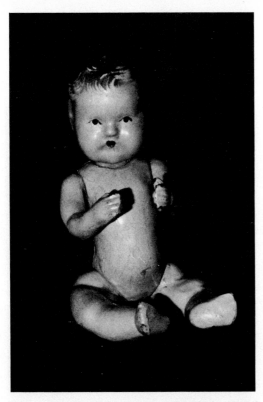

Hollywood--7" All composition. Molded painted brown hair. Painted blue eyes. Marks: Hollywood, on back. $9.00. (Courtesy Connie Snapp)

Hollywood--8" All hard plastic with glued on mohair wig. Blue sleep eyes/molded lashes. Legs are thin and spread far apart. Not a walker. Head fits high on neck. Marks: Star/A Hollywood Doll. $5.00.

Hollywood--9" All composition. Painted features. Glued on auburn wig. Marks: Hollywood Dolls on back. 1945. $6.00. (Maish Collection)

Horsman--18" "Joyce" Cloth body. Composition arms, legs and shoulderplate (unjointed) head. Glued on bright red mohair. Blue tin sleep eyes/lashes. Open mouth with six teeth. Marks: Horsman, on head. Original. 1935. $30.00.

Horsman--14" "Roberta" All composition with molded hair. Painted eyes. Right arm molded in bent position. Original. Marks: Roberta 1937 Horsman. $35.00. (Courtesy Roberta Lago)

Horsman--13" "Jojo" All composition with brown tin sleep eyes. Wig over molded, unpainted hair. Toddler. Marks: Jojo/1937 Horsman. $45.00. (Courtesy Thelma and Joleen Flack)

Horsman--15" "Bright Star" All hard plastic with glued on reddish hair. Blue sleep eyes. Original. Marks: Horsman, on head. 1952. $20.00. (Courtesy Virginia Jones)

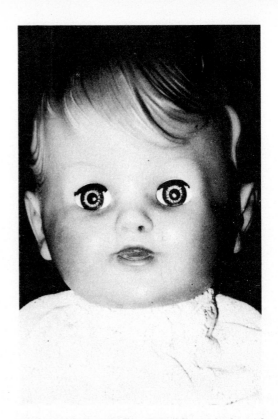

Horsman--15" "Cindy" All hard plastic. Walker, head turns. All original. Marks: 170, on head. 1953. $20.00.

Horsman--26" "Life Size Baby" Latex body with stuffed vinyl head. Blue sleep eyes. Open/closed mouth with molded tongue. 1953. $17.00. (Courtesy Dorothy Westbrook)

Horsman--17" "Cindy" All hard plastic. Bright red hair. Original clothes. Marks: Horsman, on head. 1955. $20.00.

Horsman--18" "Renee Ballerina" by Couturier, a division of Horsman. One piece stuffed vinyl body and legs. Vinyl arms with jointed elbows. Lower arm strung on wooden blocks. Vinyl head. Large blue sleep eyes. High heel feet. Original. Marks: Horsman, on head. $7.00.

139

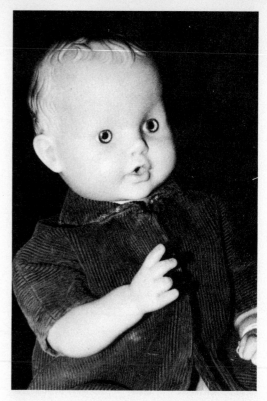

Horsman--3" "Perfume Pixie" All vinyl with rooted white hair. Painted blue eyes to the left. Original. Marks: Hong Kong, on head. Perfume Pixie, on base and other side: Horsman/Made in Hong Kong. $2.00. (Courtesy Mary Partridge)

Horsman--12" "Yvonne, a Lullabye Baby" Plastic and vinyl with molded hair. Inset stationary blue eyes. Nurser. No eyebrows or lashes. Key wind music box. Featured on Art Linkletter T.V. Show. Marks: Can't make them out. Doll designed by Couturier, a Division of Horsman. 1961. $4.00.

Horsman--11½" "Poor & Rich Cinderella" Plastic and vinyl with painted blue eyes. Flat feet. Marks: H, on heads. $5.00 each. (Courtesy Sharon Hazel)

Horsman--15" Plastic body and legs. Vinyl arms and head. Rooted blonde hair. Dark blue sleep eyes/lashes. Open/closed mouth. Marks: 2/Horsman Dolls Inc/Ogigi, on head. Horsman Dolls Inc/Pat. Pend., on back. $6.00.

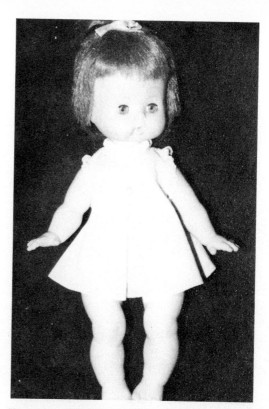

Horsman--16" "Molly" Plastic and vinyl. Brown rooted hair. Blue sleep eyes. Very posable head. Introduced in Spiegles 1961. Marks: Horsman/T 16, on head. New 16/Ball Joint/© bottom of both feet. $8.00. (Courtesy Connie Snapp)

Horsman--11" "Twin Tot" Plastic and vinyl with rooted ash blonde hair. Blue sleep eyes/molded lashes. Nurser. Baby legs. 1963. Marks: 2308/3 Eye/10/Horsman Dolls Inc/07111. $2.00.

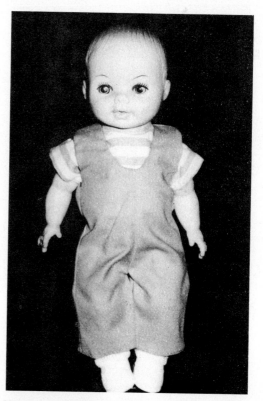

Horsman--11" "Wee Bonnie Baby" Plastic and vinyl with rooted blonde hair. Black pupiless eyes to the side. Marks: 11/11, on head. Horsman Dolls, Inc./T-11, on body. 1963. $2.00.

Horsman--12" "Teensie Baby" Plastic and vinyl. Painted blue eyes. Nurser. Dimpled cheeks. Marks: Horsman Dolls Inc./1964/SA32, on head. Horsman Doll/Pat. Pend., on back. $2.00.

141

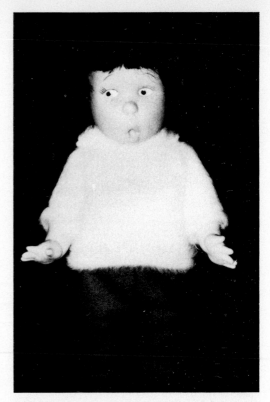

Horsman--18" "Floppy" Foam body and legs. (wire through legs) Vinyl arms and head. Rooted blonde hair. Blue sleep eyes. Dimples. Original. Marks: Horsman Dolls Inc/G6175, on head. Horsman Dolls Inc, on body. 1965. $5.00.

Horsman--12" "Anthony Pipsqueak" Plastic and vinyl with rooted dark brown hair. Painted features. Pipsqueaks came in set of four: Cleo, Mark, Anthony and Patti. Marks: Horsman Dolls Inc/1967/6712-AA/, on head. Horsman Dolls Inc/T-12, on back. $4.00.

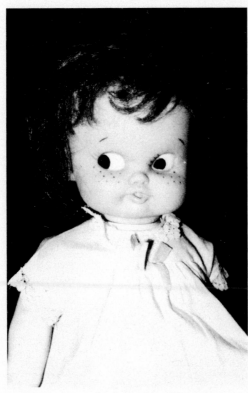

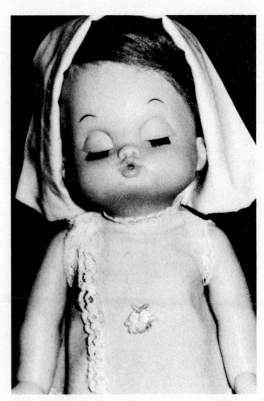

Horsman--12" "Marc Pipsqueak" Plastic and vinyl with rooted red hair. Painted blue side glancing eyes. Freckles. Marks: Horsman Dolls Inc/1967/6712-BB, on head. Horsman Dolls Inc/T12, on back. $4.00.

Horsman--13" "Cleo Pipsqueak" Plastic and vinyl with rooted dark blonde hair. Closed eyes/lashes. Marks: 2/Horsman Dolls Inc/1967/ 6712-OG, on head. Horsman Dolls Inc/T-12, on back. Not original. $4.00.

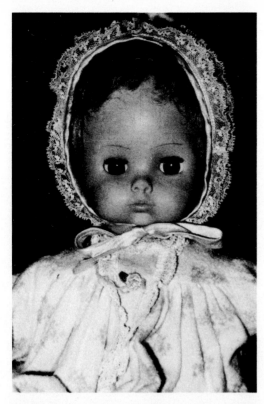

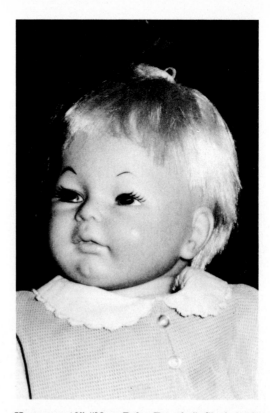

Horsman--17" "Baby Precious" Cloth stuffed body/cryer. Vinyl arms, legs and head. Rooted blonde hair. Blue sleep eyes. Original. Tag: Horsman Dolls Inc. Head: Horsman Dolls Inc/ S-175/13. 1967. $4.00.

Horsman--19" "New Baby Tweaks" Cloth body with vinyl arms, legs and head. Rooted white hair. Blue painted eyes. Open/closed mouth. Marks: 17/Horsman Dolls Inc/1967, on head. $4.00.

Horsman--6" "Tiny Baby" All vinyl. Inset, stationary blue eyes/molded lashes. Open/ closed mouth. Marks: Horsman Dolls Inc/1968, on head. Pants original to basic doll; top from extra clothes set sold with doll. $2.00.

Horsman--4" "Loonie Lite" All vinyl with red plastic eyes and nose. Battery operated. Rubber string attached to top of head. Marks: Horsman/ Doll Inc./1968, on head. 21, on back. $2.00.

143

Horsman--18" "Penny Penpal" Plastic body, arms and legs. Jointed at elbows, waist, hips and shoulders. Vinyl head with rooted white hair. Painted blue eyes. Right hand molded to hold pencil. Came with table and panograph. Marks: 38/Horsman Dolls Inc/1970, on head. Horsman/Dolls/Inc., on back. $5.00.

Horsman--16" "Softy Skin" One piece body, arms and legs of dublon. Vinyl head with rooted white hair. Blue sleep eyes/lashes. Open mouth/nurser. Marks: 3255/15 Eye/39/Horsman Dolls Inc./1971, on head. G/Horsman Dolls Inc., on back. $3.00.

144

Horsman--6½" "Bedknobs and Broomsticks" Plastic and tin bed. Battery operated to "fly." Bed will go half way over an edge and turn directions. Vinyl doll with blonde hair and painted blue eyes. Blue eyeshadow, dimples. Jointed waist. Original. Marks: Taiyo/Pat. Made in Japan, on bed. Hong-Kong, doll head and back. $7.50.

Horsman--18" "Pippi Longstocking" Cloth body vinyl arms, legs and head. Rooted orange hair. Painted features. Freckles. Dimples. Original. Marks: 3508, high on head. 25-3/Horsman Dolls Inc/1972, lower on head. $9.00. (Courtesy Leslie White)

Hubley--10" "Lone Ranger" Plastic with gauntlet vinyl hands. Molded brown hair. Painted blue eyes. Jointed knees, with a knee cap. Jointed between waist and hip. Jointed elbow and wrist. Original. Marks: 1973 Lone Ranger/Tel. Inc./Made in Hong Kong/For Gabriel Ind. Inc. Box: Hubley. $5.00.

Hubley--10" "Tonto" Same as Lone Ranger but has black molded hair and painted blue eyes. Marks: 1973 Tonto/Tel. Inc./Made in Hong Kong/For Gabriel Ind. Inc. Box: Hubley. $5.00.

Hungerford--15" "Baby Wet" Lastic plastic legs and head. Vinyl arms and body, with high neck flange. Blue sleep eyes. Nurser. Dimples. Baby legs. Marks: Hungerford, on neck. 1956. $3.00.

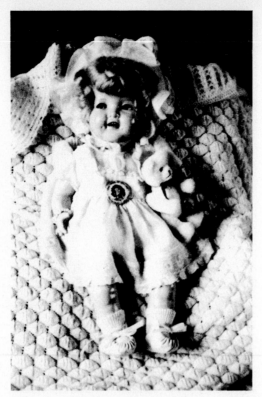

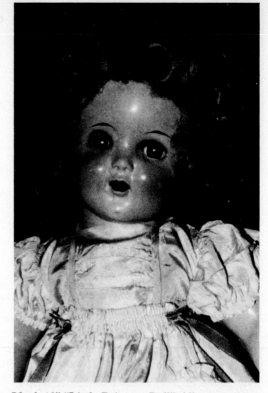

Ideal--16" "Shirley Temple Baby" Marks: Shirley Temple, on head. Original pin says: The Worlds Darling/Genuine Shirley Temple Doll. Cloth and composition. Flirty eyes. $120.00. (Courtesy Roberta Lago)

Ideal--18" "Little Princess Doll" All composition with glued on blonde hair in ringlets. Green (not flirty) sleep eyes. Open mouth/four teeth. Dimple in chin. Original minus tiara. Marks: Shirley Temple (Straight)/18, on back. Dress tag: Rayon/An Ideal Doll. 1938. $65.00. (Courtesy Alma Carmichael)

146

Ideal--18" "Snow White" All composition with glued on black wig. Flirty green eyes. Lashes painted on bottom only. Light black eyeshadow. Open mouth with four teeth. Dimple in chin. Copy of original clothes. Marks: Shirley Temple/18 on back. 1938. $75.00. (Courtesy Pearl Clasby)

Ideal--18" "Judy Garland" As Dorothy of the Wizard of Oz. All composition with glued on human hair. Hair is a red/brown. Brown sleep eyes. Open mouth with six teeth. Original dress. Marks: Ideal Doll, on head. 18/Ideal Doll/Made in USA, on back. 11/18, on upper left arm. 10, on upper arm. 18, inside both legs. Paper dress tag: 17. 1939. $85.00. (Courtesy Alice Capps)

Ideal--22" Composition head, arms and legs. Cloth body. Brown sleep eyes, four teeth. Red gold hair. Dimpled chin. 1935. In beautiful condition. $35.00. (Maish Collection)

Ideal--13" "Shirley" All composition. All jointed. Original mohair wig. All original clothing. Mint condition and never played with. Marks: Shirley Temple-13 on head and back. ca. 1936. $45.00. (Maish Collection)

Ideal--18" "Shirley" All composition, all jointed, original mohair wig, eyes. Marks: Very large lettering Shirley Temple-18 on back. Curved Shirley Temple Cap Ideal N&T Co on head. 1940. $55.00. (Maish Collection)

Ideal--16" All composition. Glued on mohair wig, blue green sleep eyes, four teeth. All original shoes, socks, underwear, dotted swiss dress and bonnet. Although this particular doll is plainly marked "Nancy" on the head, not all are and sadly has been extensively sold as "unmarked" Shirley. All mint and original. $35.00. (Maish Collection)

147

Ideal--18" All composition. Brown sleep eyes. Brown mohair braids. Shirley Temple body. Dimpled chin. Marks: none. $25.00. (Maish Collection)

Ideal--15" "First Magic Skin Baby" 1942. Latex, fully jointed. Composition head. Nurser. Blue sleep eyes. Dimples in chin. Marks: none. 1941. $6.00.

Ideal--22" "Talking Tot" Cloth and vinyl with a hard plastic head. Had wig glued on over molded hair. Blue sleep eyes. Key wind talker. Laughs and when laying down, cries. Marks: none. 1950. By Shilling Co. $12.00.

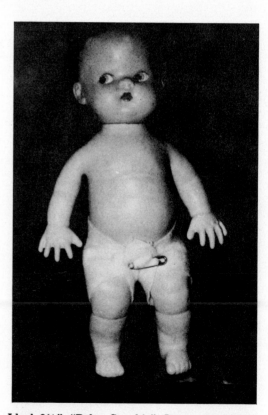

Ideal--9½" "Baby Snookie" Latex one piece body, arms and legs. Early vinyl head with molded hair. Painted blue eyes to the side. Original. Came also as twins. Marks: Ideal Doll, on head. Box: Snookie/Ideal's/Baby Doll/With the/Life Like/Features. 1950. $4.00.

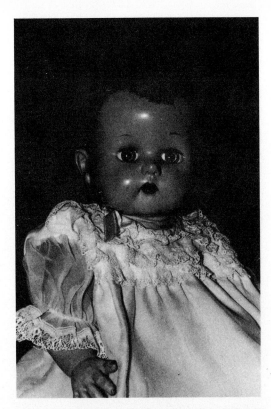

Ideal--19" "Baby Gurglee" in 1951 and "Tousle Head" in 1953. Hard plastic head. One piece latex body and legs. Latex disc jointed arms. Blue sleep eyes. Squeeze "coo" voice. Red caracul wig over molded hair. Marks: none. $9.00.

Ideal--15" "Peggy" *(unverified name) All hard plastic. Blonde very full mohair wig. Blue sleep eyes. Individual fingers, clearly defined nails. Matte complexion. $35.00. (Maish Collection)

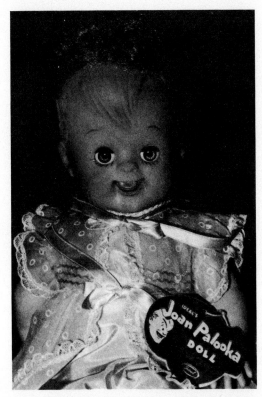

Ideal--14" 'Joan Palooka" Latex with disc jointed arms. Early vinyl head with molded blonde hair. Tuft of yellow saran hair on top. Blue sleep eyes. Original. Marks: 1952/Ham Fisher/Ideal Doll, on head. Tag: Ideal's/Joan Palooka/Doll. $18.00. (Courtesy Virginia Jones)

Ideal--21" "Sara Ann" All hard plastic with glued on yellow saran hair. Blue sleep eyes. Not a walker. Original. Marks: P93/Ideal Doll/Made in USA, on head. Ideal Doll/P93, on back. 1952. $20.00. (Courtesy Virginia Jones)

149

Ideal--15" "Mary Hartline" All hard plastic with glued on blonde wig. Blue sleep eyes. Eyeshadow over and under eyes. Original clothes. Marks: Ideal USA, head. Ideal Doll/P91, on back. 1952. $25.00.

Ideal--22" "Saucy Walker" In an original outfit. Marks: Ideal Doll, on head. 1953. $18.00.

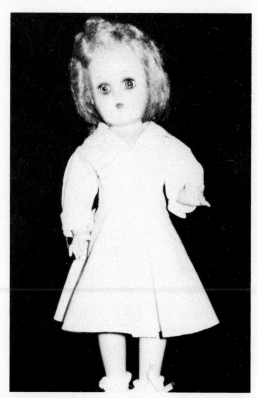

Ideal--14" "Miss Curity" All hard plastic. Blue sleep eyes. Black eyeshadow above and below eyes. Marks: P-90. Miss Curity and Mary Hartline are "Toni" dolls but have the dark eyeshadow. Original dress. $25.00.

Ideal--19" "Patty Petite" Rigid vinyl body, arms and legs. Vinyl head with rooted dark brown hair. Blue sleep eyes. Posable head. Marks: Ideal Toy Corp/G-18, on head. (Also sold as "Tiny Patti" Play Pal) $22.00. (Courtesy Irene Gann)

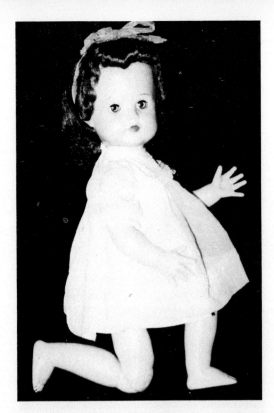

Ideal--23" "Posie" Hard plastic with vinyl head. Rooted brown hair. Blue sleep eyes. Marks: Ideal Doll/VP-23, on head. Ideal Doll, on back. Pat. Pending, on upper section of each leg. $20.00. (Courtesy Connie Snapp)

Ideal--18" "Miss Revlon" Dressed in "Cherries Ala Mode" outfit. Marks: Ideal Doll/VT-18. 1955. $22.00.

Ideal--19" "Shirley Temple" Vinyl. Flirty eyes. Marks: Ideal Dolls/ST-19, on head. Ideal Doll/ST-19, on body. Dress tag: Shirley Temple/ Made by Ideal Toy Corp. Arm tag: Twinkle eyes baby doll Ideal/Featuring/flirting rolling eyes/vinyl head/rooted hair/made by Ideal Toy Corp. $35.00. (Courtesy Roberta Lago)

Ideal--17" "Shirley Temple" Vinyl. Marks: Ideal Doll/ST17-1, on head. Ideal Doll/ST 17, on back. All original, as "Heidi." 1958. $20.00. (Courtesy Roberta Lago)

Ideal--35" "Shirley Temple" Vinyl. All original except bow in hair. Marks: Ideal Doll/ST-35-38-2 on head. Ideal/35, in oval, on back. $80.00.

Ideal--10½" "Little Miss Revlon" Vinyl head, rooted blonde hair, plastic body, swivel waist, high heel feet. Pierced ears. Marks: Ideal VT 10½. 1957. $14.00. (Maish Collection)

Ideal--12" "Mitzi" Plastic and vinyl with rooted red/brown hair. Painted blue eyes/molded lashes. Marks: Mitzi/Ideal Toy Corp/MCMLX/2 on back. $7.00.

Ideal--9" "Patti" Plastic and vinyl with rooted brown hair. Painted blue eyes. Marks: Ideal Toy Corp/G-9-L, on head. Ideal Toy Corp/G-9-W/2, on back. $5.00.

Ideal--19" Plastic body with vinyl arms, legs and head. Blue sleep eyes/lashes. Dimples in cheeks and chin. Arms are ball jointed and strung. Marks: Ideal Doll/B-19-1. $6.00.

Ideal--36" "Patti Playpal" 1961. Also sold in the talking version as "Mary Christmas" through Spiegels, 1961. Plastic and vinyl with blue sleep eyes. Rooted blonde hair. Marks: Ideal Doll/G-35, on head. Ideal (in an oval)/35, on back. $45.00. (Courtesy Marjorie Pine)

Ideal--16" "Lovely Liz" Also sold as "Jackie" 1961 (in sheath checkered dress and short jacket) Plastic and vinyl with blue sleep eyes. Very beautiful hands and fingers. Original. Marks: Ideal Toy Corp/G 15-L, on head. Ideal Toy Corp/M-15, on back. $8.00 (Courtesy Lita Wilson)

Ideal--12" "Tammy" In school outfit. Marks: Ideal Toy Corp/BS 12, head and body. Dress tag: Tammy. 1962. $5.00.

153

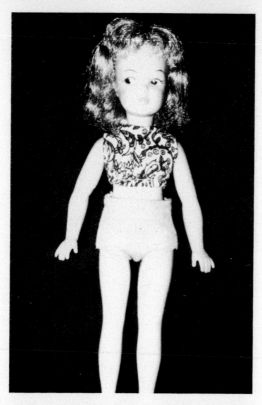

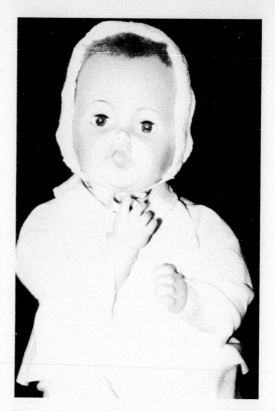

Ideal--9" "Tammy" in an original two piece bathing suit. 1962. $5.00. (Courtesy Leslie White)

Ideal--21" "Rock Baby Coo's" Cloth and vinyl with rooted ash blonde hair. Blue sleep eyes. Open, yawning mouth with molded tongue. Marks: Ideal Toy Corp/YTT-19-L-5, on head. 1962. $6.00.

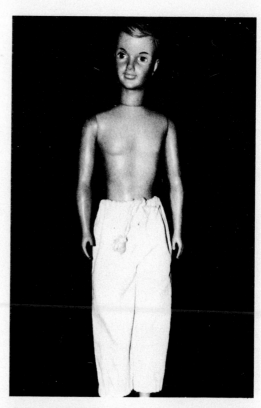

Ideal--12" "Tammy's Mom" Plastic and vinyl with rooted blonde hair. Painted blue eyes. High heel feet. Marks: Ideal Toy Corp/W-18-L, on head. Ideal Toy Corp/W-13, on back. Dress tag: Petite Fashions/By Debutante. $8.00. (Courtesy Yvonne Baird)

Ideal--12½" "Ted" Tammy's brother. Plastic and vinyl with painted brown hair. Marks: Ideal Toy Corp/B-12-U-2, on head. Ideal Toy Corp/B12½, on back. 1963. $8.00.

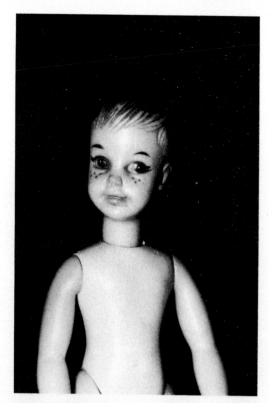

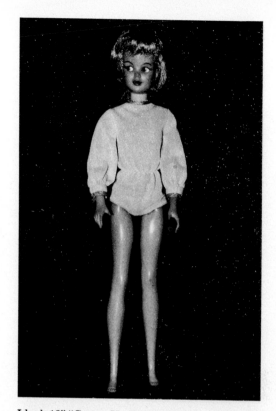

Ideal--7½" "Pos'N Pete" Plastic and vinyl with molded brown hair. Painted brown eyes. Freckles. Marks: 1964/Ideal Toy Corp/P-8, on back. 1964/Ideal Toy Corp, on head. $7.00.

Ideal--12" "Grown Up Tammy" Plastic and vinyl. Rooted blonde hair. Painted blue eyes. Medium heel feet. Marks: 1964/Ideal Toy Corp/T 12-E, on head. 1965/Ideal (in oval)/T-12, on back, with 1, lower down. $8.00. (Courtesy Yvonne Baird)

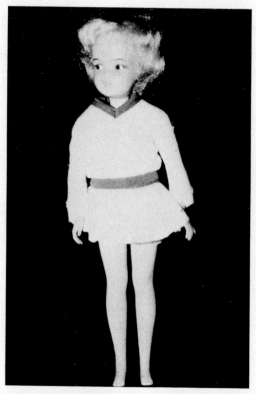

Ideal--9" "Pepper" Plastic and vinyl with rooted blonde hair. Painted features. Freckles. Original. Marks: Ideal Toy Corp/P9-3, on head. 1964/Ideal, in oval/L DO-P, on back. Tag: Pepper/Ideal. $5.00.

Ideal--9" "Dodi" Plastic and vinyl with rooted ash blonde hair. Painted blue eyes. Marks: 1964/ Ideal Toy Corp/DO-9-E, on head. 1964/Ideal Toy Corp/DO-9, on back. $7.00.

155

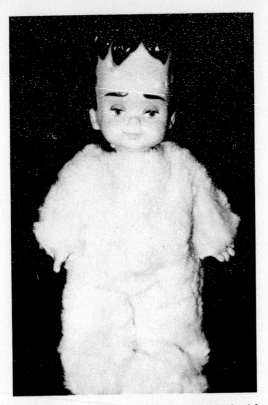

Ideal--12" "Samantha, The Witch" Plastic and vinyl with rooted white hair. Green eyes looking straight ahead. Knees do not bend. Original dress, minus hat and broom. Marks: Ideal Toy Corp/M-12-E-2, on head. 1965/Ideal (in oval)/M-12, on hip with a 1, lower down. $8.00 (Courtesy Yvonne Baird)

Ideal--9" "Baby Herman" Plastic and vinyl with molded hair. Painted features. Marks: 1965/Ideal Toy Corp/M-8¼, on head. Made in Japan, on back. $4.00.

Ideal--20" "Real Live Lucy" All vinyl with rooted white hair. Blue sleep eyes. Head on weight, whenever touched, bobs. Original dress. Marks: 1965/Ideal Toy Corp/FL-20-H-33, on head. $6.00.

Ideal--27" "Talking Goody Two Shoes" Plastic and vinyl with rooted ash blonde hair. Blue sleep eyes/long lashes. Very large feet. Battery operated. Says: "My Name is Goody Two Shoes. I know a cat named Halloween," etc. Marks: 1966/Ideal Toy Corp/WT-27-H-50, on head. $22.00.

Ideal--11½" "Captain Action" Plastic and vinyl with jointed elbows, wrists, waist, knees and ankles. This is face mask sold with separate clothes. Marks: Ideal Toy Corp/M-18 1966, on head. 1966/Ideal Toy Corp/1, on back. Tag: Captain Action/1966 Ideal, in oval/Hong/Kong. $4.00.

Ideal--Captain Action in original outfit. 1966. $4.00.

Ideal--Captain Action in Batman outfit. 1966. $4.00.

Ideal--5" "Trixy Flatsy" All vinyl with rooted black hair. Painted features. Came in frames. Set of nine: Sandy, Cookie, Candy, Bonnie, Filly, Dewie, Rally and Nancy. Marks: 1968/Ideal Toy Corp. $2.00. Doll only, $7.00 complete.

157

Ideal--5" "Casey Flatsy" All vinyl with molded red hair. Painted features. Freckles. Original. Marks: Ideal, in oval/1969/Pat. Pending/Hong Kong. $2.00 doll only. $7.00 complete.

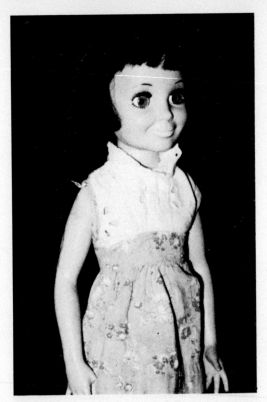

Ideal--18" "Tressy" Plastic and vinyl with rooted black hair with grow feature. Blue sleep eyes. Blue eyeshadow. Marks: 1969/Ideal Toy Corp/GH-18/US Pat 3162976, on hip. 1970/Ideal Toy Corp/SGH-17-HL6L/Hong Kong, on head. $6.00.

Ideal--18" "Kerry" Plastic and vinyl with rooted blonde hair with grow feature. Basic blue sleep eyes. Marks: 13 EYE/1970/Ideal Toy Corp/NGH-18-H-172/Hong Kong, on head. 1969/Ideal Toy Corp/GH-18/US Pat 3162976, on hip. $6.00.

Ideal--5" "Filly Flatsy" All vinyl with rooted orange hair. Painted features. Original. Marks: Ideal, in oval/1969/Pat Pend/Hong Kong. $2.00 doll only. $7.00 complete.

Ideal--4" "Baby Flatsy" All vinyl with rooted yellow hair. Painted features. Original. Marks: Ideal/1969/Pat. Pend. $2.00. (Courtesy Mary Partridge)

Ideal--5" "Spinderella Flatsy" All vinyl with rooted blonde hair. Painted features. Bendable and can be posed. Foot fits in stand that is pull string operated. Marks: Ideal, in an oval, /1969/Pat. Pend./Hong Kong, on back. 1970/ Ideal Toy Corp/Hong Kong, on stage. Original clothes. $4.00.

Ideal--2½" "Lemonade Flatsies" All vinyl. Girl: Brown hair. Green eyes. Boy: Molded yellow hair. Brown eyes. Original. 1969. $3.00.

Ideal--3" "Play Time Flatsy" Original. Pink hair/blue eyes. Black hair/brown eyes. 1970. $2.00 doll only. $7.00 complete.

Ideal--3" "Slumber Time Flatsy" Brown hair/green eyes. Blue hair/blue eyes. 1970. $2.00 doll only. $7.00 complete.

Ideal--4½" "Nancy Flatsy" Long brown hair. Painted blue eyes to the right. 1970. $2.00 doll only. $7.00 complete.

Ideal-4½" "Rally Flatsy" Green hair. Painted blue eyes to the right. 1970. $2.00 doll only. $7.00 complete.

Ideal--4½" "Bonnie Flatsy" Pink hair. Painted blue eyes to the right. 1970. $2.00 only. $7.00 complete.

Ideal--4½" "Candy Flatsy" Brown hair. Painted blue eyes to the right. 1970. $2.00 doll only. $7.00 complete.

Ideal--18" "Brandi" Plastic and vinly with rooted blonde hair with grow feature. Suntan skin tones. Painted blue eyes. Small heart painted on right cheek. Swivel waist moves back and forth as well as side to side. Marks: 1971/Ideal Toy Corp/GHB-18-H-185/Hong Kong, on head. 1971/Ideal Toy Corp/MG-18/US Pat 3-162-978, on back. $10.00.

Ideal--4½" "Cookie Flatsy" Pink hair. Painted blue eyes to the right. 1970. $2.00 doll only. $7.00 complete.

Ideal--15½" "Mia" Plastic and vinyl with rooted dark brown hair, with grow feature. Blue sleep eyes. Original. Marks: 1970/Ideal Toy Corp/NGH-15-H173, on head. $6.00.

Ideal--15½" "Cricket" Plastic and vinyl with rooted red hair with grow feature. Brown sleep eyes. Jointed waist. Original clothes. Marks: 1970/Ideal Toy Corp/CR-15-H-177/Hong Kong, on back. $6.00. (Courtesy Leslie White)

Ideal--Black and white "Velvets" Both original. 1970. $6.00.

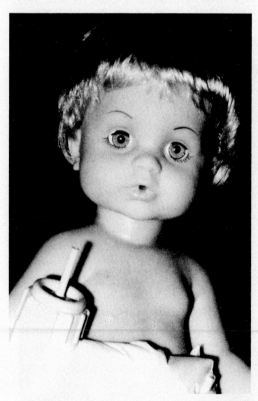

162

Ideal--13" "New Tiny Tears" All vinyl. Only jointed at neck. Rooted blonde hair. Blue inset eyes/lashes. Nurser. Special bottle fills (reservoir) as doll is upright, when on back she cries tears and stops when picked up. Dressed only in disposable diaper. Marks: 1971/Ideal Toy Corp/TNT-14-B-34, on back. $4.00.

Ideal--9" "Baby Belly Button" All vinyl with rooted black hair. Painted brown eyes. Large plastic belly button makes legs, arms and head move. Marks: 1970/Ideal Toy Corp./E9-2-H-165/ Hong Kong, on head. Ideal Toy Corp/Hong Kong/2A-0156, on back. Original clothes. $4.00.

Ideal--12" "Cinnamon" Plastic and vinyl with rooted red grow feature, hair. Painted blue eyes. Original clothes. Marks: 1971/Ideal Toy Corp/GH-12-H-183/Hong Kong, on head. 1972/Ideal Toy Corp/US Pat. 3162976, on back. $6.00.

Ideal--17" "Busy Lizy" Plastic and vinyl. Rooted white hair. Blue sleep eyes. Plug in, in back. Marks: 1971/Ideal Toy Corp/HK-18, on back. 1970/Ideal Toy Corp/HK-18-H-171, on head. $22.00.

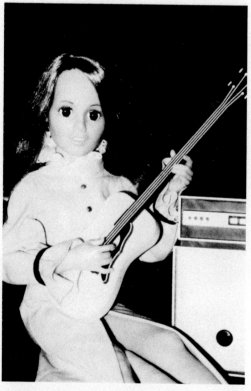

Ideal--15" "Upsy-Dazy" Foam body and legs. Vinyl head with rooted hair. Painted features. Non-removable clothes. Plastic arms. Hold upright and rock back and forth a few times, stand on head with arms and feet flat, she flips over. Marks: 1972/Ideal Toy Corp/UD-H-221/Hong Kong, on head. Tag: Upsy Dazy. $5.00.

Ideal--21" "Harmony" Plastic and vinyl with rooted frosted red hair. Brown stationary eyes/lashes. Jointed elbows. Original. Arms and head move. Battery operated. Amplifier plugs into back. Marks: H-2000/1971 Ideal, in oval, on head. 1972/Ideal Toy Corp, on back. $12.00.

163

Ideal--7" "Evel Knievel" All vinyl. Completely bendable. Plastic hands and feet/shoes, inserted by plastic rods so they are "jointed". Molded hair. Painted features. An original outfit (came in three). Marks: 1972 Ideal, in oval/Hong Kong, on hip. $4.00.

Ideal--15½" "Look Around Velvet" Plastic and vinyl. Rooted blonde hair with grow feature. Lavender sleep eyes. Pull string operated. Moves at waist and head. Original. Marks: 1969/Ideal Toy Corp/GH 15-H-157/Hong Kong, on head. 1972/Ideal Toy Corp/Hong Kong/US Pat. No. 3162976/Other Patents Pending, on back. $6.00.

Ideal--18" "Look Around Crissy" Plastic and vinyl with rooted red hair with grow feature. Painted brown eyes. Pull string moves waist and head. Marks: 1968/Ideal Toy Corp/G-H-18-H129, on head. 1972 Ideal Toy Corp/Hong Kong/US Pat. No. 3162976/Others Patents Pending. Original. $6.00.

Ideal--17" "Shirley Temples" for comparison. Left is the 1972 issue in plain unmarked box. Right is the "new" Shirley Temple, in box that is designed with many pictures of Shirley. Legs on early doll are vinyl and ones on later dolls are plastic. Left: body marks: 1971/Ideal Toy Corp/ST-14-H-213. Left: $14.00. Right: $10.00.

Imperial Toy Corp--5" "Pan Am Air Hostess" Plastic and vinyl with rooted blonde hair. Painted features. Original, non-removable clothes. Marks: none. Box: Imperial Toy Corp/1971/Made in/Hong Kong. $2.00.

Imperial Toy Corp--5" "Jal Air Hostess" Plastic and vinyl with rooted black hair. Painted features. Original, non-removable clothes. Marks: none. Box: Imperial Toy Corp/1971/Made in/Hong Kong. $2.00.

Imperial Toy Corp--5" "BOAC Air Hostess" Plastic and vinyl with rooted light brown hair. Painted features. Original, non-removable clothes. Marks: none. Box: Imperial Toy Corp/1971/Made in/Hong Kong. $2.00.

Jolly Toys--14" "Little Love" Plastic and vinyl. Rooted blonde hair. Blue sleep eyes/lashes. Original. Marks: Jolly Toys Inc./1962, on head. $3.00.

Jolly Toys--15" "Lovely Lisa" Cloth body with vinyl arms, legs and head. Rooted white hair. Blue sleep eyes/lashes. Marks: 14/4/Jolly Toy Inc., on head. Original dress. 1962. $3.00.

Jolly Toys--12" "Miss Grow-Up" Plastic and vinyl with rooted blonde hair. Inset stationary eyes. Molded, shaped lashes. Molded eyebrows that are painted over. Marks: Jolly Toys Inc/ 1963, on head. 1963/Jolly Toys Inc, on back. $4.00.

Jolly Toys--14" "Kimberly" Plastic and vinyl with rooted blonde hair. Painted blue eyes. Original. 1972. Sold as "Playmate for the Children of Aquarius" Marks: Hong Kong, on paper sticker, on head. $5.00.

Joy Doll Co.--8" All composition, painted eyes and molded hair under red mohair wig. Painted shoes. Swivel neck; arms and legs jointed. Tag: Shelia from Ireland Joy Doll Corp. NYV New York Worlds Fair 1939. $18.00 (Maish Collection)

Joy Doll Co.--8" Composition. All jointed. Swivel neck. Painted eyes and hair. Molded socks and slippers. Marks: none. Original yellow organdy dress, underclothes. 1939. $18.00. (Maish Collection)

Kay Stan--13½" "Terri Ann Meuson, Miss America 1971" Plastic and vinyl with rooted brown hair. Brown painted eyes. Dimples far out on cheeks. Original. Marks: Kaystan/1971, on head. Hong Kong, on body. Company plans on changing heads each year, to be a portrait series of beauty queens. $18.00. (Courtesy Lita Wilson)

KAYSTAN
KENNER

Kenner--9" "Steve Scout" Plastic and vinyl. Painted blue eyes. Gives Scout salute when right arm is raised. Marks: 1974 GMFGL/Kenner Prod./Cinti. Ohio 45202/NO 7000/Made In Hong Kong, lower back. $7.00.

167

Kenner--18" "Crumpet" Plastic and vinyl with rooted blonde hair. Blue sleep eyes. Jointed wrists and waist. Holds tea pot in left hand, plate in right. Battery and pull string operated. Marks: 1970/Kenner Products Co/235-225, on head. 1970. Kenner/Products Co/Cincinnati, Ohio/Patent Pending/Made in Hong Kong. $5.00.

Kenner--11½" "Blythe" Plastic and vinyl with rooted blonde hair. Jointed waist. Pull string operated, makes eyes change position and color. Green, pink, blue and yellow. Original. Marks: Blythe TM/Kenner Products/1972 General Mills/Fun Group Inc/Patents Pending/Made in Hong Kong. Dress tag: Blythe TM/By Kenner. $5.00. (Courtesy Leslie White)

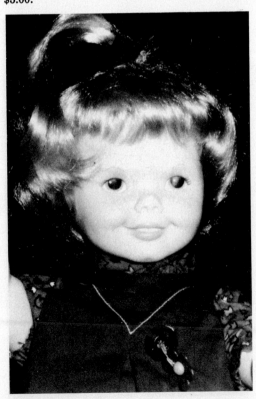

Kenner--18" "Gabbigale" Plastic and vinyl with rooted blonde hair. Painted blue eyes. Pull string in chest. Battery operated. Repeats anything you say. Marks: 1972/Kenner Products Co/99, on head. Gabbigale/1972 Kenner Products/General Mills/Fun Group Inc/Patents Pending, on back. Dress tag: Gabbigale/Made in Kong Kong. $6.00.

Kenner--7" "Meadow, of the Garden Gal Series" All vinyl with rooted brown hair. Painted brown eyes. Right arm molded bent to hold watering can. Came with pots and seeds. Original. Marks: Garden Gal/By/Kenner/Hong Kong, on back. Box: Distributed By/1972 Kenner Products/A Div. of General Mills/Fun Group, Inc. $4.00.

Knickerbacher--12" "Hy Finance" All plastic with velour face and hands. Felt features. Jointed arms and legs. Original. Marks: Tag: Hy Finance/Knickerbacher Toy Co. Set of 3 Whimsical Jointed Dolls: Terry Troll, Hy Finance and Kookie Klown. 1971. $4.00.

Knickerbacher--15" "Sleeping Beauty" All composition. All original except shoes. 1939. $48.00. (Courtesy Mary Partridge)

Libby--20" "I Dream Of Jeannie" as portrayed by Barbara Eden. Plastic and vinyl with rooted, frosted blonde hair. Blue sleep eyes. Original clothes. Marks: 4/1966/Libby, on head. Box: Sidney Sheldon Productions Inc. 1966/Libby Majorette Doll Corp/Exclusive Mfg. $18.00.

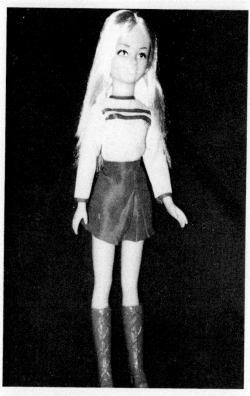

LJN--18" "Pamela" in another original outfit. 1973. $6.00.

169

LJN--12" "Mister Action" Plastic and vinyl with jointed waist. Dark skin tones. Molded hair. Painted blue eyes. Marks: Hong Kong, on back. Originally came in a camouflaged swimsuit. 1967. $4.00.

LJN--7½" "Mike, Terry and Willie of the Rookies" Plastic and vinyl. Fully jointed. Marks: ⌂ LJN Toys/Hong Kong. 1974. $3.00 each.

LJN--7½" "John and Roy of the TV Emergency Squad" Plastic and vinyl. Completely jointed. Torso, under jointed waist is actually molded white jockey shorts. Slightly open/closed mouth with unpainted teeth area. Original. Made in 1973 for the 1974 marked. Marks: ⌂LJN Toys Ltd/Hong Kong/All Rights Reserved. Brown molded hair and painted blue eyes. $3.00 each.

LJN--18" "Pamela, Fashion Doll" Plastic and vinyl. Rooted white hair. Painted blue eyes. Blue eyeshadow. Original. Marks: Hong Kong, on head. Box: Made Exclusively For L.J.N. Toys Ltd. 1973. $6.00. (Courtesy Lita Wilson)

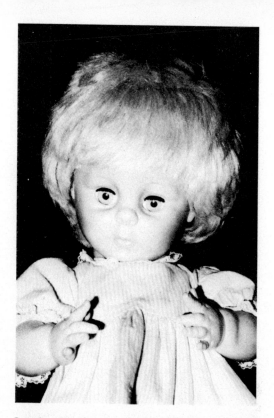

Lorrie--14" "Bonnie Jean" Plastic and vinyl with rooted blonde hair. Tiny blue sleep eyes. Nurser. Toddler legs. Marks: Lorrie Doll Inc/ 1961, on head. $4.00.

Lorrie--19" "Sweet Candy" Plastic and vinyl with rooted blonde hair. Blue sleep eyes. Crossed baby legs. Head molded in downward position. Marks: Lorrie Doll/1964, on head. $4.00.

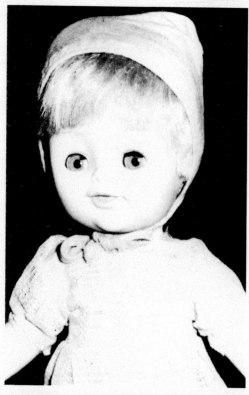

Lorrie--15" "Debbie Trix" Plastic and vinyl. Brown sleep eyes. Dimple in chin. Painted black area on head; came with three wigs: red/black/ brown. Marks: Lorrie Doll Co. Inc./1964 (backward 4). $6.00.

Lorrie--11½" "Mary Jane" Plastic body and legs. Vinyl arms and head. Rooted blonde hair. Blue sleep eyes/lashes. Open/closed mouth. Palms down. Marks: Lorrie Doll/1966, on head. $2.00.

171

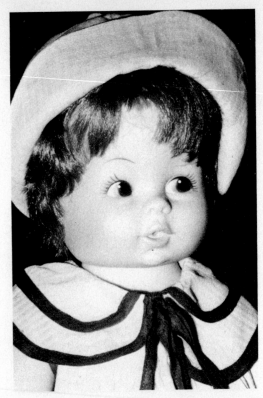

Lorrie--19" "Pretty" (Sold with 2 other "family" dolls, an 11" baby and 9½" teen) Plastic and vinyl with rooted red hair. Blue sleep eyes. Marks: Lorrie Doll/1966. $4.00.

Lorrie--15" "Powder Puff" All one piece plastic body, arms and legs. Vinyl head with rooted red hair. Painted blue eyes. Nurser. Marks: Lorrie Doll/1971, on back. Lorrie Doll/1971/11, on head. $3.00.

Unmarked--21" Composition head, arms and legs. Cloth body. Blonde mohair wig. Brown tin eyes, four teeth, felt tongue. This is obviously a Bernard Lipfert head and an unauthorized "Shirley." The hair suggests Shirley and the original dress with the stars on the bodice implies "movie star!" Same era, 1935. $45.00. (Maish Collection)

Unmarked--11" "Marie Antonnette" All composition. Glued on white wig. Painted features. 2nd and 3rd fingers molded together. Marks: none. 1935. $15.00.

Unmarked--19" Toddler. All composition. All jointed. Red brown molded hair and eyelashes. Amber brown eyes. Red corduroy jumper and bonnet. Dotted swiss blouse, panties and hat trim. Red suede shoes. All original. This doll seems to be a Lipfert design suggesting the Dionne toddler. The body is the same but the mold marks are not finished off as well as they could be. Early 1940's. All original. $45.

Unknown--8" "Chubby Kid" All composition. Wearing original crepe paper dress with metalic ribbon sash, from early thirties; we bought these dolls at the dime store, paying about 50 cents for them. 1935. Blah, but original. $15.00. (Maish Collection)

173

Unmarked--8" "Chubby Kid" All composition. Painted features, watermelon mouth. Jointed arms. Black mohair wig. Sold by Sears from 1910-1940. $18.00-$20.00. (Maish Collection)

17" All composition. Blue sleep eyes. Original blonde mohair wig. Pigtails. Two teeth, Redressed nicely, excellent condition. 1930's. $30.00. (Maish Collection)

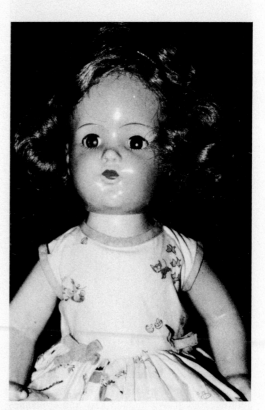

174

Unknown--7" "Twins" All composition. Fully jointed with molded hair and painted side glancing blue eyes. Original clothes. Marks: none. $18.00 pair. These dolls and clothes look very identical to Effanbee's Patsy (Baby) Tinyette.

Unknown--17" "Rosalie Teenage Doll" All composition with glued on blonde wig. Brown sleep eyes. Dimple in chin. Both arms molded bent. 1939. Marks: none. $20.00.

Unmarked--10" Composition. One piece body on pedestal. The type and color of composition used suggests the doll was intended for commercial display. Original handmade clothing. 1945-50. $20.00. (Maish Collection)

Unknown--1" "Alice In A Thimble" A whimsical miniature put-together. Hand painted "charm" doll of forties, painted thimble. (Maish Collection)

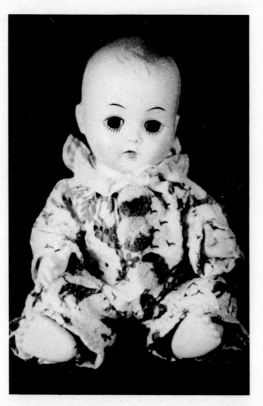

Unknown--27" "Majorette" All hard plastic with glued on yellow blonde hair. Blue sleep eyes. Lightly eyeshadowed. Open mouth/4 teeth. Walker (head does not turn) Original clothes. Marks: none. $40.00.

Unmarked--9½" Baby. All hard plastic. Molded hair. Blue sleep eyes. Unusual quality plastic, beautifully detailed hands and coloring. Marks: none. $20.00. (Maish Collection)

175

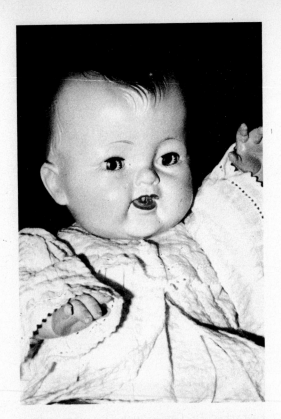

Unknown--22" "Baby Rose" Hard plastic head with glued on brown saran wig over molded hair. Blue sleep eyes. Open mouth/two upper teeth. Cloth body. Latex arms and legs. 1949. Marks: none. $7.00.

Unknown--15" Rubber body, arms and legs. Hard plastic head. Tear ducts in corner of eyes. Nurser. Eyes half closed as if it were crying. Marks: none. $15.00.

Unknown--9½" "Dude Ranch Cowgirl" One piece latex with early vinyl head. Glued on dark brown wig. Painted blue eyes. Original. 1949. Marks: none. $4.00.

Unknown--14" "Carol Brent Display Manikin" All painted mache. 1950. Marks: none. $7.00.

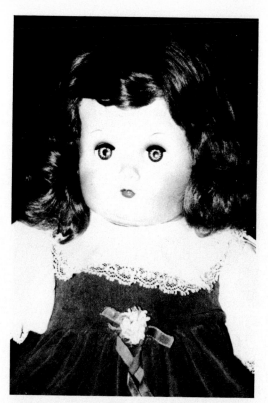

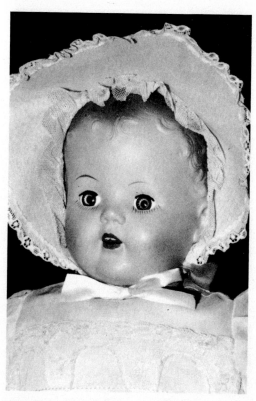

Unknown--21" "Angel Face" Cloth with vinyl arms and legs. Hard plastic head with mohair over molded hair. Blue sleep eyes. Marks: none. Sold through retailers in 1951. $10.00.

Unknown--24" "Bundle of Charm" Vinyl and cloth with hard plastic head. Blue sleep eyes. Open mouth/two upper teeth. Squeaker in both legs. Original. 1953. Marks: A Backward 650. 1951. $14.00.

Unknown--21" "Pretty Miss" All hard plastic with glued on yellow wig. Blue sleep eyes. Open mouth/four teeth. Walker, head turns. 1952. Marks: none. $18.00.

Unknown--18" "Baby Good" Cloth with latex arms and legs. Hard plastic head with molded hair. Blue sleep eyes. Open mouth/two upper teeth. Very bright red cheeks. Original. 1953. Marks: none. $14.00.

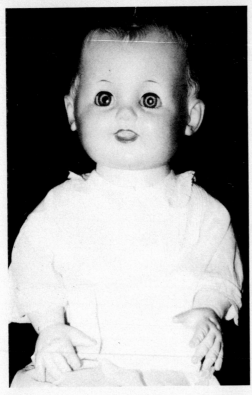

Unknown--21" "Christening Baby" One piece un-jointed, stuffed vinyl body, arms and legs. Vinyl head with squeeze cryer. Molded hair. Blue sleep eyes. Open/closed mouth with molded tongue. Very large hands, small wrists. 1953. Marks: none. $5.00.

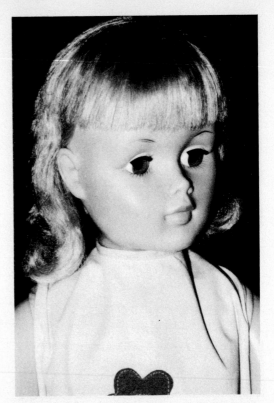

Unknown--31" "Walking Pretty Betty" Plastic and vinyl with rooted blonde hair. Blue sleep eyes. Blue eyeshadow. Marks: 5/1961, on head. $4.00. (Courtesy Allin's Collection)

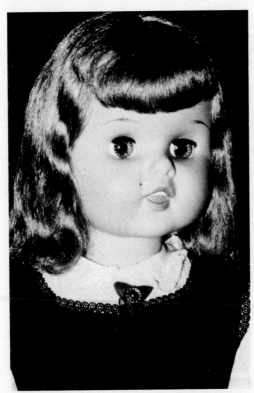

Unknown--29" "Miss Echo" Plastic and vinyl with rooted dark blonde hair. Blue sleep eyes. Open/closed mouth, painted teeth. Holds tape recorder and records voice, plays back for ½ minute and erases automatically. Battery operated. On and off knob on upper chest. 1963. (Sold for three years) Marks: 67, high on head. Original vest. $22.00.

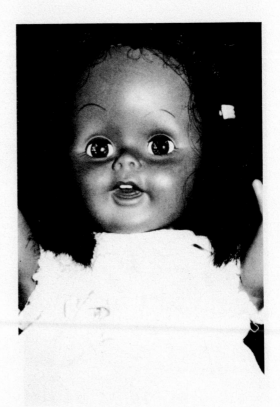

17" "Snow Baby" Plastic body and legs. Vinyl arms and head. Rooted black hair. Brown sleep eyes/lashes. Open/closed mouth with two molded upper teeth. Marks: none. 1964. $3.00.

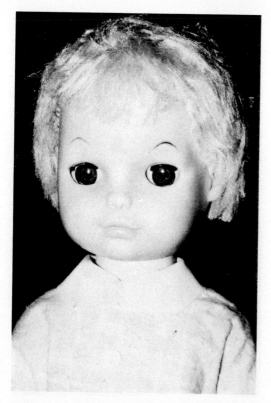

Unknown--19" "Carry Walker" Plastic and vinyl with rooted white hair. Brown sleep eyes. Walker. Dimples in cheeks. Marks: KB, in a diamond/1966/deet. $3.00.

Unknown--3½" "Mascots" These are "Cook" and "M.D." Original. 1972. Marks: none.

Unknown--3½" "Mascots" These are "Pirate and Elf" Original. Marks: none. $3.00 Set of 6.

Unknown--13" "Shelly" Plastic and vinyl with rooted blonde hair, with grow hair feature. Slot in back of head to hold hair when it is out. Year after "Miss Clarol" was introduced. Marks: none. 1966. $2.00.

179

Unknown--3½" "Mascots" These are "Police-man" and "Drum Major" Original. Marks: none.

Unknown--10" "Big Boy" All vinyl with molded and painted hair, features and clothes. Marks: Big Boy is a/Reg. U.S. Trademark/8, on bottom. Big Boy, can't make out rest, base of back. 1972. $1.00.

Unknown--16" "Lili" All excellent quality vinyl. Long yellow blonde saran hair. Blue sleep eyes. Marks: Something like MECA. Script: Lili. $5.00 (Courtesy Mary Partridge)

Unknown--11½" "Carole Channing" as Hello Dolly. Plastic and vinyl with rooted orange/blonde hair. Painted eyes. Original. Marks: AE, on head. 1971. $5.00. (Courtesy Sharon Hazel)

Unknown--Western Union Dollie Grams "Cheer-up" and "Just To Say" 1973. $1.00 each.

Unknown--12" "Johnny Hero" Foam/wire. Plastic head and gauntlet hands. Metal rod in right hand to hold football. Marks: none. $3.00.

Marlin--9" "Baby Susan" All vinyl with rooted ash blonde hair. Blue sleep eyes/molded lashes. Open mouth/nurser. 2nd and 3rd fingers molded together. Marks: Baby Susan, on head. Made by Marlin Doll Co. ca. 1950's. $3.00.

Marquette Corp--17" "Bonnie Blue Ribbon" All vinyl with ball jointed waist. Rooted blonde hair. Painted blue eyes. High heel feet. Original. Marks: Perfekta/Hong Kong, on head. Box: A Creation of/National Blue Ribbon/Freezer Food Service. 1969. $6.00.

181

Mary Hoyer--14" "Julianna" also "Sonja" Each outfit had a different name although the doll was the same. All composition with glued on brown hair. Blue sleep eyes. Light cheek dimples. Marks: The Mary Hoyer Doll, on back. Tag: Made/By/Mary Hoyer/Yarns. 1947. $35.00.

Mary Hoyer--14" "Peggy" Three piece outfit, plus purse and hat. All composition. Marks: The/Mary Hoyer/Doll, on back. 1946. $35.00.

The Mary Hoyer Company began in Reading, Pa. in 1925, and Mary Hoyer was the sole owner and designer of the business. The first Hoyer dolls were made of wood-pulp composition with sleep eyes, but, during W.W.II when tin and steel were restricted, the eyes were painted. The Mary Hoyer Company actually made their own dolls. In 1945 the change was made from composition to plastic using the Eastman Injection molds and these dolls were Unmarked. (These were of hard plastic) When it was found that the cost of Eastman Injection was much too expensive the method of molding was changed. Over the years there have been several different Hoyer dolls, including plastic and vinyl. The official publication was "Mary's Dollies" showing patterns (yarn) for the Hoyer dolls. Each outfit had a name...the dolls were the same, but the patterns were named. There were many volumes over the years. As for outfits designed and sold, there were hundreds, both crocheted and sewn. In the later plastic/vinyls each doll had her own name. For example, one of the last order forms of "Mary's Dollie," there are plastic and vinyl dolls named Becky and Margie. I was unable to get the marking information from the company and cannot even tell you what to look for! As of Spring 1974, the Mary Hoyer Co. is no longer in business.

Mary Hoyer--14" "Peggy" Shows top and skirt for the "Peggy" outfit. 1946. $35.00.

Mary Hoyer--14" "May-Belle" Majorette outfit. All composition. Marks: The/Mary Hoyer/Doll, on back. 1948. $35.00.

Mary Hoyer--14" "Caroline" Fun in the snow outfit. Hard plastic. 1950. $25.00.

Mary Hoyer--14" "Olga" Skating outfit. This is the hard plastic Mary Hoyer doll. 1950. $25.00.

Mary Hoyer--14" "Patsy" Coat and hat outfit. Hard plastic. 1951. $25.00.

Mary Hoyer--14" "Mary Hoyer" All composition with painted eyes. Made during World War II and after. Original pattern clothes. $40.00. (Courtesy Mary Partridge)

Marx--11½" "Johnny West" Marks: Louis Marx & Co. Inc./MCMLXV in circle, on back. $3.00.

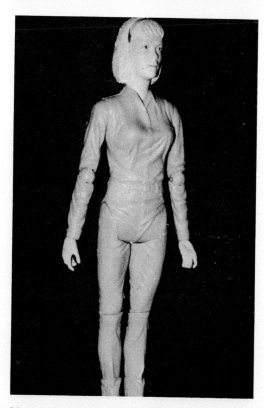

Marx--10¾" "Jane West" Marks: Louis Marx & Co. Inc./MCMLXV, in circle on back. $3.00.

Marx--18" "Miss Seventeen" All plastic with inset skull cap. Painted features. Original. Sold with 12 fashion outfits. Marks: US Patent 2925784/British Patent 804566/Made in Hong Kong. Literature: 18" Miss Seventeen Doll/Made in Hong Kong/1961 Louis Marx & Co. $8.00. (Courtesy Virginia Jones)

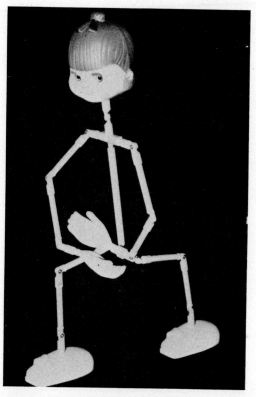

Marx--40" "Ginny Bones" All plastic. Painted features. Inter-connected pieces of plastic tubing. Marks: none. Box: Louis Marx & Co./ Patent Pending/MCMLXX. "She will pose, wear your clothes, touch her toes." The Bones family included a boy and dog. $12.00.

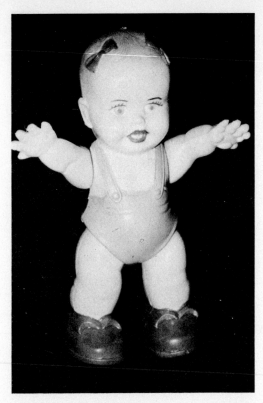

Marx--6" "Bonnie Braids Walker" All plastic. String in stomach (missing) made doll walk. Marks: Marx/Toys/Made in Hong Kong, in circle, on sticker. 1952. $4.00.

Marx--11½" "Geronimo" Marks: Louis Marx & Co./MCMLX11/Made In/USA, in circle on back. $3.00.

Marx--11½" "General Custer" Marks: Louis Marx & Co./MCMLX111/Made in/USA, in circle on back. $3.00.

Marx--6" "Shopping Anyone?, Campus Cutie" All plastic with molded clothes. Marks: MCMLXIV/Louis Marx & Co. Inc. 2nd doll is "Nitey Nite" and 3rd doll is "On the Town." $2.00 each.

EDITORS

Sibyl DeWein; recognized as an authority in the world of Barbie.

Joan Ashabraner; recognized as an authority in the world of Barbie and Kiddles.

MATTEL, INC.

Mattel, at the beginning, designed and made doll house furniture and took in partners due to the increase of business. In 1945 the company started using the name Mattel. Matt, for partner Harold Matson and El for Elliot Handler, founder. In 1947, they introduced their first musical toys, a Uke-A-Doodle and it was an instant hit. This was followed by a music box and burp gun that did not sell until Mattel became a sponsor on ABC-Tv's Mickey Mouse Club.

TV, once again, in 1959 brought the Barbie doll before millions of small viewers. Barbie was the result of studying a child, the Handler's own daughter, named Barbie. She wanted a fashion doll she could dress. The rest is history. Barbie was followed by a success in every line Mattel made including Creepy Crawlers, Fun Flowers, Icky Yuk, Plastic-goop, etc. The Mattel Toy names are the creations of a department called "Name-Makers" and in charge is Alexandra Laird.

Within the Barbie Era, there have been two "Trade-In" programs by Mattel. The first was in May of 1967. The following are quotes from a talk given by Elliot Handler, on March 14, 1968, at the Newcomer Society meeting in New York: "Last May, a trade-in program to introduce the new bendable (Twist & Turn) Barbie drew more than 1,250,000 trade-ins of the old product. That was more than the number of automobiles traded in during that month in the United States." And from "The Barbie Era-A Chronology" (A Mattel Inc. Publication) the following: "1967: Teenage make-up and hairstyles have changed drastically since 1959. Barbie changes too...and appears with a new, more youthful face, long straight hair, and a major technological change-a Twist 'N Turn waist. Little girls can trade in an old Barbie on a new one. The old dolls turned in by the millions are given to charitable organizations." This 1967 "trade in" was a Barbie doll, in any condition, plus $1.50.

Then again in 1970 when Mattel introduced Living Skipper, they had a trade in deal.

The most elusive member of the Barbie Family is a doll called Becky. When Mattel was asked about this doll they replied: "There was intent at one time to manufacture such a doll, and some costume packaging was printed and shipped with the name "Becky" before this idea was dropped. No such doll was ever made. The doll in the 1971 fashion booklet and the 1973 toy catalog is No. 1170, Twist Waist Francie." This was by Beverly Stinnett, of Mattel.

Sibyl DeWein has studied the fashion booklet very carefully and has come to this conclusion: "The doll in the 1971 booklet wearing No. 3444, 3446, 3449 and 3450 is not a Francie doll. The doll shown has a different head mold, a Casey head mold. I agree with Mrs. Stinnett that none of the dolls were ever produced for the market or sold in the stores. But I do believe that a few samples were made up. They had to be, to make the pictures for the clothing boxes and the 1971 booklet. And at least one of the sample dolls was still being used two years later. The 1973 toy catalog pictures the doll on page 40, wearing one of the Sew Magic outfits."

"There are rumors that some have seen Beckys in stores. I believe that what they saw were stacks of clothing boxes saying "Francie and Becky," but not the doll itself."

This Mattel Section is "layed out" in the following way:

1. Background information by Mattel.

2. General listing of all Mattel Fashion Dolls, 12" and under, by year.

3. 16 years with Barbie, Ken, Midge, etc. Each one done separately for quick reference.

4. Mattel historical doll list; All dolls except the Barbies, by the year and shows when each doll was first introduced.

5. Over 250 pictures of Mattel dolls, with descriptions and current prices.

Barbie's Sweet 16 Background Information

Barbie, the world's most famous doll, was introduced to the toy-buying public 16 years ago this year. The Barbie doll was created as a result of Ruth Handler, now Co-Chairman of the Board, Mattel, Inc., observing her own daughter playing with paper dolls.

Ruth Handler observed that her daughter enjoyed paper doll play, but was interested only in those paper dolls of adult figures. It became apparent to Ruth Handler that her daughter could have more fun with a "three-dimensional" doll that would have a variety of miniature outfits to wear, just like the paper dolls.

Ruth Handler's intuition was correct and, as a result, the Barbie doll in 1958 became the first adult figure doll introduced in the American marketplace.

Today there is a second generation of youngsters playing with Barbie--just like their mothers did 16 years ago. As of this date there have been more than 80 million Barbie dolls sold around the world and more than six million Barbie dolls sold every year.

Barbie outfits, of which there are approximately 36 new designs each year, sell at a rate of approximately 20 million per year--which qualifies Mattel as the largest manufacturer of women's wear.

Reprinted with permission.

The Barbie Era-A Chronology

1958: *Barbie, teenage fashion model is created and tested.
March, 1959: Toy Fair, New York. Toy buyers are not enthusiastic--large, life-size dolls are currently popular--a tiny fashion doll won't make it. But Barbie goes into the stores, little girls are enthused and the Barbie era begins.
1961: *Ken is introduced as Barbie's boyfriend. He is immediately accepted--first as an escort for Barbie--then as a personality in his own right.
1963: *Midge, freckle-faced and impish, is brought into being as Barbie's best friend. They can wear each other's clothes. Play possibilities expand. No definite ages are assigned Barbie and Midge, but little girls tend to think of the dolls as being about six years older than themselves. Barbie and her friends are receiving fan letters.
1964: *Skipper, Barbie's little sister, and *Allan, Ken's buddy, join the scene. Skipper is smaller and younger than her teenage companions and is the first to be named as part of Barbie's family. Now, it's Barbie and her family and friends.
In addition, the first variations on the original Barbie doll are introduced this year--"Miss Barbie" and "Fashion Queen Barbie" keep the same personality, but have bendable knees, eyes that open and close, and a sculptured hairstyle so that various wigs can be worn.
1965: *Skooter and *Ricky, friends for Skipper, come along. Now all the dolls have bendable legs for more lifelike play. The original concept of merely posing a fashion doll in a costume is giving way to endless imaginary play situations.
1966: *Francie, Barbie's MODern cousin, and *Tutti and *Todd, tiny twin sister and brother to Barbie and Skipper, join the growing Barbie family. Francie is especially well-received.
1967: Teenage makeup and hairstyles have changed drastically since 1959. Barbie changes too--and appears with a new, more youthful face, long straight hair, and--a major technological change--a Twist 'n Turn waist! Little girls can trade in an old Barbie on a new one. The old dolls--turned in by the millions--are given to charitable organizations.
*Casey, Francie's friend, and *Chris, little Tutti's playmate are introduced. (Identifying a newcomer as "friend of..." an existing personality indicates that he or she can wear the same clothes as the other doll.)
1968: Barbie talks! Extensive research is done to find out what kind of voice Barbie fans imagine her to have. Her newest friends are *Stacey, who is English and has the appropriate accent, and *Christie, who is black. (A black Francie doll was tried and rebuffed in 1967--Barbie and her friends have distinct personalities to their young buyers. Christie, her own person, is a success.)
*Twiggy is introduced--the first of Barbie's friends to be copied after a real-life personality.
1969: *Julia, the popular TV nurse, is now a doll, with the face of Diahann Carroll.
*P.J. is Barbie's new friend. Little girls write in: "What does P.J. stand for?" Answer: Nothing! P.J. is her name.
1970: *Brad, Ken's new buddy, is introduced and the world of Barbie has another black member.
1971: *Fluff, a playmate for Skipper, is the only new personality this year, but Barbie, Ken, Francie and Skipper bloom forth with suntans, as the "Malibu" versions of the dolls are introduced.
1972: *Steffie is Barbie's new f end, *Tiff is skipper's new playmate and *Miss America, in authentic gown and royal accessories, is also introduced--based on the popular national contest. Another technological breakthrough--the dolls now have hands that bend at the wrist, open and close to carry things.
1973: *Kelley steps on the scene with hair that can be curled without lotions, heat, water or waiting! The other dolls now have the same feature and Ken makes a dramatic change in appearance with long hair and removable beard, moustache and sideburns!
1974: Barbie is "Sweet 16." She is a contemporary "with-it" teenager--her fashions now include ski, camping, sailing, swimming and tennis outfits, as well as a ballet costume and the traditional but ever-popular wedding gown. Little girls play with cars and trucks through the world of Barbie as Barbie now enjoys a dune buggy, tent-trailer, bicycle, camper, beach bus and a United Airlines Friend Ship to fly her all over the world!

So--Barbie continues to respond not only to fashion changes, but to the changes in lifestyle of today's young women. That's why, no doubt, she has been and continues to be--the most popular doll in the world.

*U.S. registered trademarks of Mattel, Inc. for its Dolls.

The Barbie Family Tree

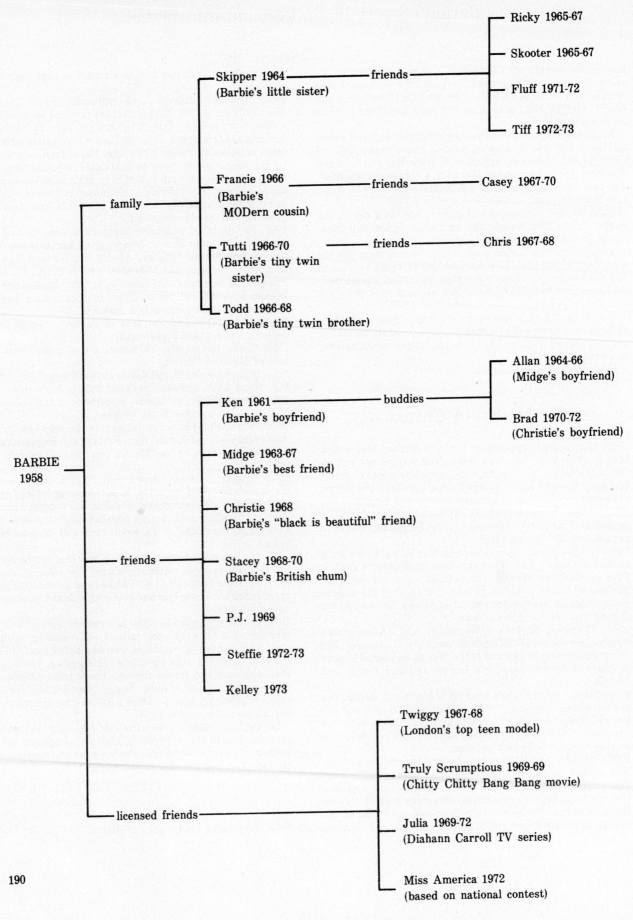

BARBIE
1958

family
- Skipper 1964
  (Barbie's little sister) —— friends
  - Ricky 1965-67
  - Skooter 1965-67
  - Fluff 1971-72
  - Tiff 1972-73
- Francie 1966
  (Barbie's MODern cousin) —— friends —— Casey 1967-70
- Tutti 1966-70
  (Barbie's tiny twin sister) —— friends —— Chris 1967-68
- Todd 1966-68
  (Barbie's tiny twin brother)

friends
- Ken 1961
  (Barbie's boyfriend) —— buddies
  - Allan 1964-66
    (Midge's boyfriend)
  - Brad 1970-72
    (Christie's boyfriend)
- Midge 1963-67
  (Barbie's best friend)
- Christie 1968
  (Barbie's "black is beautiful" friend)
- Stacey 1968-70
  (Barbie's British chum)
- P.J. 1969
- Steffie 1972-73
- Kelley 1973

licensed friends
- Twiggy 1967-68
  (London's top teen model)
- Truly Scrumptious 1969-69
  (Chitty Chitty Bang Bang movie)
- Julia 1969-72
  (Diahann Carroll TV series)
- Miss America 1972
  (based on national contest)

Sixteen Years with Barbie
(1958-1974)

This is a general listing of the Fashion Dolls, 12" and under, made by Mattel, Inc. from the introduction of the Barbie doll in 1959, through 1974. It is important to remember that dolls usually Reach the market one year after the date in the fashion booklets.

The following, and the listing of individual dolls in the following section, are listed by the date the dolls were on the market. These lists were compiled by Sibyl DeWein and Joan Ashabraner.

1958: Barbie was designed, tested and patented.

1959: 850: Barbie: Ponytail with curly bangs. White irises and pointed eyebrows. Holes in feet to fit on prongs of pedestal stand. Heavy, solid torso, marked: Barbie/Pats. Pend/MCMLVIII/by/Mattel/Inc. Bright red lips and nails. Black and white stripe bathing suit. Gold hoop earrings.

1960: 850: Barbie: Same doll as 1959 except this one does not have holes in feet because there is now a different type of stand. Bathing suit is the same but now has pearl earrings.

850: Barbie: Same doll but has blue irises and curved eyebrows.

1960: Ken was designed and patented.

1961: 850: Barbie: New hard, hollow type body but has the same Pats. Pend. markings. Some dolls still have the old soft ponytail hair and bright red lips and nails. Others have sturdier hair and more delicate lip and nail colors.

750: Ken: Fuzzy hair (flocked). Hard, hollow, plastic torso marked: Ken/Pats. Pend/MCMLX/by Mattel/Inc. Red trunks.

1962: 850: Barbie: Bubble cut. Pats. Pend. body. 1 pc. red suit.

850: Barbie: Ponytail with bangs. Pats. Pend. body. 1 pc. red suit.

750: Ken: New head mold with painted hair. Same Pats. Pend. markings. Red shorts and stripe jacket.

1963: 860: Midge: Flip hair. Freckled face. Midge/Barbie body. Marked: Midge/1962/Barbie/1958/by Mattel, Inc. These bodies are slightly taller. 2 pc. suit.

870: Fashion Queen Barbie: Molded head. 3 wigs. On Midge/Barbie body. 1 pc. gold and white stripe suit and head scarf.

850: Barbie: Bubble cut. Midge/Barbie body. 1 pc. red suit.

850: Barbie: Ponytail. Midge/Barbie body. 1 pc. red suit.

750: Ken: Same as 1962 except on newly marked body: 1960/by/Mattel, Inc./Hawthorne/Calif., U.S.A.

953: "Barbie Baby Sits:" Baby with apron. Blonde painted hair.

1964: 0850: Barbie: Swirl ponytail, no bangs. Midge/Barbie bodies. Red suit. A few were released on the Pat. Pend. bodies.

1060: Miss Barbie: Sleep eyes. First bendable legs. Molded head with orange head band. 3 wigs. Lawn swing. Pink suit and cap.

0950: Skipper: Long straight hair. Straight legs. 1 pc. red/white suit.

1000: Allan: Molded reddish hair. Straight legs. Blue trunks and stripe jacket.

0871: Barbie's Wig Wardrobe: One molded Barbie head. 3 wigs.

0953: "Barbie Baby Sits:' Baby with apron. Slight difference in hair color.

0850: Barbie: Regular ponytail. Same as 1963.

0850: Barbie: Bubble cut. Same as 1963.

0870: Fashion Queen Barbie: Same as 1963.

0750: Ken: Same as 1963.

0860: Midge: Same as 1963.

1965: 1070: Barbie: Bendable legs. 1 pc. suit, stripe/top solid bottom. Came in at least three hair styles.

1020: Ken: Bendable legs. Red shorts, blue jacket.

1080: Midge: Bendable legs. New hair style. 1 pc. stripe suit.

1010: Allan: Bendable legs. Blue shorts, red jacket.

1030: Skipper: Bendable legs. Same hair as 950. 1 pc. blue and red suit.

1040: Skooter: Straight legs. "Puppy ears" hair-do. Freckles. 2 pc. red shorts/stripe top.

1090: Ricky. Straight legs. Painted red hair. Blue shorts/stripe jacket.

4035: Color 'N Curl Set: 2 molded heads (one Barbie, one Midge). 4 wigs. Color changers. Hair dryer.

0953: "Barbie Baby Sits:" Baby now has a layette.

?: Midge's Wig Wardrobe: One molded Midge head. 3 wigs.

0871: Barbie's Wig Wardrobe: Same as 1964.

0850: Barbie: Swirl ponytail. Same as 1964.

0750: Ken: Same as 1964.

0860: Midge. Same as 1964.

1000: Allan: Same as 1964.

0950: Skipper: Same as 1964.

1966: 1150: Color Magic Barbie: Bendable legs. Color changers for hair. 1 pc. harlequin swim suit.

4038: Color 'N Curl Set: One molded Barbie head. 2 wigs. Colors.

4039: Color 'N Curl Set: One molded Barbie head. 4 wigs. Colors and dryer.

1130: Francie: Greyish tan skin. Bendable legs. Real eyelashes. 1 pc. suit has blue/green background.

1130: Francie: Pink skin. Bendable legs. Real lashes. 1 pc. suit has white background, green bottom.

1140: Francie: Pink skin. Straight legs. Painted eyelashes. 2 pc. red and white suit.

3550: Tutti: Playsuit and hat.

3580: Todd: Blue shirt, red and blue check pants and cap.

3552: Tutti: "Walkin' My Dolly"

3553: Tutti: "Night-Night"

3554: Tutti: "Me And My Dog"

3555: Tutti: "Melody In Pink"

3556: Tutti and Todd: "Sundae Treat"

1120: Skooter: Bendable legs. Greyish tan skin. Blue shorts, red top.

1120: Skooter: Later in year: Bendable legs. Pink skin. Same clothes.

1040: Skooter: Straight legs. New pink skin. Clothes same as 1965.

1030: Skipper: Bendable legs. New pink skin. Clothes same as 1965.

0950: Skipper: Straight legs. New pink skin. Clothes same as 1965.

1090: Ricky: Straight legs. New pink skin. Clothes same as 1965.

1070: Barbie: Bendable legs. Same as 1965.

0850: Barbie: Swirl ponytail. Same as 1965.

0871: Barbie's Wig Wardrobe: Same as 1965.

1020: Ken: Bendable legs. Same as 1965.

0750: Ken: Straight legs. Same as 1965.

1080: Midge: Bendable legs. Same as 1965.

0860: Midge: Straight legs. Same as 1965.

1010: Allan: Bendable legs. Same as 1965.

1000: Allan: Straight legs. Same as 1965.

1967: 1160: Barbie: Jointed waist. Bendable legs. Real eyelashes. Long straight hair. 3 pc. orange and net suit.

1162: Barbie: Trade In Doll. Same as above: 1160.

1180: Casey: Bendable legs. Short hair. Jointed waist. 1 pc. white and gold suit.

1100: Colored Francie: Bendable legs. Jointed waist. Floral and see-through suit.

1170: Francie: Jointed waist. Bendable legs. Med. long hair. 1 pc. rose bottom, stripe top.

1185: Twiggy: Jointed waist. Bendable legs. Blue and yellow mini dress.

3570: Chris: Same size as Tutti. Multi-color dress.

3550: Tutti: New clothes. Dress: floral skirt, solid pink top. This stock number was used the first part of the year. Last part of the year it was changed to: 3580.

3590: Todd: New stock number. Same clothes.

3559: Tutti Set: "Cookin' Goodies"

3560: Tutti Set: "Swing A Long"

3552, 3553, 3554, 3555 and 3556: Same as 1966.

1150: Color Magic Barbie: Same as 1966.

0850: Barbie: Same as 1966.

1030: Skipper: Same as 1966.

0950: Skipper: Same as 1966.

1140: Francie: Same as 1966.

1968: 1115: Talking Barbie: Braid ponytail to side. Mentions Stacey. Rose knit top over rose shorts. Bendable legs.

1125: Talking Stacey: Long straight hair to side. 2 pc. stripe suit. Bendable legs.

1126: Talking Christie: Brown curly hair with a part. Light brown skin. Bendable legs. Green knit top, rose shorts.

8348: Spanish Talking Barbie: Same hair and clothes of regular one.

1190: Barbie: Straight legs. Pink skin. 2 pc. pink suit. Painted eyelashes. Hair-do like No. 1160.

4042: Hair Fair Head: One Barbie head and hair pieces.

1165: Stacey: Jointed waist. Long straight hair. Red suit with white buttons.

1105: Skipper: Jointed waist. Same long straight hair. 1 pc. blue suit.

1160: Barbie: New clothes. Rose and green knitted top over rose shorts. Rest same as 1967.

0950: Skipper: Same as 1967.

1100: Colored Francie: Same as 1967.

1170: Francie: Same as 1967.

1140: Francie: Same as 1967.

1185: Twiggy: Same as 1967.

1180: Casey: Same as 1967.

3570: Chris: Same as 1967.

3580: Tutti: Same as 1967. All 6 Tutti Sets.

1969: 1111: Talking Ken: Solid red jacket and red shorts. Bendable legs.

8372: Spanish Talking Ken: Dressed same as regular one.

1128: Talking Julia: Light brown skin, short straight dark brown hair. Gold/silver jumpsuit. Bendable legs.

1127: Julia: Jointed waist. 2 pc. nurse uniform. Hair and skin same as above.

1107: Talking Truly Scrumptious: Bendable legs. Old fashioned clothes.

1108: Truly Scrumptious: Straight legs. Old fashioned clothes.

1113: Talking P.J.: Bendable legs. Rosy orange mini dress.

4043: Hair Fair: One Barbie head, hair pieces.

4042: Hair Fair: One Barbie head, hair pieces. Same as 1968.

1160: Barbie: Jointed waist. New 1 pc. diagonal striped suit. New hair in long flip style.

1165: Stacey: Jointed waist. New 1 pc. multi-colored suit. New flip hair-do.

3577: Buffy & Mrs. Beasley: Same size as Tutti.

3580: Tutti: Print top, solid skirt.

1105: Skipper: Jointed waist. New hair-do in two long curls. New 1 pc. rose and orange suit.

1170: Francie: Jointed waist. New flip hair style. New 1 pc. solid rose top/stripe bottom.

1126: Talking Christie: Same as 1968.

1190: Barbie: Straight legs. Same as 1968.

1115: Talking Barbie: Same as 1968.

8348: Spanish Talking Barbie: Same as 1968.

1125: Talking Stacey: Same as 1968.

1180: Casey: Same as 1968.

1970: 1116: Living Barbie: Gold/silver suit with orange net cover.

1117: Living Skipper: 1 pc. green, blue and rose suit.

1147: Living Skipper: Trade In Doll. Same as No. 1117 above.

0950: Skipper: Re-issue of straight leg doll. Pinker skin. Long straight hair. Same clothes as first 0950 doll.

1142: Brad: Bendable legs. Solid orange top, print shorts.

1124: Ken: Bendable legs. Solid yellow top, print shorts.

1129: Francie Growin' Pretty Hair: No extra hair pieces. Pink dress.

1122: Francie Hair Happenin's: Blue dress. Jointed waist.

1119: Christie: Jointed waist. Dark reddish brown curly hair, with part. Light brown skin color. 1 pc. multi-color suit.

1118: P.J.: Jointed waist. 1 pc. rose suit.

1114: Talking Brad: Dark brown skin. Afro top and shorts.

1132: Walking Jamie: Made for Sears. Same head mold as Barbie. Brown eyes.

1133: Lori & Rori: "Pretty Pairs." Same size as Tutti.

1134: Nan & Fran: "Pretty Pairs." Same size as Tutti.

1135: Angie & Tangy: "Pretty Pairs." Same size as Tutti.

1115: Talking Barbie: New hair, curls on nape of neck. New clothes, 2 pc. red and net jacket. In some dolls, the old voice box was used. In others, the new (mentioning P.J.) was used.

8348: Spanish Talking Barbie: Same as regular doll.

1115: Talking Barbie (Stacey head mold). New words, mentions P.J. Curls at nape of neck.

8348: Spanish Talking Barbie: (Stacey head mold). Same as regular doll.

1160: Barbie: Jointed, hair same as 1969, turned up on ends. New rose and white 1 pc. suit.

1190: Barbie: Straight legs. New 1 pc. rose and green suit. Painted eyelashes.

1111: Talking Ken: New blue and orange jacket and orange shorts. New words.

8372: Spanish Talking Ken: Dressed same as 2nd issue No. 1111.

1125: Talking Stacey: New blue/silver suit.

1165: Stacey: Jointed. New blue and rose 1 pc. floral suit.

1126: Talking Christie: New Afro top and shorts. New darker skin. New black modified Afro hair-do.

1105: Skipper: Jointed. New orange and vinyl suit. Doll same as 1969.

1170: Francie: New floral top over rose shorts. Rest of doll same as 1969.

3580: Tutti: Same as 1969.

1128: Talking Julia: Same as 1969.

1127: Julia: Jointed. New 1 pc. white uniform. Rest same as 1969.

4043: Hair Fair: One Barbie head, hair pieces. Same as 1969.

1180: Casey: Same as 1969.

1113: Talking P.J.: Same as 1969.

1971: 1174: Barbie Hair Happenin's: Extra hair pieces. Rose skirt, white blouse.

1152: Barbie Live Action on Stage.

1155: Barbie: Live Action.

1172: Ken Live Action on Stage.

1159: Ken: Live Action.

1153: P.J. Live Action on Stage.

1156: P.J.: Live Action.

1175: Christie: Live Action: Long straight black hair, dark brown skin.

1067: Barbie: Malibu: 1 pc. blue suit. Suntan. Long blonde hair.

1088: Ken: Malibu: Orange shorts. Suntan. Yellow painted hair.

1069: Skipper: Malibu: 2 pc. orange suit. Suntan. Long blonde hair.

1068: Francie: Malibu: 1 pc. rose and red suit. Suntan. Casey head mold.

4044: Hair Fair: One Barbie head, hair pieces. New, eyes in center.

1143: Living Fluff: 1 pc. stripe top, solid skirt.

1144: Barbie Growin' Pretty Hair: Extra hair pieces. Pink dress.

1074: Francie Growin' Pretty Hair: Extra hair pieces. Same dress as No. 1129.

1116: Living Barbie: New long skirt and 1 pc. suit. Eyes in center.

1115: Talking Barbie: Mentions P.J. Eyes in center. New 2 pc. white suit, long gold coat.

8348: Spanish Talking Barbie: Same as regular doll.

1190: Barbie: (Chef Boy-ar-dee Labels) Eyes in center. 1 pc. rose and green suit.

1160: Barbie: Jointed waist. New stripe knit suit. New, eyes in center. Same hair style.

1117: Living Skipper: New 2 pc. yellow suit.

1170: Francie: Jointed waist. New hair brushed back. New orange pleated dress.

1128: Talking Julia: New skin which is darker. New black modified Afro hair-do. Same clothes.

1127: Julia: Jointed waist. Same as 1970.

1111: Ken: Talking: Same as 1970.

1124: Ken: Same as 1970.

1132: Walking Jamie: Same as 1970.

1113: Talking P.J.: Same as 1970.

1118: P.J.: Same as 1970.

1126: Talking Christie: Same as 1970.

1119: Christie: Jointed waist. Same as 1970.

1114: Talking Brad: Darker skin. Same clothes as 1970.

1142: Brad: Darker skin. Same clothes as 1970.

1105: Skipper: Jointed waist. Same as 1970.

1122: Francie Hair Happenin's: Same as 1970.

3580: Tutti: Same as 1970.

1972: 1179: Skipper Pose 'N Play: Gym. Blue check suit.

1199: Tiff Pose 'N Play: Blue jeans, white shirt.

1182: Barbie Walk Lively. Red jumpsuit.

1184: Ken Walk Lively: Plaid pants, blue shirt.

1183: Steffie Walk Lively: Rose and reddish jump suit.

1187: P.J. Malibu: 1 pc. lavender suit.

3200: Miss America Walk Lively: Royal robes. Real eyelashes.

3194-9991: (Kelloggs Labels) Miss America: Same as 3200, but no walking stand.

3269: Barbie "Forget Me Nots" (Kelloggs labels): Same as Malibu Barbie.

3210: Barbie: Montgomery Wards re-issue of ponytail in black and white stripe suit. On Midge/Barbie body. Straight legs.

3311: Busy Barbie: Check skirt over denim sun suit. Open and close hands.

1195: Talking Busy Barbie: Blue hot pants, rose blouse. Open and close hands.

?: French Talking Busy Barbie: Dressed same as 1195. Open and close hands.

3314: Busy Ken: Blue jeans, red top. Open and close hands.

1196: Talking Busy Ken: Red pants, red and blue shirt. Open and close hands.

3312: Busy Steffie: Long sun back dress. Open and close hands.

1186: Talking Busy Steffie: Blue hot pants, pink and white blouse. Open and close hands.

3313: Busy Francie: Jeans and green top. Open and close hands.

1144: Barbie Growin' Pretty Hair: New long dress, blue top/red stripe skirt. Hair-do slightly different.

1067: Malibu Barbie: Same as 1971.

1088: Malibu Ken: Same as 1971.

1069: Malibu Skipper: Same as 1971.

1068: Malibu Francie: Same as 1971.

1115: Talking Barbie: Same as 1971.

8348: Spanish Talking Barbie: Same as 1971.

1111: Talking Ken: Same as 1971.

1113: Talking P.J.: Same as 1971.

1126: Talking Christie: Same as 1971.

1114: Talking Brad: Same as 1971.

1128: Talking Julia: Same as 1971.

1155: Live Action Barbie: Same as 1971.

1159: Live Action Ken: Same as 1971.

1156: Live Action P.J.: Same as 1971.

1175: Live Action Christie: Same as 1971.

1119: Christie: Same as 1971.

1142: Brad: Bendable legs. Same as 1971.

1074: Francie Growin' Pretty Hair: Same as 1971.

1973: 8697: Quick Curl Miss America: Different body but same clothes as 1972. Painted eyelashes.

4220: Quick Curl Barbie: Pink dress. Painted eyelashes.

4221: Quick Curl Kelley: Green dress. Painted eyelashes.

4223: Quick Curl Skipper: Blue dress. Painted eyelashes.

4222: Quick Curl Francie: Yellow dress: Painted eyelashes.

4224: Mod Hair Ken: Rooted hair. Tan pants, check coat. Coats came in two size checks.

7745: Malibu Christie: Long straight black hair. Dark skin. 1 pc. red suit.

1067: Malibu Barbie: Suit is deeper blue. Eyes are brighter.

3194-9991: Miss America: New Kelloggs labels. Some dolls same as 1972. Some were brunette Quick Curl dolls.

3311: Busy Barbie: Same as 1972.

3314: Busy Ken. Same as 1972.

3312: Busy Steffie: Same as 1972.

1195: Talking Busy Barbie: Same as 1972.

1179: Pose 'N Play Skipper: Same as 1972.

1182: Walk Lively Barbie: Same as 1972.

1184: Walk Lively Ken: Same as 1972.

1183: Walk Lively Steffie: Same as 1972.

1088: Malibu Ken: Same as 1972.

1187: Malibu P.J.: Same as 1972.

1069: Malibu Skipper: Same as 1972.

1068: Malibu Francie: Same as 1972.

1974: 7796-8: Barbie's Sweet 16 Promotion. Long, blonde hair. Long, pink dress. Free outfit included (jeans and blouse)

7796: Barbie's Sweet 16: Same doll and pink dress as above.

7806: Sun Valley Barbie: Suntan. Skiing gear and outfit.

7807: Newport Barbie: Suntan. Boating outfits and boat.

7808: Yellowstone Kelley: Long straight red hair. Suntan. Camping gear and outfit.

7809: Sun Valley Ken: Suntan. Orange painted hair. Skiing gear and outfit.

8697: Quick Curl Miss America: New blonde hair. Rest same as 1973.

3194-4: Miss America: Kelloggs offer. New blonde Quick Curl. Rest same as 1973.

4220: Quick Curl Barbie: Same as 1973.

4222: Quick Curl Francie: Same as 1973.

4223: Quick Curl Skipper: Same as 1973.

4221: Quick Curl Kelley: Same as 1973.

4224: Mod Hair Ken: Same as 1973.

1067: Malibu Barbie: Same as 1973.

1088: Malibu Ken: Same as 1973.

1068: Malibu Francie: Same as 1973.

1069: Malibu Skipper: Same as 1973.

1187: Malibu P.J.: New green suit. Rest of doll same as 1973.

7745: Malibu Christie: Same as 1973.

7803: Francie and her Ten Speeder: This doll and bicycle set was shown in the early 1974 toy catalog. The later catalog did not show the set. As this goes to press, none of these have been found in the stores.

<u>1958:</u> Patented. 11½" doll.

<u>1959:</u> 850: Ponytail with curly bangs. White irises and pointed eyebrows. Holes in feet to fit on stand with prongs. Heavy solid torso marked: Pat. Pend.* Bright red lips and nails. Black and white strip swim suit. Hoop earrings.

<u>1960:</u> 850: Same as above except no holes in feet because of new stand design. Pearl earrings. Also: 850: same except Blue iris and curved eyebrows. No holes in feet.

<u>1961:</u> 850: New type hard, hollow body but same markings.* Blue iris and pearl earrings. Some dolls still have the old soft ponytail hair and bright red lips and nails. Others have sturdier hair, more delicate lip and nail colors.

<u>1962:</u> 850: Bubble cut hair and 850: Ponytail/bangs: both on hard hollow, Pat. Pend.* bodies. Both wear one piece red bathing suit.

<u>1963:</u> 870: Fashion Queen. Molded hair/3 wigs. Gold and white stripe suit and head scarf. Bodies now marked: Midge/Barbie.** 850: Bubble cut and ponytail now on Midge/Barbie bodies.**

<u>1964:</u> 0850: Swirl ponytail, no bangs. One piece red suit. A few are on the Pat. Pend.* bodies, but most on the Midge/Barbie bodies.**

0871: Wig Wardrobe: One molded head/3 wigs.
1060: Miss Barbie: Sleep eyes. One piece pink suit. First bendable legs. Molded hair/3 wigs.
0870: Fashion Queen: Same as 1963.
0850: Regular ponytail and 0850 Bubble cut: Same as 1963.

<u>1965:</u> 1070: Bendable legs. Came in at least three hair styles. One piece stripe top, solid bottom suit.
4035: Color 'N Curl Set: Set had one Barbie and one Midge head; both with molded hair/4 wigs/colors/one dryer.
0850: Swirl ponytail: Same as 1964.
0871: Wig Wardrobe: Same as 1964.

<u>1966:</u> 1150: Color Magic: Bendable legs. Color changes. One piece harlequin swim suit.
4038: Color 'N Curl Set: One molded head. 2 wigs. Colors.
4039: Color 'N Curl Set: One molded head. 4 wigs. 1 dryer. Colors.
1070: Bendable legs. Same as 1965.
0850: Swirl ponytail: Same as 1965.
0871: Wig Wardrobe: Same as 1965.

<u>1967:</u> 1160: Twist 'N Turn: Long straight hair. Real eyelashes. Bendable legs. 3 piece orange and net suit.
1162: Trade In: Same as above Twist 'N Turn.
1150: Color Magic: Same as 1966.
0850: Swirl Ponytail: Same as 1966.

<u>1968:</u> 1115: Talking: Braid ponytail to side. Rose knit top over shorts. Mentions Stacey.
8348: Spanish Talking: Dressed and looks like 1115.
1190: Straight legs. Hair like No. 1160. Painted eyelashes. 2 pc. pink suit.
4042: Hair Fair: One head with extra hair pieces.
1160: Twist: New clothes. Knitted top over rose shorts. Rest same as 1967.

<u>1969:</u> 1160: Twist: New 1 pc. diagonal stripe suit. New long flip hair-do.
4043: Hair Fair: 1 head with extra hair pieces.
4042: Hair Fair: 1 head. Extra hair pieces.
1115: Talking: Same as 1968.
8348: Spanish Talking: Same as 1968.
1190: Straight legs: Same as 1968.

<u>1970:</u> 1116: Living: Gold/silver, orange net cover.
1115: Talking: New clothes and hair. 2 pc. red suit, net jacket. Curls on nape of neck. New words, mentions P.J. In some, the old voice box was used, in others the new one was used.
8348: Spanish Talking: Same clothes and hair as 1115.
1190: New Clothes: 1 pc. rose and green suit. Rest same as 1969.
4043: Hair Fair: Same as 1969.
1160: Twist: New clothes: 1 pc. rose and white suit. Same hair as 1969.
1115: Talking with Stacey head mold: 2 pc. suit/net jacket. New words mention P.J. Curls at nape of neck.
8348: Spanish Talking with Stacey head mold. Same hair and clothes as above.

<u>1971:</u> 1190: Chef Boy-ar-dee Labels. New eyes in center. 1 pc. rose and green suit. Painted eyelashes.
1152: Live Action on Stage.
1155: Live Action.
1067: Malibu: 1 pc. light blue suit. Suntan. Long blonde hair. Painted eyelashes.
1174: Hair Happenin's: Rose skirt, white blouse. Extra hair pieces.
4044: Hair Fair: 1 head. New eyes in center. Extra hair pieces.
1144: Growin' Pretty Hair: Pink dress. Extra hair pieces.
1116: Living: New long skirt over 1 pc. suit. New eyes in center.
1115: Talking: New 2 pc. white, long gold coat. New eyes in center.
8348: Spanish Talking Barbie: Same as 1115 above.
1160: Twist: New stripe knit suit. New eyes in center. Same hair as 1970.

<u>1972:</u> 1182: Walk Lively: Red jumpsuit.
3210: Montgomery Wards Re-issue: Ponytail with bangs. Midge/Barbie body. Black and white suit.
3269: "Forget-Me-Nots." Kelloggs labels. Same as No. 1067.
3311: Busy: Check skirt over denim sun suit. Open and close hands.
1195: Talking Busy: Blue hot pants, rose blouse. Open and close hands.
?: French Talking Busy: Dressed and looks same as 1195.
1144: Growin' Pretty Hair: New long dress, blue top. New slight difference in hair-do.
1067: Malibu: Same as 1971.
1115: Talking: Same as 1971.
8348: Spanish Talking: Same as 1971.
1155: Live Action: Same as 1971.

<u>1973:</u> 4220: Quick Curl: Pink dress. Painted eyelashes.
1067: Malibu: Suit is a brighter blue. Eyes brighter.
1182: Walk Lively: Same as 1972.
3311: Busy: Same as 1972.
1195: Talking Busy: Same as 1972.

<u>1974:</u> 7796.8: Sweet 16 Promotion. Doll and a free outfit.
7796: Sweet 16. Long, blonde hair. Long pink dress. Painted eyelashes.
7806: Sun Valley: Ski outfit. Suntan. Painted eyelashes.
7807: Newport: Sailing outfit. Suntan. Painted eyelashes.
4220: Quick Curl: Same as 1973.
1067: Malibu: Same as 1973.

KEN, BARBIE'S BOYFRIEND (12")

<u>1960:</u> Patented.
<u>1961:</u> 750: Fuzzy hair, flocked. Red trunks. Hard hollow torso marked***
<u>1962:</u> 750: Painted hair. New head mold. Red shorts. Stripe jacket. Marked***
<u>1963:</u> 750: Painted hair. Same as 1962 except new marking****
<u>1964:</u> 0750: Same as 1963.
<u>1965:</u> 1020: New bendable legs. Red shorts, blue jacket.
0750: Same as 1964.
<u>1966:</u> 1020: Same as 1965.
0750: Same as 1965.
<u>1969:</u> 1111: Talking. Solid red top, red shorts. Bendable legs.
8372: Spanish Talking. Looks and is dressed same as 1111.
<u>1970:</u> 1111: Talking. New blue and orange jacket, orange shorts. New words.
8372: Spanish Talking. Dressed and looks like one above.
1124: Bendable legs. Solid yellow top. Print shorts.
<u>1971:</u> 1172: Live Action on Stage.
1159: Live Action.
1088: Malibu. Orange shorts. Suntan. Yellow painted hair.
1111: Talking. Same as 1970.
1124: Bendable legs. Same as 1970.
<u>1972:</u> 1184: Walk Lively. Plaid pants. Blue shirt.
3314: Busy: Blue jeans, red shirt. Open and close hands.
1196: Talking Busy. Red pants, red/blue shirt. Open and close hands.
1088: Malibu. Same as 1971.
1111: Talking. Same as 1971.
1159: Live Action. Same as 1971.
<u>1973:</u> 4224: Mod Hair. Rooted hair. Brown check jacket, solid pants.
1184: Walk Lively. Same as 1972.
3314: Busy. Same as 1972.
1088: Malibu. Same as 1972.
<u>1974:</u> 7809: Sun Valley. Ski outfit. Suntan. Orange painted hair.
4224: Mod Hair. Same as 1973.
1088: Malibu. Same as 1973.

"BARBIE BABY SITS" BABY (3")

<u>1963:</u> 953: Has an apron. Blonde painted hair.
<u>1964:</u> 0953: Has an apron. Slight difference in hair.
<u>1965:</u> 0953: Has a layette.

MIDGE, BARBIE'S BEST FRIEND (11½")

<u>1963:</u> 860: Flip hair. Freckles. On Midge/Barbie body.** 2 pc. suit.
<u>1964:</u> 0860: Same as 1963.
<u>1965:</u> 4035: Color 'N Curl Set. One molded Midge and one Barbie head. 4 wigs, colors and one dryer.
?: Wig Wardrobe. One molded head. 3 wigs.
1080: Bendable legs. New hair-do. One piece stripe suit.
0860: Same as 1964.
<u>1966:</u> 1080: Same as 1965.
0860: Same as 1965.

SKIPPER, BARBIE'S LITTLE SISTER (9¼")

<u>1964:</u> 0950: Straight legs. Long straight hair. 1 pc. red/white suit.
<u>1965:</u> 1030: New bendable legs. Same hair-do. New 1 pc. blue suit.
0950: Same as 1964.
<u>1966:</u> 1030: New pinker skin. Rest same as 1965.
0950: New pinker skin. Same as 1965.
<u>1967:</u> 1030: Same as 1966.
0950: Same as 1966.
<u>1968:</u> 1105: Twist 'N Turn. Same long hair as 950. New 1 pc. blue suit.
0950: Same as 1967.
<u>1969:</u> 1105: Twist 'N Turn. New 1 pc. rose and orange suit. New hair-do, two long curls.
<u>1970:</u> 1105: Twist 'N Turn. New orange and vinyl suit. Same hair as 1969.
1117: Living. 1 pc. green, blue and rose suit.
1147: Living (Trade In). Same as 1117.
0950: Re-issue of straight leg. Pinker skin.
<u>1971:</u> 1069: Malibu. Bendable legs. 2 pc. orange suit. Suntan.
1117: Living. New 2 pc. yellow suit.
1105: Twist 'N Turn. Same as 1970.
<u>1972:</u> 1179: Pose 'N Play. With gym. Blue check suit.
1069: Malibu. Same as 1971.
<u>1973:</u> 4223: Quick Curl. Blue dress.
1069: Malibu. Same as 1972.
1179: Pose 'N Play. Same as 1972.
<u>1974:</u> 4223: Quick Curl. Same as 1973.
1069: Malibu. Same as 1973.

ALLEN, KEN'S BUDDY (12")

<u>1964:</u> 1000: Reddish painted hair. Straight legs. Blue trunks, striped jacket.
<u>1965:</u> 1010: Bendable legs. Same hair. Blue shorts. Red jacket.
1000: Same as 1964.
<u>1966:</u> 1010: Same as 1965.
1000: Same as 1965.

SKOOTER, A PLAYMATE FOR SKIPPER (9¼")

<u>1965:</u> 1040: 2 pc. red suit. "Puppy ears" hair-do. Freckles. Straight legs.
<u>1966:</u> 1120: Bendable legs. Same hair-do as 1965. Red top, blue shorts.
1120: Same except has new pinker skin.
1040: Same as 1965, except has new pinker skin.

RICKY, SKIPPER'S FRIEND (9¼")

<u>1965:</u> 1090: Reddish painted hair. Straight legs. Blue shorts and jacket.
<u>1966:</u> 1090: Same as 1965, except has pinker skin.

FRANCIE, BARBIE'S MOD COUSIN (11")

1966: 1130: Greyish skin. Hair is curlier on ends. Bendable legs. Real eyelashes. 1 pc. suit has blue/green background.
1130: Pink skin. Rest same as above, except suit has white background.
1140: Pink skin. Straight legs. Painted eyelashes. 2 pc. red/white suit.
1967: 1100: Colored Twist 'N Turn: Long straight dark hair. Floral and see-through suit.
1170: Twist 'N Turn. Long hair. 1 pc. rose bottom, stripe top.
1140: Same as 1966.
1968: 1100: Colored. Same as 1967.
1170: Twist 'N Turn. Same as 1967.
1140: Straight legs. Same as 1967.
1969: 1170: New hair-do, flip style. New suit 1 pc. rose solid top, stripe bottom.
1970: 1170: Same hair-do. New suit, floral top over pink shorts.
1122: Hair Happenin's. Extra hair pieces. Blue dress.
1129: Growin' Pretty Hair. No extra hair pieces. Pink dress.
1971: 1068: Malibu. 1 pc. red and rose suit. Suntan. Casey head mold.
1074: Growin' Pretty Hair. Extra hair pieces. Same dress as No. 1129.
1122: Hair Happenin's. Same as 1970.
1170: New hair-do, brushed back. New orange pleated dress.
1972: 3313: Busy. Jeans and green top. Open and close hands.
1074: Growin' Pretty Hair. Same as 1971.
1068: Malibu. Same as 1971.
1973: 4222: Quick Curl. Yellow dress. Painted eyelashes.
1068: Malibu. Same as 1972.
1974: 7803: Ten Speeder. Doll and Bike. (This may not have been on the market.)
4222: Quick Curl. Same as 1973.
1068: Malibu: Same as 1973.

TUTTI, TWIN TO TODD,
BARBIE'S LITTLE SISTER (6¼")

1966: 3550: Playsuit and hat.
3552: "Walking My Dolly"
3553: "Night Night"
3554: "Me and My Dog"
3555: "Melody In Pink"
3556: "Sundae Treat" (Also with Todd)
1967: 3550: New clothes. Floral shirt, solid pink top dress.
3559: "Cookin' Goodies"
3560: "Swing A Ling"
3552 Through 3556. Same as 1966.
3580: New Stock Number. Same dress.
1968: All Tutti sets.
3580: Same as late 1967.
1969: 3580: Dress now has floral top, solid skirt.
1970: 3580: Same as 1969.
1971: 3580: Same as 1970.

TODD, TWIN TO TUTTI
BARBIE'S LITTLE BROTHER (6¼")

1966: 3580: Blue shirt, check pants and cap.

3556: "Sundae Treat" (Also has Tutti)
1967: 3590: New stock number. Same clothes.
3556: "Sundae Treat." Same as 1966.

CASEY, FRANCIE'S FRIEND (11")

1967: 1180: Bendable legs. Short straight hair. Gold and white suit.
1968: 1180: Same as 1967.
1969: 1180: Same as 1968.
1970: 1180: Same as 1969.

CHRIS, LITTLE TUTTI'S PLAYMATE (6¼")

1967: 3570: Multicolored dress. Same size as Tutti.
1968: 3570: Same as 1967.

BUFFY & MRS. BEASLEY

1969: 3577: Same size as Tutti.

TWIGGY, LONDON TEEN MODEL (11")

1967: 1185: Knitted-like mini dress. Very short blonde hair. Painted teeth.
1968: 1185: Same as 1967.

STACEY, AN ENGLISH FRIEND (11½")

1968: 1125: Talking. Long straight hair to side. 2 pc. stripe suit.
1165: Twist 'N Turn. Long straight hair drawn to back. 1 pc. red suit with white buttons.
1969: 1125: Talking. Same as 1968.
1165: Twist 'N Turn. New 1 pc. mulit-color suit. New hair, short flip.
1970: 1125: Talking. New clothes, blue/silver 1 pc. suit.
1165: Twist 'N Turn. New clothes, 1 pc. blue and rose floral suit.
1971: 1125: Talking. Same as 1970.
1165: Twist 'N Turn. Same as 1970.

CHRISTIE, (BLACK) BARBIE'S FRIEND (11½")

1968: 1126: Talking. Green knit top over rose shorts. Light brown skin. Brown curly hair with a part.
1969: 1126: Talking. Same as 1968.
1970: 1119: Twist 'N Turn. 1 pc. multi-color suit. Same hair and skin.
1126: Talking. New darker skin. New black modified Afro hair-do. New clothes, Afro top and shorts.
1971: 1175: Live Action. Long straight black hair. Dark skin.
1119: Twist 'N Turn. Same as 1970.
1126: Talking. Same as 1970.
1972: 1175: Live Action. Same as 1971.
1119: Twist 'N Turn. Same as 1971.
1126: Talking. Same as 1971.
1973: 7745: Malibu. Long straight black hair. Dark skin. 1 pc. red suit.
1974: 7745: Malibu. Same as 1973.

TRULY SCRUMPTIOUS
(CHITTY, CHITTY BANG, BANG) (11½")

<u>1969:</u> 1107: Talking. Old fashioned rose colored dress.
1108: Straight legs. Old fashioned pink dress.

JULIA, TV NURSE
(DIAHANN CARROLL) (11½")

<u>1969:</u> 1127: Twist 'N Turn. Light brown skin, short straight hair. 2 pc. white uniform.
1128: Talking. Same hair and skin. Gold and silver jumpsuit.
<u>1970:</u> 1127: Twist 'N Turn. New 1 pc. white uniform. Rest same as 1969.
1128: Talking. Same as 1969.
<u>1971:</u> 1128: Talking. New darker skin. New modified Afro hair-do. Same clothes as 1970.
1127: Twist 'N Turn. Same as 1970.
<u>1972:</u> 1128: Talking. Same as 1971.

P.J., BARBIE'S NEW FRIEND (11½")

<u>1969:</u> 1113: Talking. Floral mini dress. Bendable legs.
<u>1970:</u> 1113: Talking. Same as 1969.
1118: Twist 'N Turn. 1 pc. rose suit.
<u>1971:</u> 1153: Live Action on Stage.
1156: Live Action.
1113: Talking. Same as 1970.
1118: Twist 'N Turn. Same as 1970.
<u>1972:</u> 1187: Malibu: 1 pc. lavender suit.
1113: Talking. Same as 1971.
1156: Live Action. Same as 1971.
<u>1973:</u> 1187: Malibu. Same as 1972.
<u>1974:</u> 1187: Malibu. New green suit.

PRETTY PAIRS (6¼")

<u>1970:</u> 1133: Lori & Rori. Blonde doll and a teddy bear.
1134: Nan & Fran. Black doll and a small black doll.
1135: Angie & Tangie. Brunette doll and a small blonde doll.

BRAD (BLACK) KEN'S NEW BUDDY (12")

<u>1970:</u> 1114: Talking. Dark brown skin. Afro top and shorts.
1142: Bendable legs. Solid orange top, print shorts.
<u>1971:</u> 1114: Talking. Skin is darker. Same clothes as 1970.
1142: Bendable legs. Skin is darker. Same clothes as 1970.
<u>1972:</u> 1114: Talking. Same as 1971.
1142. Bendable legs. Same as 1971.

WALKING JAMIE
(MADE FOR SEARS ROEBUCK & CO.) (11½")

<u>1970:</u> 1132: Walks. Knitted-like dress. Same head mold as Barbie. Brown eyes.
<u>1971:</u> 1132: Same as 1969.
<u>1972:</u> 1132: Same as 1970.

FLUFF (9¼")

<u>1971:</u> 1143: Living. 1 pc. stripe top, solid skirt.

TIFF, SKIPPER'S NEW FRIEND (9¼")

<u>1972:</u> 1199: Pose 'N Play. Jeans and white shirt.

STEFFIE, BARBIE'S NEW FRIEND (11½")

<u>1972:</u> 1183: Walk Lively. Red and rose jumpsuit.
3312: Busy. Long, sun back dress. Open and close hands.
1186: Talking Busy. Blue hot pants, pink and white blouse. Open and close hands.
<u>1973:</u> 1183: Walk Lively. Same as 1972.
3312: Busy. Same as 1972.

MISS AMERICA (11½")

<u>1972:</u> 3200: Walk Lively. Royal robes. Real eyelashes.
3194-9991: Same as above but no walking stand. (Laurie Lea Schaefer) This was a Kelloggs offer.
<u>1973:</u> 8697: Quick Curl. Painted eyelashes. Different body, same clothes.
3194-9991. Same as 1972 but paler lips. (Terry Anne Meeuwsen). This was a Kelloggs offer. Some dolls were brunette Quick Curls.
<u>1974:</u> 8697: Quick Curl. New blonde hair.
3194-4: Same clothes. Blonde Quick Curl. A Kelloggs offer.

KELLEY

<u>1973:</u> 4221: Quick Curl. Green dress. Painted eyelashes.
<u>1974:</u> 7808: Yellowstone. Camping gear and clothes. Suntan. Long red hair.
4221: Quick Curl. Same as 1973.

MARKS:

*	**
BARBIE	MIDGE
PATS. PEND.	C 1962
©MCMLVIII	BARBIE (R)
BY	©1958
MATTEL	BY
INC.	MATTEL, INC.
***	****
KEN	©1960
PATS. PEND.	BY
©MCMLX	MATTEL, INC.
BY	HAWTHORNE
MATTEL	CALIF., USA
INC.	

Mattel Historical Doll List (Does Not Include Barbie's)

1960: *Chatty Cathy: Says 11 different phrases. Released in two different outfits. Red and white pinafore and blue party dress.

1961: *Matty, The Talking Boy: TV Character. Says 11 different phrases.

*Sister Belle, The Talking Girl. TV Character. Says 11 phrases.

*Casper, The Friendly Ghost: TV cartoon character. 11 phrases.

Chatty Cathy: Additional costumes now available.

1962: *Black Chatty Cathy: Same as 1960.

*Chatty Baby: (Blonde and brunette) Talking. Says 18 different phrases.

*Black Chatty Baby: Same as above.

*Talking Beany: TV character. 17½".

*Beany Boy Doll: Non-talking. 15"

*Talking Cecil, Seasick Sea Serpent: Beany's friend. 18"

*Cecil, Seasick Serpent: Non-talking. 14½"

*Slim Cecil: 22" Twistable plush.

*Talking Bugs Bunny: 26½"

*Bugs Bunny Doll: 19" Non-Talking.

Chatty Cathy: Same as 1961.

Matty: Same as 1961.

Sister Belle: Same as 1961.

Casper: Same as 1961.

1963: *Chatty Cathy: New Doll: 18 phrases. Dress is red velvet bodice, white lace skirt. Auburn hair, as well as blonde and brunette.

*Charmin' Chatty: Blonde and brunette. Plays 5 records.

*Tiny Chatty Baby: Smaller 15" version. 11 phrases. Blonde and brunette.

*Black Chatty Baby: Same as above. 15"

*Tiny Chatty Brother: Boy.

*Casper, The Talking Ghost: Same as 1962 Casper, but terrycloth body.

Talking Plush Casper. Same as 1962.

Matty: Same as 1962.

Sister Belle: Same as 1962.

Talking Bugs Bunny: Same as 1962.

Bugs Bunny, Non talking: Same as 1962.

Talking Beany: Same as 1962.

Beany: Same as 1962.

Talking Cecil: Same as 1962.

14½" Non Talking Cecil: Same as 1962.

Slim 22" Cecil: Same as 1962.

1964: *Baby Pattaburp: "burps" when patted. 16"

Chatty Baby: Same as 1963.

Chatty Cathy: Same as 1963.

Charmin' Chatty: Same as 1963.

Tiny Chatty Baby: Same as 1963.

Tiny Chatty Brother: Same as 1963.

*Shrinkin' Violette: Eyes close. Mouth moves.

*Talking Bozo, The Clown: 18" TV character.

Talking Bugs Bunny: Same as 1963.

Talking Cecil: Same as 1963.

Talking Plush Casper: Same as 1963.

*First introduction

*Animal Yackers: Larry The Talking Lion: Plush. Mouth moves.

*Animal Yackers: Cracker, The Talking Parrot: Plush. Beak moves.

1965: *Baby First Step: Battery operated walking doll. 18". Sleep eyes.

*Baby Cheryl: Says nursery rhymes in baby talk. 16." Sleep eyes.

*Dee Dee: Comes with costumes to make without sewing. Sleep eyes. 15"

*Drowsy: Talking doll. 15½"

*Singing Chatty: Blonde and brunette. Sings long phrases of "Row, Row, Row, Your Boat," "Farmer In The Dell" and others. 17".

*Baby Colleen: Made only for Sears. Drowsy type doll with carrot red hair. Says 11 "bedtime" things.

Chatty Cathy: Same as 1964.

Baby Pattaburp: Same as 1964.

*Scooba-Doo: Blonde and brunette. "Beatnik" rag doll. Rooted hair. 23".

*Tatters: Talking. Says 11 phrases. 19".

*T-Bone: Talking dog with Southern accent. 11"

*Porky Pig: Talking cartoon character. 17"

*Woody Woodpecker: Talking cartoon character. 18"

*Herman Munster Rag Doll: Talking TV character. 21"

*Talking Bugs Bunny Plush Doll: Now 24" tall.

Shrinkin' Violette: Same as 1964.

Talking Bozo, The Clown: Same as 1964.

*Animal Yackers, Chester O'Chimp: Talking plush chimp. Bendable hands. 14"

Larry The Talking Lion: Same as 1964.

Crackers The Parrot: Same as 1964.

*Talking Hand Puppets: Herman Munster, Porky Pig, Bugs Bunny, Bozo The Clown, Woody Woodpecker, T.V.S Mr. Ed. (Talking Horse)

1966: *Baby Teenie Talk: Blonde hair. Painted blue eyes. Talking. 17".

*Baby Secret: Lips move as she whispers. Red hair. Blue eyes. 18"

*Cheerful-Tearful: Face changes. Nurser. Cries real tears. Blonde hair. 13"

*Tiny Baby Pattaburp: Same as 1965 except only 14½"

*Teachy Keen: Sears only. Talker. Tells child to use accessories. 16"

*Babystep: Sears only. Similar to Baby First Step. Short straight hair. 18"

Baby Pattaburp: Same as 1965.

Baby Cheryl: Same as 1965.

Dee-Dee: Same as 1965.

Talking Drowsy: Same as 1965.

Singin' Chatty: Same as 1965.

Talking Baby Colleen: Same as 1965.

*Patootie: Talking clown/with a sad face mask extra. 16"

*Tom & Jerry: TV and Movie characters. Talking. 19" Tom and a tiny Jerry.

*Biff Bear: Talker. Moves lips. 14".

*Linus, The Lionhearted: TV Lion rag doll. Talker. 21"

Talking Bozo The Clown: Sears only this year.

Tatters: Same as 1965.

T-Bone: Same as 1965.

Porky Pig: Same as 1965.

Bugs Bunny: Same as 1965.

*Bernie Bernard, Animal Yackers: St. Bernard dog/keg on collar. 13"

Larry, The Talking Plush Lion: Same as 1965.

Chester O'Chimp: Same as 1965.

Talking Hand Puppets: *Linus, The Lionhearted, *Tom & Jerry, *Popeye: For Sears only, Herman Munster, Porky Pig, Bugs Bunny, Mr. Ed.

1967: *Baby's Hungry: Battery operated. Eyes move and mouth "chews." Also wets. 17½"

*Black Baby Say 'N See:

*Baby Cheerful-Tearful: Press tummy to change expression. 6".

*Talking Baby First Step: Same as 1965 but says 10 phrases.

*Baby Walk 'N See With Skates: Sears Only. Head similar to Baby Say 'N See. Body similar to Baby First Step. Battery operated, walks, skates, eyes move.

*Little Sister Look 'N Say: Sears Only. Similar to Baby Say 'N See.

Baby First Step: Same as 1966.

Talking Drowsy: Same as 1966.

Baby Teenie Talk: Same as 1966.

Baby Secret: Same as 1966.

Cheerful-Tearful: Same as 1966.

Tiny Baby Pattaburp: Same as 1966.

Teachy Keen: Sears Only: Same as 1966.

Babystep: Sears Only: Same as 1966.

Singin' Chatty: Sears Only: Same as 1966.

*Talking Mrs. Beasley: TV's "Granny" doll. Rag. Square black glasses. 22".

*Captain Kangaroo: Sears Only: Talking TV character. 19".

*Fusby Bear: Talking, says baseball things. 17".

*Montana Mouse: Talking, says cowboy things. 17".

*Lambie Pie: Talking plush girl lamb. 17".

*King Kong & Bobby Bond: Talking TV characters. Rag, King Kong holds vinyl Bobby Bond in hand. 12".

Talking Bozo The Clown: Sears Only. Same as 1966.

Tatters: Same as 1966.

T-Bone: Same as 1966.

Porky Pig: Same as 1966.

Bugs Bunny: Same as 1966.

Patootie: Same as 1966.

Tom & Jerry: Same as 1966.

Biff Bear: Same as 1966.

Linus The Lionhearted: Same as 1966.

*Flexi-Pets:

Monkey Shines: 19" brown bear.

Leapin' Leopard: 15" Brown and white leopard.

Sporty Spaniel: 12" Pink dog.

Spunky Schnauzer: 12" Red dog.

Houn' Dawg: 16" Yellow dog.

Elegant Elephant: 16" Pink elephant.

*Googlies: 14/15" plush animals. As tummy is squeezed eyes go around.

Googli Kitty: Orange.

Googli Puppy: Blue.

Googli Bunny. Pink.

Googli Bear: Yellow.

*Talking Patter Pillows: Puppy Patter, Choo-Choo Patter, Tugboat Patter, Dolly Patter, Bunny Patter.

*Lilac, Animal Yacker: Talking Skunk, with a scent. Lavender.

*Sniffy-Mint: Talking skunk with a scent. Red.

Larry The Talking Plush Lion: Same as 1966.

Chester O'Chimp: Same as 1966.

Bernie Bernard: Same as 1966.

Talking Hand Puppets: *Monkees Finger Puppet. *King Kong *Bobby Bond, *Bozo (Sears only), Bugs Bunny, Tom & Jerry.

1968: *Baby Whisper: Talking doll that whispers 11 phrases. 17½"

*Tippee Toes: Battery operated to ride horse or tricycle. 17"

Randi Reader: Battery operated to recite 15 nursery rhymes, eyes move side to side. 19½"

*Baby Smile 'N Frown: Like Cheerful-Tearful (1966) but 9" and auburn straight hair.

*Talking Baby First Step: New doll. 19". Says 11 things. Restyled hair.

*Baby First Step: New doll. 19". Restyled hair.

*Baby Small Talk: 8 phrases in infant's voice. 10¾"

*Sister Small Talk: Talking little girl. 10¾"

*Baby Small Walk: 11¼" doll who walks with help.

Talking Drowsy: Same as 1967.

*Black Talking Drowsy:

*Spanish Speaking Drowsy:

Babystep: Sears Only: Same as 1967.

Teachy Keen: Sears Only: Same as 1967.

Sister Look 'N Say: Sears Only: Same as 1967.

Baby's Hungry: Same as 1967.

Baby Say 'N See: Same as 1967.

Baby Cheerful Tearful: Same as 1967.

*Doctor Dolittle Doll: Talking Rex Harrison rag doll. 24". Plastic head.

*Talking Pushmi-Pullyu: Two headed animal from movie.

*Talking Gentle Ben: Plush TV bear. 17½"

Larry The Talking Plush Lion: Same as 1967.

Bozo: Sears Only: Same as 1967.

Bugs Bunny: Same as 1967.

Talking Mrs. Beasley: Same as 1967.

Captain Kangaroo: Sears Only: Same as 1967.

*Plush Animal Talkers: Cloth arms and legs.

Lancelot Lion: Yellow.

Tim Tim Tiger: Pink.

Rascal Rabbit: Green.

Flexi-Pets: Monkey Shines, Leapin' Leopard, Sporty Spaniel, Spunky Schnauzer, Houn' Dawg, Elegant Elephant.

Googlies: *Googli Pig: deep pink.

Googli Elephant, Puppy, Bear, Bunny and Kitty: Same as 1967.

Talking Patter Pillows: *Mickey Mouse Patter, Donald Duck Patter, Off To See The Wizard Patter, Pink Pussycat, Nite-Nite Patter.

Puppy, Doll and Bunny: Same as 1967.

Talking Hand Puppets: *Off To See The Wizard Finger Puppet, Doctor Dolittle.

Popeye, Bugs Bunny: Same as 1967.

1969: *Dancerina: Battery operated. Dances with operation of control knob in crown. 24"

*Swingy: Battery operated walking doll. 20"

*Black Swingy: Same as above.

*Baby Fun: Blows up balloons, bubbles, toots horn, when squeezed. 8".

*First introduction

*Bouncy Baby: "Jiggles" when picked up. 11".
*Black Bouncy Baby: Same as above.
*Talking Buffy and Mrs. Beasley: Buffy holds a tiny rag Mrs. Beasley. 10¾".
*Baby Sing A Song: Sears Only. Sings first line of 10 songs. 16½".
Talking Drowsy: Same as 1968.
Teachy Keen: Sears Only: Same as 1968.
Baby Whisper: Same as 1968.
Tippee Toes: Same as 1968.
Talking Baby First Step: Same as 1968.
Black Talking Drowsy: Same as 1968.
Spanish Speaking Drowsy: Same as 1968.
Baby Small Talk: Same as 1968.
Black Baby Small Talk: Same as 1968.
*Spanish Speaking Baby Small Talk:
Sister Small Walk: Same as 1968.
Baby Small Walk: Same as 1968.
*Storybook Small Talk Dolls: Similar to Sister Small Talk, with costumes and phrases appropriate to character. Cinderella, Little Bo Peep and Goldilocks.
*Mr. Potts: Talking Dick Van Dyke.
*Buzzy Bear Plush Doll: Sears Only.
Bugs Bunny: Same as 1968.
Captain Kangaroo: Same as 1968.
Talking Mrs. Beasley: Same as 1968.
Talking Gentle Ben: Same as 1968.
Bozo Rag Doll: Sears Only: Same as 1968.
*Roaring Twenties Rag Dolls: Sears Only: Flappers with dangling jewelry. 11½", Flo and Flossie.
*Talking Cuddle Snuggles: Plush dolls in costumes. 11", Nibbles The Mouse, Lovely The Lamb, Biffy The Bear.
Talking Patter Pillows: *Brown Bear Patter, Circus Clown Patter, Tinker Bell Patter, Puppy Patter (S&H Green Stamps Only)
Bunny, Nite Nite, Pink Pussycat, Mickey Mouse and Donald Duck: Same as 1968.
Talking Hand Puppets: *Larry Lion, Maurice Monkey, Bernardo, Popeye For S&H Green Stamps Only.
1970: *Baby Go Bye Bye: Doll sits in car (Bumpety Buggy) which is battery operated, and can do 12 maneuvers. 11" doll.
*Black Baby Go Bye Bye.
*Sketchy: Came with drawing table and follows templates to draw. 19".
*Baby Dancerina: Smaller doll, no batteries.
*Tiny Swingy: Battery operated with her own 33⅓ rpm record. 11½".
Talking Drowsy: Same as 1969.
Teachy Keen (Sears Only) Same as 1969.
Tippee Toes: Same as 1969.
Baby First Step: Same as 1969.
Black Drowsy: Same as 1969.
Randi Reader: Same as 1969.
Dancerina: Same as 1969.
Swingy: Same as 1969.
Baby Fun: Same as 1969.
Bouncy Baby: Same as 1969.
Baby Sing A Song (Sears Only): Same as 1969.
Talking Buffy and Mrs. Beasley: Same as 1969.
*Chatty Dolls: Reintroduction of 2nd issue dolls. New Phrases.
Chatty Cathy, Black Chatty Cathy, Chatty Baby, Tiny Chatty Baby.

*Pretty Pairs: Bendable, posable dolls with their own tiny dolls. Lori 'N Rori, Angie 'N Tangie, Nan 'N Fran.
*Wet Noodles: Squeeze tummies, their arms move and shampoo their hair. Came with 2 oz. of shampoo. 5" Fuchsia, Lime Green and Orange.
Storybook Small Talk Dolls: *Snow White.
Cinderella, Little Bo Peep, Goldilocks: Same as 1969.
*Great Big Beautiful Bertha: 40" Talking rag dolls. Feet straps for dancing.
*Somersalty: Clown that can stand on his flat head.
*Baby Flip Flop: Penny's Only: Talking doll. Can stand on head.
*Gramma Doll: Sears Only: Grey yarn hair. Talking doll.
*Puff: Talking fluffy white 18" dog from "To Rome With Love."
*Curly Pup: Sears Only: Talking poodle with long eyelashes.
*Barry Bear: Talking brown bear. 16".
*Talking Cat In The Hat: 23" Dr. Seuss character.
Bozo Rag Doll: Same as 1969.
Bugs Bunny: Same as 1969.
Talking Gentle Ben: Same as 1969.
Talking Mrs. Beasley: Same as 1969.
Buzzy Bear Plush Doll: Sears Only: Same as 1969.
Roarin' Twenties: Sears Only: Same as 1969.
*Patter Pal Dolls: Similar to Patter Pillows but with arms and legs.
Pep Talk, Happy Talk, Beddie Bye Talk.
Talking Patter Pillows: *Red Riding Hood & Wolf Turnover. Rest same as 1969.
Talking Cuddle Snuggles: Nibbles The Mouse, Lovely The Lamb: Same as 1969.
Talking Hand Puppets: Same as 1969, except the following:
*Myrtle: "My Three Son's" TV Show Doll. Freckles, blonde yarn hair.
1971: *Shoppin' Sheryl: One magnetized hand and one hand with flexible thumb for holding supermarket products and pushing shopping cart. 14".
*Busy Becky: Same principal as Shoppin' Sheryl.
*Timey Tell: Talking doll. Set wristwatch and she tells time. 17½".
*Talking Baby Tender Love: Says 8 phrases in babytalk. Safe for bathing.
*Living Baby Tender Love: Has movable arms and legs. 19".
*Baby Lovelight: Eyes light up when hand is squeezed. Battery operated.
*Valerie With Growin' Pretty Hair: 11" doll with hair that pulls out.
*Black Valerie.
*Baby Beans: 12" Bean rag dolls. Bedsie Beans, Yawning: Booful Beans, Grinning: Bitty Beans, Smiling.
*Talking Bean Bag: Penny's Only: Talking Baby Beans-type doll.
Talking Drowsy: Same as 1970.
Black Drowsy: Same as 1970.
Dancerina: Same as 1970.
Talking Buffy and Mrs. Beasley: Same as 1970.
Baby Tender Love: Same as 1970.
Baby Go Bye Bye: Same as 1970.
Tiny Swingy: Same as 1970.
Chatty Cathy: Same as 1970.
Chatty Baby: Same as 1970.
Tiny Chatty Baby: Same as 1970.
*Small Shots: Dolls on skates and Hot Wheels Track. 5".
Daffy Taffy & Dizzie Lizzie: Boy, Taffy, has dark brown hair.

*First introduction

Lizzie is blonde.

Red Hot Red & Sillie Millie: Red has red hair. Millie, dark brown hair.

Nifty Nan: Blonde hair.

Breezy Bridget: Red hair.

Daredevil Dexter: Blonde hair.

*Talking Mother Goose: Says 10 different nursery rhymes. 20".

*Talking Twosome: Sears Only: 16" rag doll with 12 phrases holding 8" rag doll that says 8 different things.

*Paula Bear: Talking polar bear. 16".

*Humpty Dumpty Turnover: 17" pillow with arms and legs.

*Bozo Patter Pal: Sears Only: Bozo, The Clown talking pillow.

*Talk-A-Littles: 6-7" rag characters. 8 phrases.

Toofums: Baby girl with one tooth.

Roscoe: Yellow dog with brown spots.

Sassie: Red yarn hair, freckles.

Dr. Seuss Characters: *Talking Cat In The Hat, *Talking Hedwig Bird, *Horton The Elephant, *Talking Yertle The Turtle, *The Cat In The Hat Hand Puppet, 23" Talking Cat In The Hat: Same as 1970.

Bozo Talking Rag Doll: Same as 1970.

Bugs Bunny: Same as 1970.

Talking Woody Woodpecker: Same as 1970.

Great Big Beautiful Bertha: Same as 1970.

Talking Mrs. Beasley: Same as 1970.

Curli Pup: Sears Only: Same as 1970.

Gramma Doll: Sears Only: Same as 1970.

Baby Flip Flop: Penny's Only: Same as 1970.

1972: *Hi Dottie: Came with two telephones, one for her and one for child. 17".

*Baby Play A Lot: Came with 20 toys. Pull string. Can hold things. 15".

*Baby Kiss & Talk: 15" doll talks when kissed.

*Tearful Baby Tenderlove: Expression changes as head is turned. 15".

*Tiny Baby Tenderlove: 11½".

*Cynthia: 19". Came with 3 double sided records.

*Cuddly Beans: Larger bean bag type.

Talking Drowsy: Same as 1971.

Black Drowsy: Same as 1971.

Baby Tenderlove: Same as 1971.

Living Baby Tenderlove: Same as 1971.

Talking Baby Tenderlove: Same as 1971.

Timey Tell: Same as 1971.

Shoppin' Sheryl: Same as 1971.

Baby Love Light: Same as 1971.

Valerie: Same as 1971.

*Super Small Shots: Same as 1971 except now has vehicle instead of skates.

*Talk Ups: 4½" dolls talk when heads are pulled up.

Funny Talk: Brown hair.

Silly Talk: Blonde hair.

*Teachy Talk: Says 10 things about good grooming.

*Bean Pals: Animal like Baby Beans. *Bear Pal and *Puppy Pal.

*Small Talkers: 9-11" rag. Talking Bullwinkle, Yertle The Turtle.

Talking Bugs Bunny, Talking Cat In The Hat.

Talking Cat In The Hat: 23": Same as 1971.

Talking Mother Goose: Same as 1971.

Talk A Littles: Same as 1971.

*First introduction

*Talking Party Liners: Rag Elephant and Donkey. Election year dolls.

Talking Mrs. Beasley: Same as 1971.

Larry Lion: Same as 1971.

Bugs Bunny: Same as 1971.

Bozo Talking Rag Doll: Same as 1971.

1973: *Cry Baby Beans: 12" Cries tears. Dressed in yellow.

*Biffy Beans: 12" dressed in blue.

*Bitty Beans: 12" dressed in pink.

*Talking Baby Beans: 12" dressed in pale blue.

*Booful Beans: 12" dressed in yellow.

*Black Bitty Beans: 12" dressed in pink.

*Puffin (red) and Punky (Blue): Bean puppets. Both puppet and doll.

Bean Pets: Puppy Dog and Cubby Bear: Same as 1972.

*Splash Happys: 18". 1 pc. molded vinyl. Blonde girl, Sal and Brunette boy, Hal.

*Walk A Bye Baby: 13½". Rag walker with hobby horse.

*Bedtime Baby and Ballerina Baby: 12½" cloth. Posable.

Talking Mrs. Beasley: Same as 1972.

Drowsy: Same as 1972.

Black Drowsy: Same as 1972.

Spanish Drowsy: Same as 1972.

*New Born Baby Tenderlove: 13".

*Little Baby Tenderlove: 11½".

Talking Baby Tenderlove: Same as 1972.

Baby Tenderlove: Same as 1972.

Black Baby Tenderlove: Same as 1972.

Tearful Baby Tenderlove: Same as 1972

*Peachy and Her Puppets: 18".

*Black Peachy and Her Puppets: 18".

*Saucy: 15". Changes facial expressions.

Cynthia: Same as 1972.

Hi Dottie: Same as 1972.

Talking Bugs Bunny. Same as 1972.

Bugs Bunny: Same as 1972.

Talk Ups: Funny Talk, Casper, Silly Talk: Same as 1972.

Talk A Littles: Toofums, Sassie: Same as 1972.

Small Talkers: Talking Bugs Bunny (11"): Same as 1972.

Bozo Talking Rag Doll: Same as 1972.

Larry Lion: Same as 1972.

1974: *Jimmy Jeaner: Denim rag boy.

*Jibby Jeaner: Denim girl rag doll.

*Itsy Bitsy Beans: Poofum (Yellow), Pidgy (Blue), Piffle (Pink).

Baby Beans: Booful (Yellow), Biffy Beans (Blue), Bitty Beans (Pink): Same as 1973.

*Show Offs: Lionhearted and Scarycrow: Puppets on a stand. 13".

*Sunshine Family: Mother, Father and Baby. Extra clothes, house and accessories.

*Pedal Pretty: 15" Has wagon and trike.

*Sweet Sounds Tenderlove: 13". Coos and gurgles. Cries tears.

*Dreamtime Tenderlove: 13". 2 pc. blue layette outfit.

*Sunshine Tenderlove: Yellow romper suit.

*Rosie Tenderlove: Pink dress and pants.

*Cathy Quick Curl: 15"

Talking Mrs. Beasley: Same as 1973.

Black Drowsy: Same as 1973.

Drowsy: Same as 1973.

Spanish Speaking Drowsy: Same as 1973.

Talking Bugs Bunny: Same as 1973.

Talk Ups: Funny Talk, Casper, Silly Talk: Same as 1973.

Mattel--"Barbie" In the 1959-61 "Floral" petticoat, bra and panties. Doll: $10.00. Outfit: $1.00.

Mattel--"Barbie" in "Cotton Casual" 1959. Doll: $10.00. Outfit: $3.00.

Mattel--"Barbie" Leather car coat and hooded T shirt are from "Winter Holiday," jeans from "Picnic Set" 1959. Doll: $7.00. Outfit: $3.00.

Mattel--"Barbie" in the blue "Knitting Party" outfit. 1963. In 1959 the skirt was gray and sweater peach. In 1964 the outfit was pink. Doll: $10.00. Outfit: $5.00.

Mattel--"Barbie" shown in "Sheath Sensation" that came with white/red hat. 1961. Doll: $7.00. Outfit: $2.50.

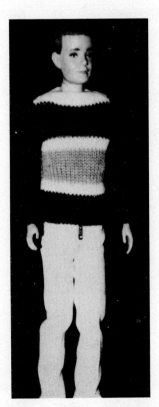

Mattel--Doll is the first "Ken" sold in 1961. Outfit is "Campus Hero" 1961. Flocked hair Ken: $9.00. Outfit: $3.00.

Mattel--1962 "Ken" with the jacket and shirt from "Saturday Date" and pants from "Campus Hero," both 1961. Doll: $7.00. Outfit: $3.00.

Mattel--"Ken" wearing the "Dreamboat" suit of 1961 with a different shirt. Doll: $7.00. Outfit: $3.00.

Mattel--"Ken" in the "Sportsman" outfit of 1961 and 1962. Came with yellow bermuda shorts, long socks and oxford shoes. Doll: $5.00. Outfit: $2.00.

Mattel--"Ken" dressed in the "Campus Hero" outfit that came with a pennant, trophy and letter "U" for sewing on. 1961. Flocked hair Ken: $9.00. Outfit: $3.00.

 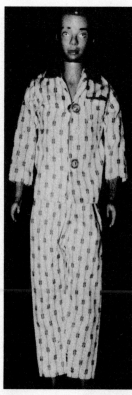 

Mattel--"Ken" in "Tuxedo" that came with a cummerbund and a corsage for Barbie. 1961. Doll: $7.00. Outfit: $5.00.

Mattel--"Ken" in "Sleep Set" #781. 1962. Doll: $7.00. Outfit: $2.00.

Mattel--"Barbie" in "Friday Nite Date" #0979. 1961. Doll: $7.00. Outfit: $3.00.

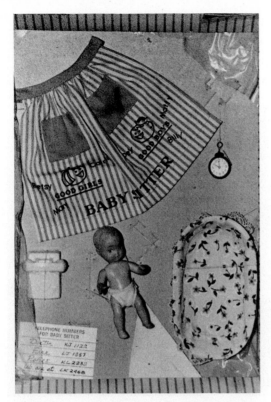

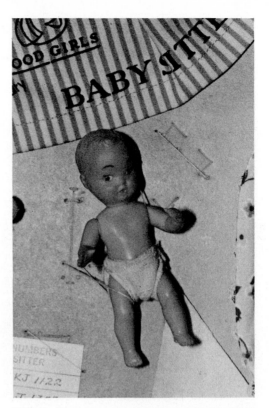

Mattel--3" "Baby From Barbie Baby Sits" Yellow painted hair. Painted blue eyes. Original. Marks: none. 1962. 1963 version had a different baby bassinet. $15.00 complete. (Courtesy Margaret Biggers)

Mattel--Close up of baby from "Barbie Baby Sits."

Mattel--"Barbie" case. 1961. $2.00.

Mattel--"Barbie" case. 1961-62. $3.00.

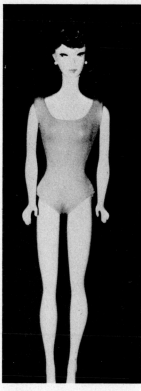

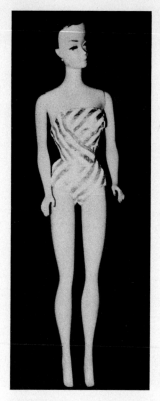

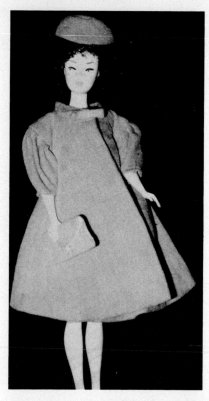

Mattel--11½" "Fashion Queen Barbie" Molded brown hair. Came with three wigs on a stand. Unjointed knees. Marks: Midge/1962/Barbie/1958/ By Mattel Inc/Patented. 1962. Doll: $7.00.

Mattel--Basic "Barbie" 1962. Came with sunglasses, earrings and shoes. Doll: $7.00.

Mattel--"Barbie" in "Red Flare" outfit. 1962. Doll: $7.00. Outfit: $5.00. (Courtesy Allin's Collection)

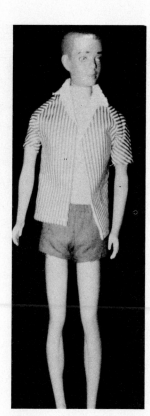

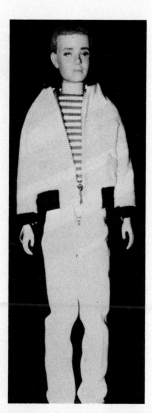

Mattel--"Barbie" Ready for tennis. 1962. Came with tennis balls, sunglasses and tennis booklet. Doll: $7.00. Outfit: $5.00. (Courtesy Allin's Collection)

Mattel--Basic "Ken" doll. 1962. Doll: $7.00.

Mattel--"Ken" in the 1962 "Yachtsman" outfit. Came with yachting booklet. This is one of the older "Kens" but not the first. The first had "flocked" hair and this one has "fuzzy" hair. Doll: $7.00. Outfit: $3.00.

Mattel--1962 Barbie Wardrobe. Made for Barbie but not by Mattel. $4.00.

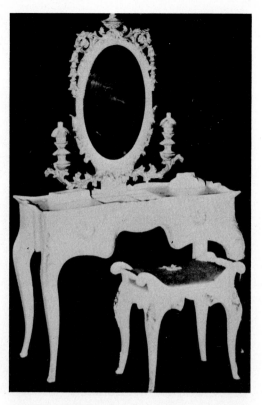

Mattel--Dressing table and bench. 1962. Made for Barbie but not manufactured by Mattel. $4.00. (Courtesy Allin's Collection)

Mattel--Barbie Case 1962. $2.00.

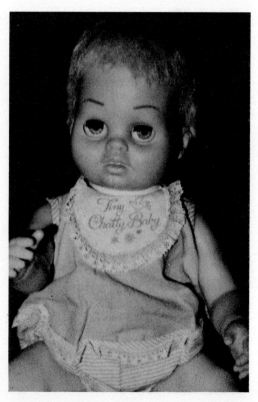

Mattel--15" "Tiny Chatty Baby" Plastic and vinyl with rooted white hair. Blue sleep eyes. Pull string talker. Marks: Tiny Chatty Baby/ Tiny Chatty Brother/1962 Mattel Inc/Hawthorne, Calif. USA/US Pat. 3017187/Other US & Foreign Patents Pending. $15.00.

207

Mattel--"Barbie" in the green "Swinging Easy" dress of 1963. This same dress in blue was "Let's Dance" of 1962. Doll: $7.00. Outfit: $3.00.

Mattel--"Barbie" dressed as "Career Girl" 1963. Doll: $7.00. Outfit: $5.00. (Courtesy Allin's Collection)

Mattel--"Barbie" in "Movie Date" dress. 1963. Doll: $7.00. Outfit: $3.00.

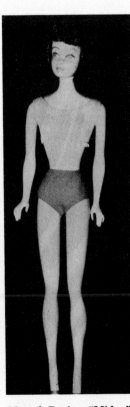

Mattel--"Barbie" in "Ski Queen" outfit that also included skis, pole and sunglasses. 1963. Doll: $7.00. Outfit: $4.00. (Courtesy Allin's Collection)

"Barbie" in "Knit Sheath" 1963. Doll: $7.00. Outfit: $1.00.

Mattel--Basic "Midge" 1963. Doll: $7.00.

Mattel--"Ken" in the shirt from "Goin' Hunting" made in 1963 for the 1964 market. Came with blue jeans. Doll: $7.00. Outfit: $2.00.

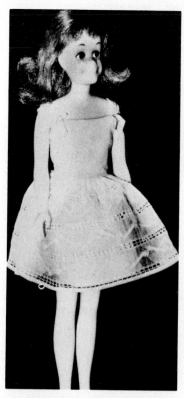

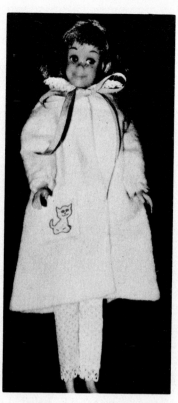

Mattel--"Skooter" wears Skipper's "Flower Girl" dress #1904. 1963. Doll: $8.00. Outfit: $2.00.

Mattel--"Midge" in "Fancy Free" dress. 1963. Doll: $7.00. Outfit: $2.00.

Mattel--"Skooter" in Skipper's "Dreamland" flannel peignoir. #1909. 1963. Doll: $8.00. Outfit: $1.00.

Mattel--"Ken" in "Ski Champion" outfit that included cap, sun glasses, skis and pole. 1963. Doll: $7.00. Outfit: $3.00.

Mattel--"Ken" in "Masquerade." 1963. Outfit: $6.00.

Mattel--"Midge" in raincoat outfit. 1963. Doll: $7.00. Outfit: $3.00. (Courtesy Allin's Collection)

Mattel--"Skooter" In "Ballet Les-
sons" Also called "Ballet Class."
Made in 1963 for market in 1964.
Doll: $8.00. Outfit: $4.00.

Mattel--"Barbie" in "Midnight Blue"
Made in 1964 for market in 1965.
Doll: $7.00. Outfit: $5.00. (Courtesy
Allin's Collection)

Mattel--"Barbie" in "Drum
Majorette" outfit. 1964.
Doll: $7.00. Outfit: $5.00.

Mattel--11½" "Miss Barbie" (#1060) Hard plastic
body and head. Molded brown hair/hair band.
Vinyl arms and legs. Snapping knees. Blue sleep
eyes/molded lashes. Blue eyelids. Painted
fingernails. 1964. Dress: "Benefit Performance" 1966. Marks: 1958 Mattel Inc/US
Patented/US Pat. Pend, on hip. M.I., on head.
Doll: $18.00.

Mattel--11½" "Miss Barbie" The sleep eyed
Barbie of 1964. Doll: $18.00.

Mattel--"Barbie" in the Little Theater "Before Cinderella" outfit. 1964. Doll: $7.00. Outfit: $6.00. (Courtesy Leslie White)

Mattel--"Barbie" in the Little Theater "Cinderella Ball" outfit. Called the "After Cinderella." 1964. Doll: $7.00. Outfit: $6.00. (Courtesy Leslie White)

Mattel--"Ken" in "Victory Dance" outfit. 1964. Doll: $7.00. Outfit: $5.00.

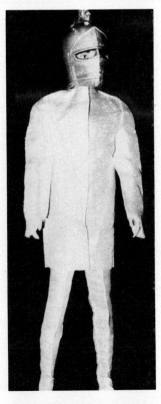

Mattel--One of the first "Kens" with flocked hair. Shown in "Roller Skate Date" outfit. Came with tam and skates. 1964. Doll: $7.00. Outfit: $3.00.

Mattel--"Barbie" in the Little Theater "Red Riding Hood" outfit. (Cape only). 1964. Came with a small polka dotted dress and wolf mask. Doll: $7.00. Outfit: $5.00. (Courtesy Leslie White)

Mattel--"Ken" in the Little Theater "King Arthur" basic outfit and face mask. 1964. Doll: $7.00. Outfit: $7.00. (Courtesy Leslie White)

Mattel--"Ken" in the Little Theater "King Arthur" outfit without mask. 1964. Doll: $7.00. Outfit: $7.00. (Courtesy Lucille Kimsey)

Mattel--"Barbie" in the Little Theater "Guinevere" outfit. 1964. Doll: $7.00. Outfit: $7.00. (Courtesy Leslie White)

Mattel--"Allan" 1964. Shirt from "Dreamboat" 1961 and pants from a pak. Doll: $9.00. Outfit: $2.00.

Mattel--"Ken" shown as "The Prince" from the 1964 Little Theater Costumes. Cape is missing. Doll: $7.00. Outfit: $7.00. (Courtesy Leslie White)

Mattel--"Ken" as "Arabian Nights" from the "Little Theater" costume. 1962-65. Doll: $7.00. Outfit: $7.00.

Mattel--"Ken" Jacket from "Ken In Mexico" of the 1964. "Travel Costumes" Sold from 1962-65. Doll: $7.00. Outfit: $5.00.

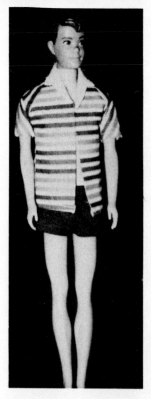  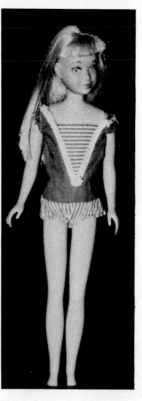 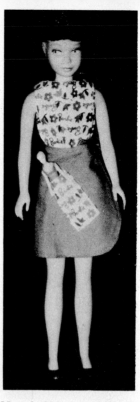

Mattel--Basic "Allen" Buddy for Ken and boyfriend for Midge. 1964. Doll: $9.00.

Mattel--"Midge" shown in "It's Cold Outside" outfit. 1964. Doll: $7.00. Outfit: $5.00. (Courtesy Allin's Collection)

Mattel--Basic "Skipper" 1964. Doll: $5.00. (courtesy Leslie White)

Mattel--'Skipper" Shown in "Day At The Fair" Made in 1964 for the 1965 market. Tiny Barbie doll in pocket. Doll: $5.00. Outfit: $5.00.

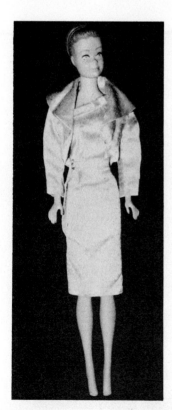  

Mattel--"Midge" With molded hair came with the head only in "Wig Wardrobe" with three wigs. Shown here in the 1964 "Satin Separates" Also the three pieces came separately in Paks, in 1963. The 1964 Gift set was called "Sparkling Pink." Also sold as "Satin 'N Rose" in 1964. Doll: $7.00. Outfit: $5.00.

Mattel--Same "Midge" is shown with her wig. 1964.

Mattel--"Francie" In skirt from "Barbie in Mexico" from the 1964 Travel costumes and jacket from one of the Paks "Going To The Ball" 1964. Doll: $5.00. Outfit: $3.00.

213

Mattel--Barbie Case, 1963. $2.00.

Mattel--Skipper Case 1964. $2.00.

Mattel--Ken case. 1964. $3.00.

Mattel-"Skipper" in the 1964 "Silk 'N Fancy" party dress. Came in a gift set, with the doll, and included red velvet coat, hat and purse. The gift set was called "Party Time." Doll: $5.00. Outfit: $3.00. (Courtesy Leslie White)

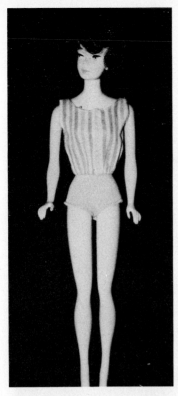

Mattel--"Barbie" in basic swimsuit. This Barbie with a bubble cut hairdo (#0850) with straight legs came in a red jersey swimsuit and the bendable leg Barbie (#1070) came in a suit. 1965. Doll: $7.00.

Mattel--"Skipper" in coat that goes with "Silk 'N Fancy" party dress. 1964. Doll: $5.00. Outfit: $2.00.

Mattel--"Barbie" in "Miss Astronaut" 1965. Came with a helmet, gloves, boats and an American Flag. Doll is a "Fashion Queen" Barbie. Doll: $7.00. Outfit: $4.00.

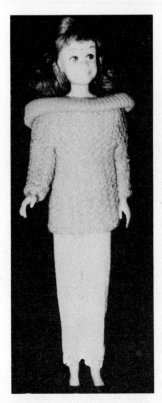

Mattel--"Skooter" Skipper's playmate. Shown in "Outdoor Casual." 1965. Doll: $9.00. Outfit: $2.00. (Courtesy Leslie White)

Mattel--"Twist 'N Turn Barbie" 1967-68 in "Lunchtime" made in 1965 for 1966 market. Material same as the "Fair Flowers" and "Barbie Learns to Cook" Made in 1964 for the 1965 market. Doll: $5.00. Outfit: $3.00.

Mattel--"Skipper" shown in "Can You Play" Made in 1965 for the 1966 market. Doll: $5.00. Outfit: $1.00.

Mattel--"Posable Skipper" Basic doll. 1965. Doll: $5.00. (Courtesy Leslie White)

215

Mattel--"Skipper" in her "Ship Ahoy" dress. Came with a sleeveless jacket. 1965. Doll: $5.00. Outfit: $1.00.

Mattel--"Kiddles Case" 1965. $2.00.

Mattel--3½" "Telly Viddle Kiddle" All vinyl with rooted brown hair. Original. Marks: 1965/Mattel Inc./Japan/15, on back. Mattel/1965, on head. $2.00.

Mattel--2½" "Calamity Jiddle" All vinyl. Rooted blonde hair. Painted blue eyes. Marks: 1965/Mattel Inc./Japan. Came with horse and large cowboy hat. $2.00.

Mattel--3½" "Soapy Siddle" Brown hair and blue eyes. 1965. Marks: Mattel Inc, on head. $2.00.

"Cycling Cheri" A beautiful quality doll. Refer to
the Tomy section for full description.

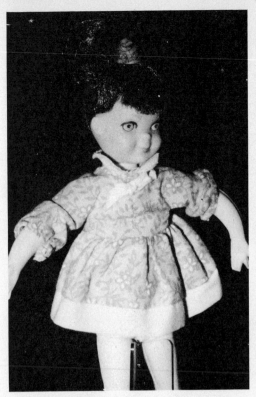

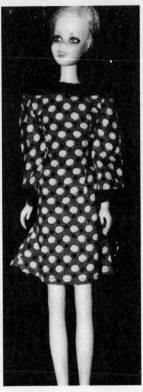

Mattel--6" "Tutti" Marks: Tutti/1965 Mattel, on dress tag. This one came in one of the play settings called "Cookin' Goodies." Missing is her apron, stove and pots. $4.00.

Mattel--11" "Twiggy" Same body as Francie. Snapping knees. Rooted short cut hair. Painted blue eyes/lashes. Open mouth with painted teeth. Dress not Mattel's. Marks: 1966/Mattel Inc/US Patented/US Pat. Pend./Made In/Japan. $9.00.

Mattel--6" "Tutti" One piece body, legs and arms of solid vinyl. Vinyl head with rooted blonde hair. Painted blue eyes. Original dress. Marks: SN/221, head. 1965/Mattel Inc/Japan, lower back. Dress tag: Tutti/1965 Mattel. $4.00. (Courtesy Leslie White)

218 Mattel--6" "Chris" Tutti's friend. One piece body, arms and legs. Brown eyes. Bangs have been cut off. Wears Tutti's dress from "Swing A Ling." 1966. $5.00.

Mattel--"Barbie" in the outfit "Benefit Performance" made in 1965 for the 1966 market. Doll: $7.00. Outfit: $7.00.

Mattel--"Skipper" in the 1966 "Dog Show" top. Pants are from "Sledding Fun." Doll: $5.00. Outfit: $2.00.

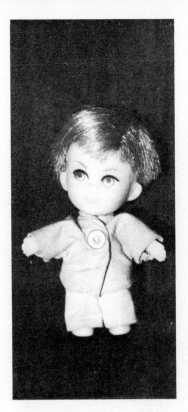

Mattel--"Skipper" in "Sledding Fun" 1966 outfit. Outfit included boots and sled. Doll: $5.00. Outfit: $2.00. (Courtesy Leslie White)

Mattel--3" "Bunson Burnie" Red hair. Marks: 1966/Mattel Inc. From the first group of Little Kiddles. 1965, repeated in 1966 (Group 2) $2.00.

Mattel--3" "Rosemary Roadster" Original. Marks: 1966/Mattel Inc. $7.00 complete with car.

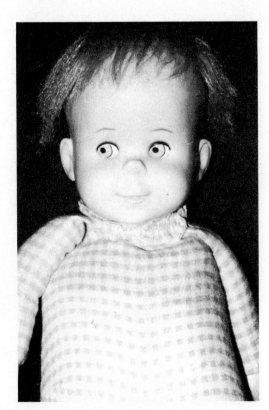

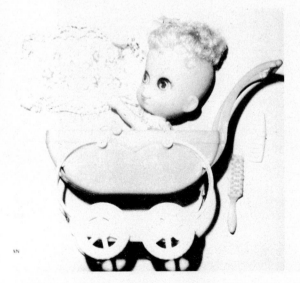

Mattel--14" "Baby Colleen" Cloth body, arms and legs. Vinyl head with rooted orange hair. Painted blue eyes. Pull string talker. Marks: Baby Colleen/1965 Mattel Inc, on tag. Made for Sears only. $5.00.

Mattel--2" "Baby Liddle" All original. 1966. $9.00 complete. (Courtesy Margaret Weeks)

19" "Charlie Chaplin" Cloth body, arms and legs. Vinyl hands, feet (shoes) and head. Molded on vinyl hat. Painted features. Original removable clothes. Very well made and of good quality materials. Marks: Bubbles Inc/1972, on head. (Courtesy The Treasure Trove)

25" "Polly Pond's Beauty Doll" Refer to Citro Mfg. Co. section for description.

"Ginger" in outfit #1003. All hard plastic doll. Not marked. Paper tag: Ginger in her official/ Walt Disney/Mickey Mousketeer Outfit.

11" "Hotten Tot" A Cameo doll by Strombecker Corp. Original. Marks: 733/1 Cameo JLK, on neck. Cameo, on back. Kewpie/JLK, on right foot. (Courtesy Verena Holzhey)

Vogue "Jill" in a "Dolls From Historyland" outfit "The Gibson Girl." The other outfit is "The Pilgrim" (Courtesy Virginia Jones)

"Ginny" shown in the 1962 Nun outfit. (Courtesy Virginia Jones)

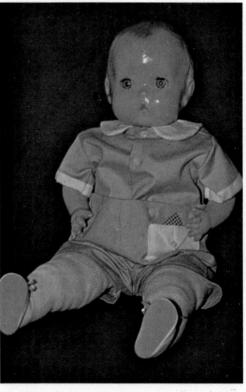

"Ginny" in her Alaskan outfit. Refer to Vogue section for full description. (Sled, courtesy of Rua Belle Green)

22" Marks: Brother/1937 Horsman. Composition and cloth.

Mattel--3" "Sleeping Biddle" All original. 1966. $8.00 complete. (Courtesy Margaret Weeks)

Mattel--3" "Liddle Biddle Peep" All original. 1966. $8.00 complete. (Courtesy Margaret Weeks)

Mattel--3" "Little Middle Muffet" All original. 1966. $8.00 complete (Courtesy Margaret Weeks)

Mattel--3" "Peter Paniddle" Original. 1966. Tinkerbell is a tiny Barbie doll. $8.00 complete. (Courtesy Margaret Weeks)

Mattel--3½" "Liddle Red Riding Hiddle" All vinyl with rooted blonde hair. Original. Marks: 1966/Mattel Inc. $8.00 complete.

Mattel--3" "Sizzly Friddle" All original. 1966. $7.00 complete. (Courtesy Margaret Weeks)

Mattel--4" "Howard "Biff" Boodle" All vinyl Rooted blonde hair. Painted features. Original. Marks: 1966/Mattel, Inc., on back. $7.00 complete. (Courtesy Lucille Kimsey)

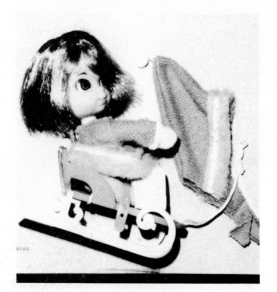

Mattel--3" "Freezy Sliddle" All original. 1966. $7.00 complete. (Courtesy Margaret Weeks)

"Cricket" shown in outfit #14108 "Shutter-Bug."

"Cricket" by American Character, in outfit called "Just Pals" #14105.

19" "Elise Denny, Honolulu Doll" Marks: 20, on head. (Courtesy Karan Penner)

16" "Terrie Lee." (Courtesy Jay Minter)

Mattel--"Cinderiddles Palace" Marks: 1966. Mattel, Inc. $4.00.

Mattel--"Sleeping Biddle's Castle" 1966. $6.00. (Courtesy Sibyl DeWein)

Mattel--Babe Biddle's Automobile, 1966. Calamity Jiddle's Horse, 1966. $4.00.

Mattel--2" "Lolli Lemon" Kiddle. Yellow hair. Lavender eyes. Original. Marks: Mattel/Inc, on back. 1966. $3.00.

225

Mattel--2" "Lolli Mint" Kiddle. White hair with painted blue eyes. Original. Marks: M, on head. Mattel/Inc., on back. 1966. $3.00. (Courtesy Leslie White)

Mattel--2" "Frosty Mint Kone" Kiddle. Green hair. Painted blue eyes. Original. Marks: Mattel/Inc, on back. 1966. (Courtesy Leslie White). $3.00.

Mattel--2" "Orange Ice Cone" Kiddle. Orange hair. Painted blue eyes. Original. 1966. Marks: Mattel/Inc., on back. $3.00.

Mattel--2½" "Violet Kiddle Kolognes" All vinyl with lavender hair. Came in set of six: Lily of Valley, Apple Blossom, Rosebud, Honeysuckle, Sweet Pea and Violet. Marks: Mattel, on back. 1966. $2.00.

Mattel--2" "Lily of the Valley Kiddle" All vinyl with rooted white hair. Painted features. Original. 1966. $2.00.

Mattel--2" "Rosebud" Kiddle Kologne. Red hair. Painted blue eyes. Original. Marks: 1966/Mattel, on back. $2.00. (Courtesy Virginia Jones)

Mattel--2" "Honeysuckle Kiddle Kologne" All vinyl with rooted yellow hair. Painted features. Original. Marks: Mattel, 1966, on back. $2.00.

Mattel--2" "Sweet Pea" Kiddle Kologne. Yellow hair. Original. Marks: Mattel Inc./Toymaker, on bottle. 1966. $2.00.

Mattel--2" "Apple Blossom" Kiddle Kologne. Green hair. Blue painted eyes. Marks: Mattel/ 1966. Original. $2.00.

Mattel--2" "Windy Fliddle" All vinyl with rooted blonde hair. Original. Marks: 1966/Mattel Inc. $8.00 complete.

Mattel--2" "Larky Locket" Kiddle. Blonde with painted blue eyes. Original. Marks: Mattel/1966, on back. $3.00.

Mattel--2" "Lou Locket" Kiddle. Red hair with painted brown eyes. Original. 1966. Marks: Mattel/Inc., on back. $3.00.

Mattel--2" "Lorelie Locket" Kiddle. Blonde with painted blue eyes. Original. Marks: 1966/Mattel/Inc, on back. $3.00.

Mattel--2" "Lorna Locket" Kiddle. Blonde with painted blue eyes. Original. 1966. Marks: Mattel/Inc., on back. $3.00.

Mattel--2" "Lilac Locket" Kiddle. White hair. Blue painted eyes. Original. Marks: 1966 Mattel Inc, on head. $3.00.

Mattel--2" "Lucky Locket" Brown hair and green eyes. Original. Marks: M.I., on head. 1966. $3.00.

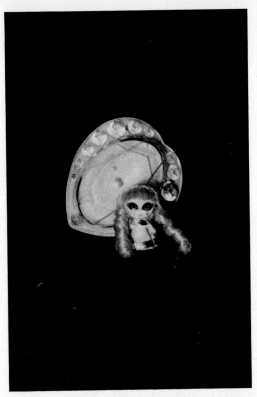

Mattel--1" "Heart Pin Kiddle" All vinyl. Yellow hair. Marks: Mattel/Hong Kong, on back. Original. 1966.

Mattel--1" "Lorelie Bracelet Kiddle" All vinyl with lavender hair. Painted blue eyes. Marks: Mattel/Hong Kong, on back. Original. 1966. $3.00.

Mattel--1" "Flower Pin Kiddle" All vinyl with painted features. 1966. $3.00.

Mattel--4" "Suki Skediddle" Vinyl and plastic. Rooted blonde hair. Painted features and socks. Original. Marks: 1966/Mattel Inc., on back. $4.00. (Courtesy Mary Partridge)

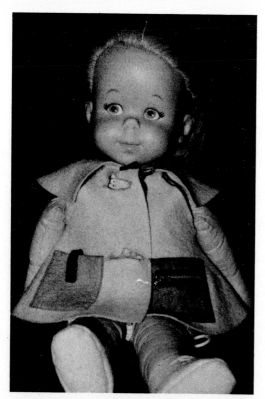

Mattel--17" Teachy Keen" Stuffed cloth body, arms and legs. Vinyl head with rooted blonde hair. Painted features. Dressed to teach opening zippers, buckling shoes, tieing and buttoning coat. Marks: Mattel/Teachy Keen/1966 Mattel, Inc., on tag. $8.00.

Mattel--Kiddle Kastle. 1966. $4.00.

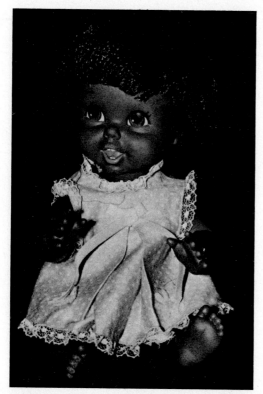

Mattel--11" "Baby Small Talk" Plastic and vinyl. Rooted black hair. Painted brown eyes. Two upper and two lower painted teeth. Pull string talker. Original. Marks: 1967 Mattel/Japan, on head. 1967 Mattel Inc/US & For/Pats. Pend./ USA, on back. Baby Small Talk/1967 Mattel Inc, on dress tag. $6.00.

Mattel--Alice in Wonderliddle Castle. 1967. Complete. $12.00. (Courtesy Sibyl Dewein)

Mattel--10½" "Valerie" Plastic body with vinyl arms, legs and head. Rooted blonde hair, floor length in back. Painted blue eyes. Two painted upper and lower teeth. Marks: 1967 Mattel Inc./US & For./Pats. Pend/Hong Kong. $4.00.

Mattel--11½" "Talking P.J." Plastic body. Vinyl arms, legs and head. Rooted blonde hair. Brown eyes/heavy lashes. Snapping knees. Pull string talker. Marks: 1967/Mattel Inc/US & Foreign/ Pats. Pend/Hong Kong. Dress is "Pink Sparkle" 1966. Doll: $8.00. Outfit: $3.00.

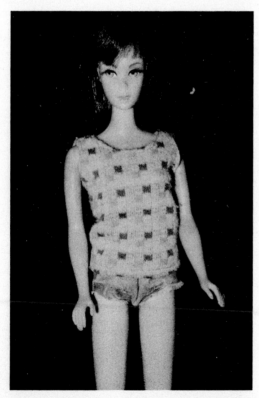

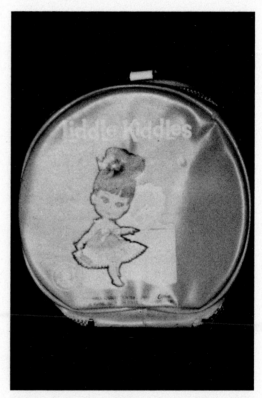

Mattel--"Twist 'N Turn Barbie" 1967-68. Hair has been re-combed. Doll: $5.00.

Mattel--Lavender Kiddle Case. 1967. $1.00. (Courtesy Roberta Lago)

Mattel--2" "Laverne Locket" 1967. Marks: Mattel, on head. $3.00.

Mattel--2" "Louise Locket" Blonde hair and brown eyes. Marks: 1966/Mattel, Inc., on back. $3.00.

Mattel--1" "Hearts" Kiddle ring, bracelet and ring. 1967. $7.00 complete. (Courtesy Virginia Jones)

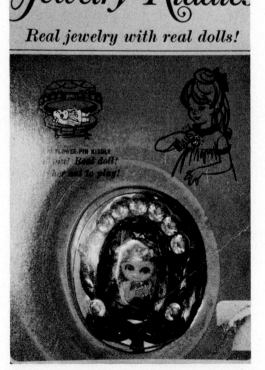

Mattel--1" "Hearts 'N Flowers" Jewelry Kiddles. This is a "Flowers" pin. Orange hair. 1967. $3.00. (Courtesy Virginia Jones)

Mattel--2" "Laffy Lemon Kola Kiddle" All vinyl with yellow hair. Original. 1967. $3.00. (Courtesy Virginia Jones)

Mattel--2" "Luscious Lime Kola Kiddle" All vinyl. Green hair. Original. Came in set of six: Kleo Kola, Olivia Orange, Laffy Lemon, Greta Grape and Shirley Strawberry. 1967. $3.00. (Courtesy Mary Partridge)

Mattel--2" "Greta Grape" All vinyl. Purple hair. Purple painted eyes. 1967. $3.00.

Mattel--2" "Shirley Strawberry Kola Kiddle" Original. 1967. $3.00. (Courtesy Virginia Jones)

Mattel--4" "Anabelle Autodiddle" All original. 1967. $6.00. (Courtesy Margaret Weeks)

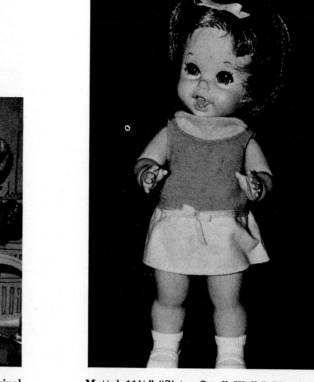

Mattel--11½" "Sister Small Walk" Plastic and vinyl with rooted brown hair. Painted blue eyes. Two upper and lower painted teeth. Molded on shoes and socks. Battery operated walker. Original dress. Marks: 1967 Mattel Inc./US & Foreign Patented/Other Patents Pending/USA. $5.00.

Mattel--"Lickety Spliddle Skediddle," with her "Fun New Traveliddle" 1967. $6.00. (Courtesy Sibyl DeWein)

Mattel--4" "Heather Hiddlehorse Skediddle" Red hair. Blue eyes. Came with horse. Same group as Tessie Tractor. Marks: 1967/Mattel Inc. $4.00.

Mattel--2" "Olivia Orange" Original. 1967. $3.00. (Courtesy Virginia Jones)

Mattel--3" "Lady Lavender" Tea Party Kiddle. Marks: Mattel, Inc. 1967. Hong Kong. $6.00 with cup and saucer.

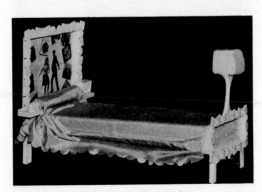

Mattel--Francie's TV Bed. 1966. Made by Susie Goose for Mattel Inc. $5.00.

Mattel--4" "Rah Rah Teeny Boppin' Skediddle" Original. 1967. $4.00. (Courtesy Margaret Weeks)

Mattel--3½" "Cherry Blossom Skididdle" on her "trikediddle." Brown almond shaped eyes. Marks: 1967/Mattel Inc/Mexico/US Patent Pend., on back. Original. $5.00.

Mattel--4" "Tessie Tractor Skediddle" All vinyl with rooted blonde hair. Painted brown eyes. Freckles. Skediddle machines included a horse and tractor. Marks: 1967/Mattel Inc. $4.00.

Mattel--4" "Shirley Skediddle" Plastic and vinyl with rooted blonde hair. Painted blue eyes. Arms, legs and head move by Skiddle machine plugged into back. Original. Marks: 1967/Mattel Inc/Mexico/US Patent Pending. $4.00. (Courtesy Leslie White)

Mattel--4" "Harriet Helididdle" All vinyl with rooted brown hair. Walker when attached to skididdle machine. Snap jointed hips so doll will sit in helicopter. Original. Marks: 1967/Mattel Inc./Mexico/Pat. Pending, on back. $5.00 complete.

237

Mattel--"Lickety Spliddle Skeddiddle & Her Traveliddles." 1967. $5.00 complete. (Courtesy Sibyl DeWein)

Mattel--4" "Tracy Skediddle" and her "Trikediddle" Original. Marks: 1967/Mattel Inc/Mexico/US Pat. Pend, on back. $5.00 complete.

Mattel--4" "Annabelle Autodiddle Skediddle" Original. Marks: 1967/Mattel Inc/Mexico/US Pat. Pend., on back. $5.00 complete.

Mattel--12½" "Captain Lazer" All plastic with vinyl head. Molded brown hair. Brown inset eyes. All clothes and back lazer pack molded on. Jointed knees. Battery operated. Eyes light up and lazer gun shoots. Marks: 1967/Mattel Inc./Hawthorne USA/Made In Mexico. $7.00.

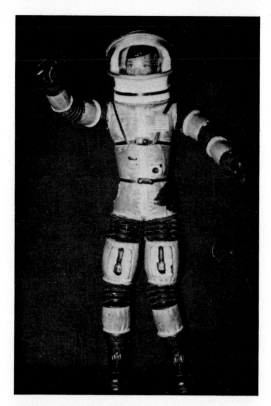

Mattel--6" "Doug Davis, Spaceman" All vinyl and posable. Dark brown hair. Marks: Mattel Inc/1967/Hong Kong, on head. $3.00.

Mattel--6" "Sgt. Storm" Light brown molded hair. Marks: Mattel Inc/1967/Hong Kong., on head. $3.00.

Mattel--6" "Major Matt Mason" Brown crew cut hair, molded. Marks: Mattel--Inc/1967/Hong Kong, on head. $3.00.

Mattel--2" "Dainty Deer Animiddle" All vinyl, orange hair. Painted brown eyes. Marks: 1967 Mattel Inc. Original. Came in set of four: Lucky Lion, Miss Mouse and Tiny Tiger. $3.00.

239

Mattel--11" "Baby Walk N Play" Plastic and vinyl with rooted yellow hair. Painted blue eyes. Two upper and lower painted teeth. Battery operated to play with yoyo, paddle ball, hankerchief and walks. Original. Marks: 1967 Mattel Inc/Hong Kong, on head. Tag: 1968 Mattel Inc. 1967 Mattel Inc/US & Foreign Patented, on back. $9.00.

Mattel--2" "Flossy Glossy, The Upsy Fire Chiefess" came with her "Elewetter Fire Engine" (Elephant type). Yellow vinyl with glued on orange/pink/yellow yarn hair. Original. Marks: 1967 Mattel Inc/Hong Kong. $3.00 complete. (Courtesy Edith Goldsworthy)

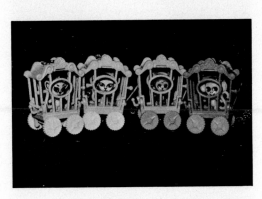

Mattel--"Zoolery Kiddles" with Little Lion, Brawny Bear, Playful Panther and Chummy Chimps. These are Circus Wagon necklaces. 1968. $3.00 each. (Courtesy Sibyl DeWein)

Mattel--2½" "Lucky Lion" Animiddle Kiddle. 1968. $3.00. (Courtesy Sibyl DeWein)

"Tenderella" See Foreign (Furga) section for full description.

14" "Lauria" by Italicremoma. Original. Marks: IC, in square/1970. (Courtesy Irene Gann)

18" "Nun" by Valentine Doll Co. Walker with jointed knees. Has no hair. Marks: 17VW, on head. Made in USA, on back. (Courtesy Virginia Jones.)

1971 "School Girl Doll" is 7" and sold with a 1972 Date Book.

Mattel--2½" "Tiny Tiger" Animiddle. 1968.
$3.00. (Courtesy Sibyl DeWein)

Mattel--2½" "Miss Mouse" Animiddle. 1968.
$3.00. (Courtesy Sibyl DeWein)

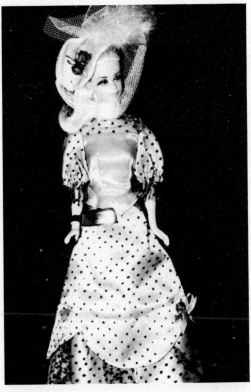

Mattel--2" "Funny Bunny" Animiddle Kiddle.
Orange yarn hair attached to cap. Original. 1968.
Made for Easter. $4.00.

Mattel--11½" "Truly Scrumptious" (Talking)
1968. Marks: 1967/Mattel Inc/US &
Foreign/Pats Pend/Mexico, on back. Genuine
Truly Scrumptious/By Mattel, on wrist paper
tag. Truly Scrumptious/1968 Gledrose Prod.
Ltd/and Warfield Prod. Ltd/Made in Japan/
1968 Matttel Inc. $9.00.

Mattel--"Barbie Family House" #1066 Marks: 1968 Mattel Inc. $4.00.

Mattel--2" "Mr. Potts" & "Truly Scrumptious" & 1" "Jemimi" & "Jeremy" All original. From "Chitty, Chitty Bang, Bang" 1968. $7.00. (Courtesy Virginia Jones)

Mattel--3" "Lenore Limosine" Original. 1968. $7.00. (Courtesy Margaret Weeks)

Mattel--3" "Henrietta Horseless Carriage" Original. 1968. $7.00. (Courtesy Margaret Weeks)

243

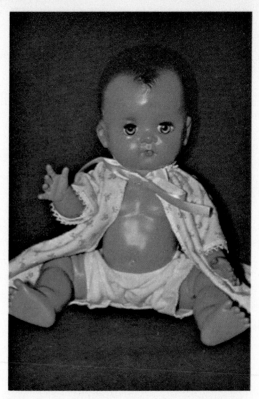

12" "Tiny Tears" Vinyl with a hard plastic head. Tear ducts and pierced nostrils. Original. Marks: Made in USA/Pat. No. 225207, on head. (Courtesy Virginia Jones)

11" "Sunbabe" by Sun Rubber Co. Rubber body with a hard plastic head. (Courtesy Jay Minter)

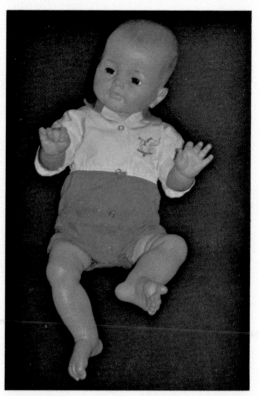

16" "Herby Hippie" by Remco Ind. Inc. Has stomach button and winks his right eye. Green sleep eyes. Freckles. Original, minus beads. Marks: Remco Inc. Inc./1968, on head. (Courtesy Irene Gann)

25" "Life Size Infant" by Ideal. Sold with "high chair." Vinyl and soft plastic body. Doll is strung. Blue sleep eyes. Nurser. Beautiful detailed hands and feet. Marks: Ideal Toy Corp/25N9, on head. Ideal Toy Corp/NB25, on back. 1963.

244

10½" "Toni" by American Character. Marks: American Character/1958, in a circle.

19" "Betsy McCall". Marks: McCall Corp 1958, in circle on head. McCall Corp, on inside upper legs. Doll is strung. Blue flirty eyes. Posable head. Original. (Courtesy Virginia Jones)

19" "Little Max" of the Joe Palooka series. Original. Squeeker in head. ca. late 1950's, or early 1960's. (Courtesy Virginia Jones)

16" All original composition. Sold to original owner as "Snow White." Unmarked. (Courtesy Jay Minter)

Mattel--4" "Snoopy Skididdler" Original. 1968. $3.00. (Courtesy Margaret Weeks)

Mattel--4" "Donald Duck Skediddler" Original. 1968. $3.00. (Courtesy Margaret Weeks)

Mattel--4" "Goofy Skididdler" Original. 1968. $3.00. (Courtesy Margaret Weeks)

Mattel--4" "Lucy Skididdler" Original. 1968. $3.00.

Mattel--Kiddles Case. 1968. $4.00. (Courtesy Mary Partridge)

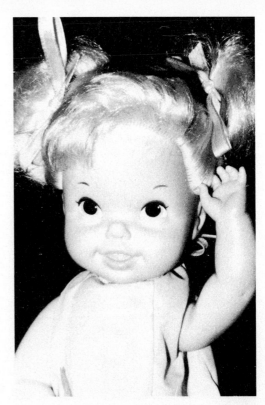

Mattel--10" "Baby Go Bye Bye" Plastic body with vinyl arms, legs and head. Rooted white hair. Painted blue eyes. Open/closed mouth with two painted upper teeth. Doll is strung. Marks: 1968 Mattel Inc/Hong Kong. $5.00.

Mattel--"Liddle Kiddles Open House" & "Snap Happy Patio" Furniture. Marks: 1968 Mattel Inc/Printed in USA. $6.00.

Mattel--11" "Small Talk Cinderella" Marks: Japan, on head. 1967 Mattel Inc/US & For/Pats Pend./Mexico, on back. Small Talk/1968 Mattel Inc/Hong Kong, on tag. $8.00.

247

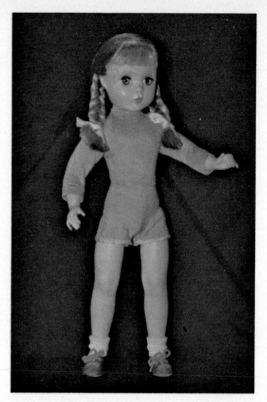

15" "Binnie Walker" by Alexander. All hard plastic with straight legs. Walker, head turns. Tag: Binnie Walker/By Madame Alexander. (Courtesy Jay Minter)

17" "Maggie" by Alexander. Original **tagged** bodysuit. (Courtesy Jay Minter)

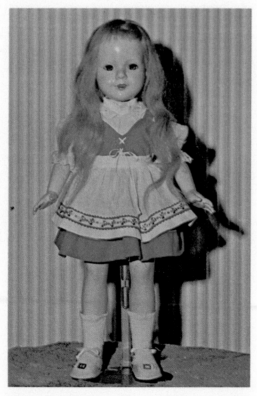

22" "Anne Shirley" All composition. Original. Called the "Open mouth" Anne Shirley, also same mold as "The Ice Queen" by Effanbee Doll Co. (Courtesy Ruth Lane)

19" "Shirley Temple" Never wigged and in original clothes. Cloth body with composition arms, legs and shoulder-plate head. ca. 1939. (Courtesy Ruth Lane)

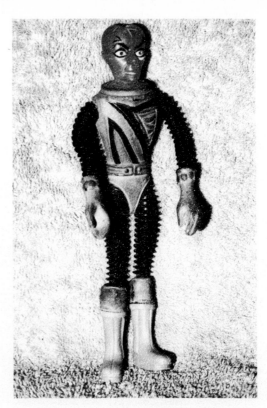

Mattel--"Kiddle Snap Happy Living Room" Came in three sets that could be set on top of each other. 6 piece bedroom, 8 piece living room and 7 piece radio. 1968. $3.00.

Mattel--6" "Callisto, from Jupiter" Transparent skull. Marks: 1968/Mattel Inc/Hong Kong/US & For/Pat. Pend/US Patented. $4.00.

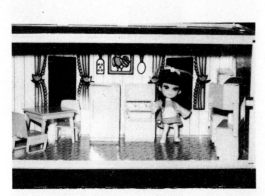

Mattel--"Cookin' Hiddle Set" All original. 1968. $5.00.

Mattel--9" "Living Fluff" Skipper's playmate. Posable head. Elbows bend. Waist bends, twists and turns. Knees bend. 1969. $7.00.

Mattel--"Kiddle Mobile" Marks: 1968 Mattel Inc. USA. Printed in USA. $4.00.

Mattel--"Twist 'N Turn Francie" 1969, in the 1967 dress called "Extravaganza." Doll: $5.00. Outfit: $4.00.

Mattel--"Living Barbie" 1970 shown in "Romantic Ruffles" made in 1968 for 1969 marked. Doll: $5.00. Outfit: $5.00. (Courtesy Lucille Kimsey)

Mattel--"Barbie" (#1070) Bendable legs. 1965. Wearing "See Worthy" made in 1968 for 1969 market. Doll: $7.00. Outfit: $5.00. (Courtesy Lucille Kimsey)

Mattel--"Twist 'N Turn Barbie" 1969-70. In "Yellow Mellow" made in 1968 for 1969 market. Doll: $5.00. Outfit: $2.00.

Mattel--"Playhouse Kiddles" Living Room with "Pretty Parlor Kiddle" 1969. $5.00.

Mattel--"Rosemary Roadster Kiddle" with Limousine, Roadster and Horseless Carriage. 1969. Part of the Kiddles 'N Kars series. This set is the Antique Fair. Original. $9.00 complete.

Mattel--"Playhouse Kiddles," Bedroom with "Good Night Kiddle" 1969. $5.00.

Mattel--2" "Baby Din Din" Set included: "Teeter-Time Baby" in a duck walker, "Baby Rockaway" (Colored) in a rocker and "Nappy-time Baby" in a Bunny bed. 1969. $4.00. (Courtesy Margaret Weeks)

Mattel--3½" "Lady Lace Tea Party Kiddles" All vinyl with rooted dark blonde hair. Painted blue eyes. Original. Marks: 1969/Mattel Inc/Made In/Hong Kong, on back. $6.00.

Mattel--2½" "Liddle Baby Kiddle-Baby Rock-away" 1969. $5.00. (Courtesy Sibyl DeWein)

Mattel--6" "Nan" and 3½" "Fran" Original. 1969. Others in this group were: "Angie N' Tangie," "Lori 'N Rori" Angie is brunette and Lori is blonde. Tangie is a rag doll and Rori is is a Teddy bear. $7.00 set.

Mattel--3½" "Wet Noodles" Orange hair. Marks: 1969 Mattel Inc/Taiwan. Hair can be washed. $1.00.

Mattel--3½" "Wet Noodles" Lavender hair and green eyes. Marks: 1969 Mattel Inc/Taiwan. Hair can be washed. $1.00.

Mattel--4½" "Bugs Bunny Skediddle" Marks: 1969/Warner Bros/Seven Arts Inc. $3.00. (Courtesy Sibyl DeWein)

Mattel--"Barbie" case. 1969. $3.00.

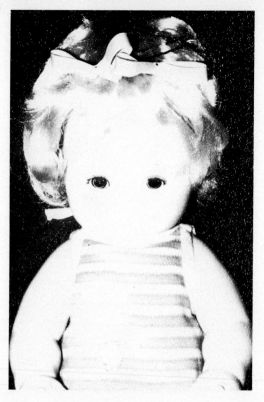

"Barbie" case (#1002) 1969. $2.00.

Mattel--16" "Talking Baby Tenderlove" All one piece dublon. Inset scalp with rooted white hair. Painted brown eyes. Open mouth/nurser. Talker with pull string in plastic hair ribbon on back of head. Marks: 677K/1969 Mattel Inc/ Mexico, on head. $4.00.

Mattel--17" "Sing A Song" Plastic and vinyl with rooted blonde hair. Painted blue eyes. Pull string. Marks: 1969 Mattel Inc Mexico, on head. 1968 Mattel Inc/Made in Hong Kong, dress tag. 1964 Mattel Inc/Hawthorne, etc, on back. $12.00. (Courtesy Connie Snap)

Mattel--2½" "Baby So High" Came with her "Airo-Zoomer" plane. All blue vinyl with rooted blue yarn hair. Original. Marks: 1969/Mattel Inc/Hong Kong. $3.00 complete with plane.

Mattel--2½" "Tickle Pinkle" All vinyl with rooted pink yarn hair. Large painted blue eyes. Original. Marks: 1969 Mattel Inc/Hong Kong, on head. One of the Upsys. $3.00 complete.

Mattel--3" "Downy Dilly and Foot Mobile" Vinyl and plastic. Marks: 1969 Mattel Inc/Hong Kong. $3.00.

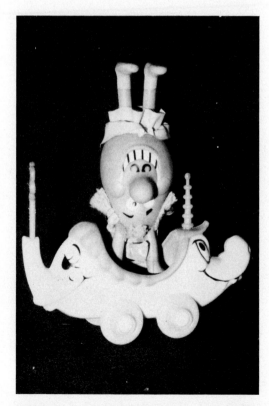

Mattel--3½" "Pocus Hocus and His Dragon Wagon" The "Downsy" mixed up magician. Vinyl and plastic. Marks: 1969 Mattel Inc/Hong Kong. $3.00.

Mattel--3" "Mother, What Now and Go Getter" Vinyl and plastic. One of the "Downsy" group. Marks: 1969 Mattel Inc/Hong Kong. $3.00.

Mattel--3" "Miss Information & Miss Information Booth" Vinyl and plastic. One of the "Downsy" group. Marks: 1969 Mattel Inc/Hong Kong. $3.00.

Mattel--3½" "Red Hot Red" One of the Small Shots Twins. Red molded hair. Marks: Mattel, Inc. 1970, on head. $2.00.

Mattel--3½" "Nitty Nan Small Shot" Marks: 1970 Mattel Inc, on head. In 1970 there were: Breezy Bridget, Funny Fran, Lively Lucy & Daredevil Dexter. In 1971: Sillie Millie, Fearless Fred, Flirty Gertie. In 1972: Dartin' Darlene, Roaring Rita, Hasty Harriet, Dashin' Dora & Reckless Richard. $2.00.

Mattel--6½" "Lilac Rockflower" Rooted red hair. Painted brown eyes. Original. Marks: 1970/Mattel Inc/Hong Kong/US and For Pat'd/Pat'd in Canada/1970. Made market, 1971. $4.00.

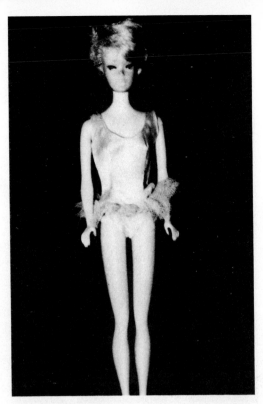

Mattel--6½" "Heather Rockflower" All vinyl with rooted blonde hair. Painted blue eyes. Posable. Marks: Mattel Inc/1970 Hong Kong. Original. Market 1971. $4.00.

Mattel--1962 "Barbie" Shown in the 1970 "Prima Ballerina" Doll: $7.00. Outfit: $3.00. (Courtesy Lucille Kimsey)

Mattel--Barbie's "Sun N' Fun" Buggy. Marks: 1970 Mattel Inc./Mexico/US Patent Pending. $6.00.

Mattel--6½" "Rosemary Rockflower" All vinyl with one piece body, arms and legs that are completely posable. Rooted black hair. Painted features. Came with 45 rpm record and attachment so doll will "dance" to music. Original. Marks: Hong Kong/Mattel Inc/1970, on head. 13/Hong Kong/1970 Mattel Inc/US and For Pat'd/Pat'd in Canada, on back. Market 1971. $5.00.

257

Mattel--"Twist 'N Turn Barbie" 1967-70. Dressed in "Ruffles 'N Swirls" 1970. This was a free costume for joining Barbie's Fan Club in 1970. Doll: $5.00. Outfit: $2.00. (Courtesy Kathy and Barbie Allin)

Mattel--"Fashion Queen Barbie" 1963, in "Skate Mates" 1970. Doll: $7.00. Outfit: $5.00. (Courtesy Lucille Kimsey)

Mattel--"Twist 'N Turn Barbie" 1967-68 in "Salute To Silver." The Silver Stockings not included. They came in a Pak "Finishing Touches" 1969. Dress also sold in regular fashion set "Silver Sparkle." Doll: $5.00. Outfit: $5.00. (Lucille Kimsey)

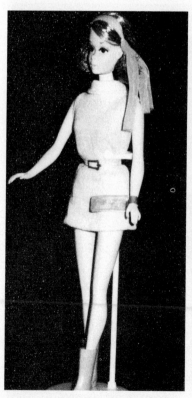

Mattel--"Walking Jamie" in the basic outfit. Made for Sears 1969 for the 1970 market. $9.00. (Courtesy Lucille Kimsey)

Mattel--"Talking Stacey" 1968 Shown in "Maxi 'n Mini" 1970. Doll: $9.00. Outfit: $7.00. (Courtesy Lucille Kimsey)

Mattel--"Christie" 1968-1972. Shown in "Great Coat" made in 1969 for the 1970 market. Doll: $7.00. Outfit: $5.00. (Courtesy Lucille Kimsey)

Mattel--14½" "Shoppin' Sheryl" Plastic body, arms and legs. Jointed waist, left wrist and thumb. Magnetic in right palm. Buttons on both sides of body that operate thumb. Vinyl head with rooted white hair. Painted blue eyes. 1970 Mattel Inc/Hong Kong, on head. 1970 Mattel Inc./Hong Kong/US Patent Pending, on back. Market 1971. $5.00.

Mattel--11" "Baby Beans" Bean bag body, arms and legs. Vinyl head with one row blonde rooted hair. Sewn on clothes. Painted blue eyes. Pull string on back of head. Talker. Marks: Mattel/Baby Beans/1970, on tag. Original clothes. Market 1971. $3.00.

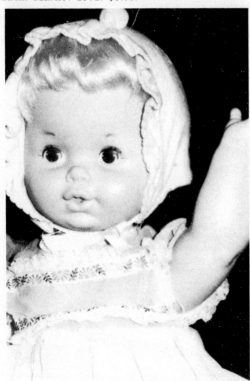

Mattel--20" "Living Baby Tenderlove" One piece dublon body and head. Jointed shoulders and hips. Arms and legs encased in plastic holders that fit into plastic shoulder and hip plates. Rooted white hair in vinyl skull cap. Painted blue eyes. Open mouth/nurser. Marks: 140/1970 Mattel Inc. Mexico/US and Foreign Patented. Other Patents Pending. Market 1971. $4.00.

Mattel--16" "Baby Love Light" Cloth body, arms and legs. Vinyl head and gauntlet hands. Battery operated, eyes light up when hands are pressed. Hands hinged so they will "hold" on. After child falls asleep and hand falls away from the doll, the lights go out. Marks: 1970 Mattel Inc. Mexico, on head. Mattel/Baby Love Light 1970 Mattel Inc., on tag. Market 1971. $6.00.

259

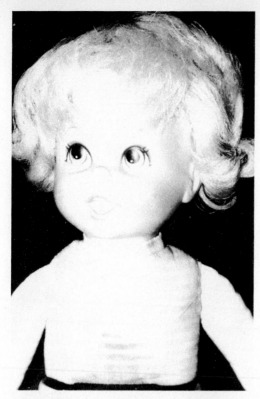

Mattel--12" "Talking Twin, Kip" Cloth body with vinyl head. Rooted blonde hair. Painted blue eyes. Open/closed mouth with two painted upper and lower teeth. Pull string talker, says: "Hi, my name is Kip," "Would you like to brush my hair," etc. Marks: Mattel/Talking Twins/ 1970 Mattel Inc., on tag. 1967 Mattel Inc/Japan, on head. Market 1971. $4.00.

Mattel--5" "Casper, The Friendly Ghost" Plastic head with talker inside. Vinyl body. Hand strap in back of head. Pull head away from body and it says 8 things like: "Boo! O! I scared myself." Marks: Harvey Famous Cartoons/Hong Kong, on head. 1971/Mattel Inc/Hong Kong, on back. $4.00.

260

Mattel--20" "Cynthia" Plastic and vinyl with rooted blonde hair. Painted blue eyes. Painted teeth. Takes records. Battery operated. Original. Marks: 1971 Mattel Inc/Hong/Kong, on head. 1971 Mattel Inc/USA/US Patent Pending, on back. $8.00.

Mattel--16" "Baby Play-A-Lot" Plastic and vinyl with rooted white hair. Painted blue eyes and teeth. Soft vinyl hands with jointed wrists. Pull string and start switch in back. Doll does many things including: comb hair, brush teeth, do dishes, play with her clown. Came with 20 toys in storage table. Marks: 1971 Mattel Inc/Hong Kong/US Patent Pending, on back. 1971 Mattel Inc./Hong/Kong, on head. $6.00.

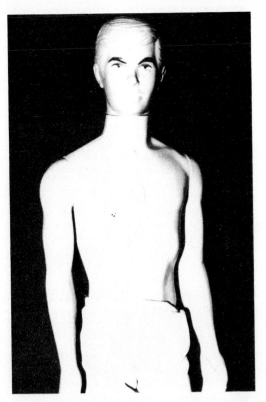

Mattel--"Malibu Ken" Not jointed at waist. Made in 1970 for 1971 market. $6.00. (Courtesy Leslie White)

Mattel--"Living Fluff" Made in 1970 for the 1971 market. Dressed in "Flower Power." 1972. Doll:$7.00. Outfit: $1.00.

Mattel--"Living Barbie" 1970 in the 1971 Sears Gift set called "Live Action P.J. Fashion 'N Motion." Doll: $8.00. Outfit: $4.00 (Courtesy Lucille Kimsey)

Mattel--11½" "Walk Lively Barbie" Original. 1971. Marks: 1967 Mattel Inc/US Pat. Pend/ Taiwan. $7.00.

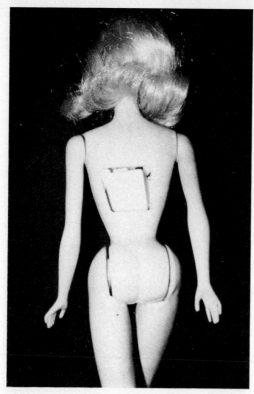

Mattel--11½" "Walking Jamie" Mattel made doll for Sears 1969 for the 1970 market. Press button and makes head turn and arms, legs move. Marks: 1967 Mattel Inc./US Patented/Pat'd Canada 1967/Other Pats. Pend./Japan. $9.00.

Mattel--12" "Ken" and "P.J." (Live Action) Original. 1971. $9.00 each. (Courtesy Lucille Kimsey)

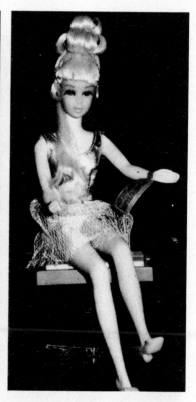

262

Mattel--Basic "Growin' Pretty Hair" Barbie. 1971. $7.00. (Courtesy Lucille Kimsey)

Mattel--11½" "Live Action Christie" Plastic and vinyl with rooted black hair and brown eyes. Bendable elbows, knees and ankles. Original. Marks: 1968 Mattel Inc/US & Foreign Patented/Pat. in Canada 1967 /Other Pats. Pending/Taiwan. $9.00. Made 1970, market 1971.

Mattel--"Francie with Growin' Pretty Hair" First one in 1970 (#1129) did not have extra hair pieces. In 1971 doll and dress were same, plus extra hair pieces. (#1074). Made in 1970. #1129: $7.00. #1074: $8.00.

Mattel--"Living Barbie" 1970 wearing "Silver Serendade" 1971. Doll: $8.00. Outfit: $6.00. (Courtesy Lucille Kimsey)

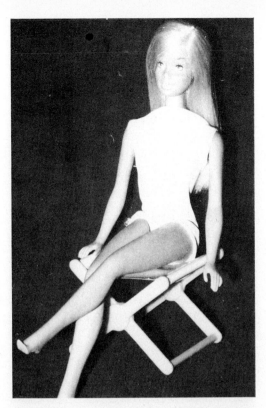

Mattel--"Malibu Barbie" 1971. Malibu Barbie, Ken, Francie and Skipper came out in 1971 but P.J. was a year later in 1972 and in 1973 Mattel introduced Malibu Christie. $2.00. (Courtesy Leslie White)

Mattel--"Malibu P.J." On market in 1972. $2.00. (Courtesy Leslie White)

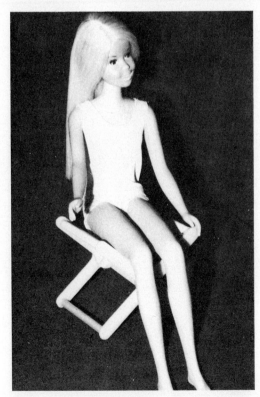

Mattel--"Malibu Francie" On market in 1971. $2.00. (Courtesy Leslie White)

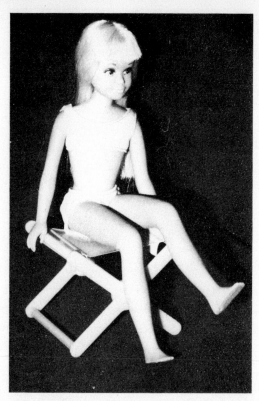

Mattel--"Malibu Skipper" 1971. $2.00. (Courtesy Leslie White)

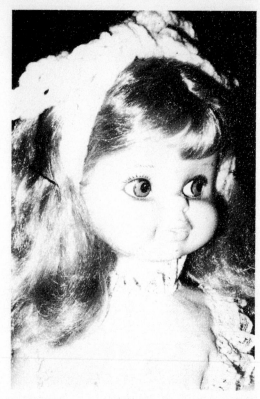

Mattel--17" "Hi Dottie" Plastic body and right arm. Left arm and head vinyl. Rooted blonde hair. Painted brown eyes. Plug in left hand to connect phone. Marks: 1969 Mattel Inc. Mexico, on head. 1971/Mattel/Inc/Mexico/US Patent Pend., on back. Made for 1972 market. Not original clothes. $4.00.

Mattel--1962 Barbie dressed in 1972 "Silver Blues." Doll: $7.00. Outfit: $5.00. (Courtesy Lucille Kimsey)

Mattel--11½" "Miss America" Barbie doll. Walker, arms move and head turns. Original. 1972. Also offered for two box tops and $3.00 from Kelloggs Cornflakes. Marks: 1967 Mattel/US Pat. Pend./Taiwan. $8.00. (Courtesy Leslie White)

264

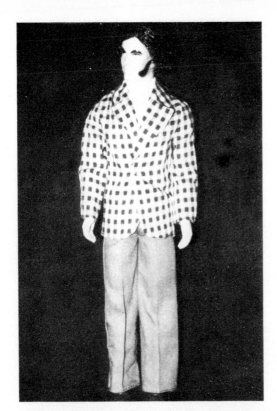

Mattel--"Mod Hair Ken" Marks: 1968/Mattel Inc./US and For Pat'd/Others/Pending/Hong Kong. Made in 1972 for the 1973 market. $4.00. (Courtesy Leslie White)

Mattel--11½" "Tiny Baby Tenderlove" All dublon molded in one piece. Glued on vinyl golden wig. Painted blue eyes. Open/closed mouth. Marks: none. 1972. $6.00.

Mattel--17" "Peachy and Her Puppets" Plastic and vinyl. Pull string operated. You hear voice of each puppet, clown, girl, dog and monkey. Original. Marks: 1972 Mattel Inc/Mexico, on head. 1964 Mattel Inc/Hawthorne, Etc, on back. $12.00.

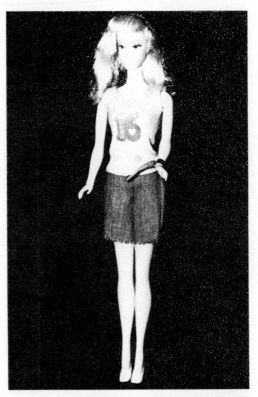

Mattel--11½" "Sweet 16 Barbie" Outfit was issued in a special limited edition for the 16th year Mattel has made the Barbie doll. (1958-1974) This Special Happy Birthday Doll came with cosmetics and magic barrettes for soft scented hair. $5.00.

265

Mattel--"Barbie" In "Sweet 16" dress. 1974.
$5.00.

Mattel--"The Sunshine Family" Steve (9½"),
Stephie (9") and Sweets (3"). Plastic body and
legs with jointed knees. Vinyl arms and heads.
Steve has inset brown eyes. Stephie and Sweets
have inset blue eyes. Original. Marks: 1973
Mattel Inc, on head. 1973/Mattel Inc/Taiwan,
center back. Wrist tag: S The Sunshine/Family.
$7.00.

Mattel--"Barbie's Ten Speeder" Also for
Francie, Kelley and P.J. 1973. $4.00.

Mattel--Barbie's Horse "Dancer" Marked on
inside back leg. 1970 Mattel Inc. 3 leg joints. To
use with Live Action Dolls.

Mattel--16" "Saucy" Plastic and vinyl. Rotating the left arm makes the mouth and eyes change positions. Original. Marks: 1972 Mattel Inc Mexico, on head. 1972 Mattel Inc/Mexico/US Patent Pending, on back. (Courtesy Mary Partridge)

Mattel--16" "Saucy" shows another face she makes. There are a total of eight different expressions. $9.00.

Mattel--"Stacey" (red haired) is wearing "Maxi 'N Mini" #1799 (1970 booklet). (Courtesy Ruth Lane) Photo by Bud Lane.

Mattel--P.J. is wearing "Fun Flakes" #3412. (1971 booklet) (Courtesy Ruth Lane) Photo by Bud Lane.

Mego--11" "Tanya" Plastic and vinyl with rooted yellow hair. Painted black eyes/lashes. Dimples. Jointed waist. Tanya is Mego's "Maddi Mod" with a suntan. Very small high heel feet. Original. Marks: Mego Corp MCMLXX/Hong Kong. Box: Mfg'd in Hong Kong/For S.S. Kresge Co. $4.00.

Mego--7½" "Action Jackson" Plastic and vinyl with jointed elbows, wrists, waist, knees and ankles. Tag: AJ, on chest. Marks: Mego Corp/ Reg. U.S. Pat. Off./Pat. Pending/Hong Kong/ MCMLXX1, on back. Clothes tag: Action Jackson/Mego Corp. This is same doll and clothes used as "Don," Dinah-Mites "Boy friend." $4.00.

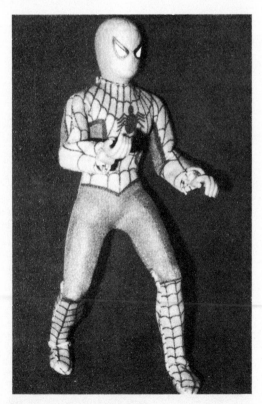

Mego--8" "Spider Man" Plastic and vinyl. Full jointed. Marks: Marvel CG 1971, on head and hip. $2.00.

Mego--8" "Tarzan" Fully jointed. Plastic and vinyl. Marks: ERB Inc 1972, on head and hip. $2.00.

Mego--7½" "Batman" Plastic and vinyl. Fully jointed. Marks: Mego Cor/Reg. US Pat Off./Pat Pending/Hong Kong/MCMLXXL. Box: National Periodical/Publications, Inc. 1972. $2.00.

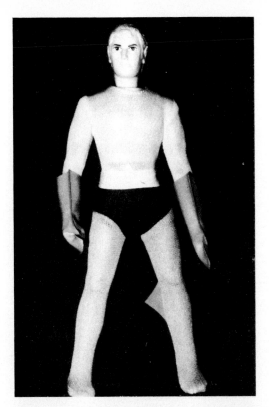

Mego--7½" "Aquaman" Plastic and vinyl. Fully jointed. Marks: Mego Corp/Reg. US Pat Off./Pat. Pending/Hong Kong/MCMLXX1. Box: 1972 Marvel Comics Group. $2.00.

Mego--7" "Robin, The Boy Wonder" Plastic and vinyl. Fully jointed. Marks: Mego Corp/Reg. US Pat. Off./Pat. Pending/Hong Kong/MCMLXX1. Box: National Periodical/Publications, Inc. 1972. $2.00.

Mego--7½" "Superman" Plastic and vinyl. Fully jointed. Marks: Mego Corp/Reg. US Pat. Off/Pat. Pending/Hong Kong/MCMLXX1. Box: National Periodical/Publications, Inc. 1972. $2.00.

Mego--7½" "Dinah-Mite" Plastic and vinyl. Suntan skin tones. Blonde with painted features. Jointed waist, elbows, waist, knees and ankles. Original. Marks: Mego Corp/MCMLXX11/Pat Pending/Made in/Hong Kong, on back. Mego Corp/1972, on head. $4.00.

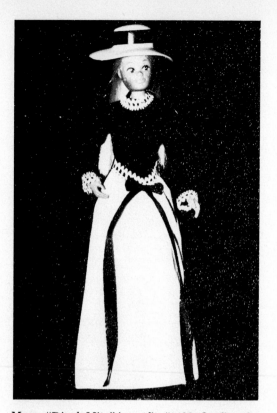

Mego--"Dinah-Mite" in outfit. #1423. Outfit only: $2.00.

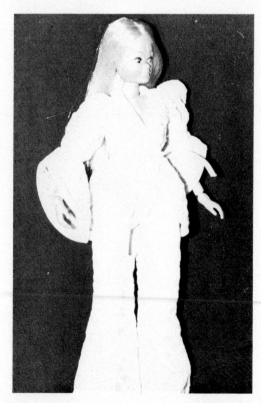

Mego--"Dinah-Mite" in outfit #1431. Outfit only: $2.00.

Mego--24" "MS Fashion" Plastic and vinyl with jointed waist. Rooted white hair. Stationary blue eyes/lashes. Blue eyeshadow. Small waist and large hips. Original. Marks: Hong Kong, on head and lower and upper back. 1973. $9.00. (Courtesy Lita Wilson)

Mego--8" "Riddler" an Arch Enemy. Purple hands and mask. Marks: NPP Inc 1973, on head. $2.00.

Mego--8" "Shazam" Plastic and vinyl. Fully jointed. Marks: Mego Corp/Reg. US Pat. Off./ Pat. Pending/Hong Kong/MCMLXXI. N.P.P. 1973, on head. $2.00.

Mego--8" "Captain America" Plastic and vinyl. Fully jointed. Marks: Mego Corp/Reg. US Pat. Off/Pat. Pending/Hong Kong/MCMLXXI, on back. MCG 1973, on head. $2.00.

Mego--8" "Penguin and Joker" Batman's arch enemy. Plastic and vinyl. Fully jointed. Marks: NPP Inc 1973, on head. $2.00 each.

271

Mego--8" "Mr. Mxyzptlk" Purple hands. An Arch Enemy. 1973. $2.00.

Mego--19" "Lainie, The Dancing Doll" Plastic and vinyl with jointed waist. Rooted blonde hair. Painted blue eyes. Battery operated. Loosley jointed. Lift arm and she goes faster. Marks: Mego Corp 1973/Made in Hong Kong, on head. Mego (in circle) Mego Corp 1973/N.Y. N.Y. 10010/Pat. Pend. 327,304/Made in USA, on back. Original clothes. $15.00.

Mego--8" "Cornelius and Zira" of Planet of the Apes and played by Roddy McDowell. Arms and legs are strung. Marks: APJAC Productions/ 20th Century Fox Films Corp. $3.00 each.

Mego--8" "Astronaut" of Planet of the Apes. Goggles are movable in helmet. Marks: Mego Corp/1972, on head. Mego Corp/Reg. U.S. Pat. Off/Pat. Pending/Hong Kong/MCMLXX1, on back. Shown, also, are 8" "Dr. Zaius" and 8" "Soldier Ape" $3.00 each.

Miller Rubber Co.--14" "New Born Baby" One piece body, arms and legs of latex. Early vinyl head. Molded hair. Blue sleep eyes. Open/closed mouth. Puckered expression. Original. Marks: MRP, on head. 1951. $6.00.

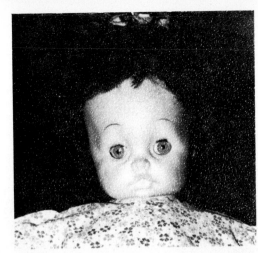

Montgomery Wards--17" "Sweet & Cuddly" Cloth and vinyl with rooted brown hair. Blue sleep eyes. Small neck with roll of fat in back. Cryer. Came with hair setting accessories and curlers. 1971. Marks: Montgomery/Wards/Made in Hong Kong. $4.00.

Monica-Marion Dolls by Margaret Groninger

The following is reprinted with the permission of Elizabeth Andrews Fisher: taken from The Toy Trader, Volume 23, February 1970.

Dolls by Monica Studios are considered, by many collectors, to be rare, unique, and quite lovely. At the same time, little is known about these dolls.

The guiding light behind the creations of Monica Studios seems to have been their originator and manufacturer, Mrs. Hansi Share, of Hollywood, California. According to a 1941 issue of Toys & Novelties magazine (which contains the first announcement of Monica dolls), Mrs. Share had always been bothered as a child because she could not comb her doll's hair as she could her own. So she created the Monica doll with human hair embedded in the scalp in such a manner that it could withstand rough treatment. Her first two dolls were 20 and 24 inches tall, featuring "beautifully molded heads on cloth of composition bodies" (whatever that means), and were fancily dressed, as were most later models. Monica was always The Complete Doll!

Every year brought some minor changes, it seems. In 1942, Monica models were called Veronica, Rosalind and Joan, and were 17 inches tall--but still with human hair rooted in the scalp. In 1943, 17 and 20 inch models were advertised, offered in a choice of 36 styles of attire. The same sizes were available in 1944, but with only 24 styles of clothing. The ads stressed the point that Monica was "the only doll made that has real human hair 'growing' out of the scalp of the doll." Today most all vinyl dolls feature hair "rooted" in the scalp, but Monica appears to have been the only composition (and later, hard plastic) doll with this characteristic.

Although the 1940's were war years and many doll makers were unable to buy supplies needed for their manufacturing, lovely Monica dolls continued to be turned out during that period and after. They received much notice and high praise from many quarters, including New Yorker magazine, which said that Monica "has few rivals as the Miss America of dolls, it seems to us." (Dec. 14, 1946)

According to Collier's magazine, "The year 1946 will usher in the first all-plastic dolls." But not until 1949 did Monica Studios advertise a hard plastic doll. At the same time, the composition version was apparently still being manufactured, though not in the same size as the plastics. The all plastic doll was called Marion, and she came in a choice of platinum blonde, golden blonde or auburn hair shades. She

was one of the last Monicas to appear, for the final Monica ad appeared in the Febuary, 1951, issue of Toys & Novelties. It would seem from the evidence that the company must have gone out of business around that time, or at least suddenly stopped its earlier extensive advertising. Thus Monica Studios was apparently in existence for only about 10 years, from 1941 to 1951.

During this short period, the firm manufactured composition dolls in at least six different sizes: 11", 15", 17", 20", 22", and 24". The two largest were early models, while the 11" doll appeared at a later date, in 1949. I have seen a doll dealer's ad for a 26" Monica; the company's ad does not verify a doll in this size, though it's certainly possible it may have existed.

In the later hard plastic versions, Monica (alias Marion) apparently came in two sizes only. 14" and 18". The 18" had sleep eyes, and the smaller one probably did, too. As far as I can determine, the composition versions always had painted eyes, usually (if not always) blue. Both composition and plastic models had pronounced eye-shadowing. In addition, both had "imported human hair" rooted in the scalp, a rare feature at the time.

How does one recognize a Monica doll? My evidence indicates that the dolls were never marked on either head or body with the firm's name. However, the composition versions are not hard to identify, due to their distinctive long, rather mature faces, painted eyes and eye-shadow, painted nostrils, somewhat large mouths, rooted human hair, and quite heavy weight. The picture of my blonde 17" Monica gives a good idea what the doll looks like.

The hard plastic dolls are harder to identify, as the faces do not resemble the composition Monicas at all, but look more like dolls made by other firms. We know, of course, that they had real human hair rooted in the scalp in a choice of only three colors (two blondes and a redhead), and that they were about 14" and 18" tall. I own what appears to be a hard plastic Monica/Marion. This doll has beautiful auburn hair (rooted in the scalp, in the same manner of the composition dolls), blue sleep eyes, rather round face, and is 18" tall.

Although manufactured in California, Monica dolls were sold throughout the country. Even Georg Jensen, the elegant New York jewelry store, sold them! And Monica was indeed a jewel among jewels."

Author's note: The above article was printed in 1970 and,

273

to date, all information it contained is still factual. There is only one item that I would like to add: From the demise of the Monica Studio (this was a doll "studio," not a Motion Picture Studio) in 1951, it took The American Character Doll Company four years to perfect their "rooted hair, in the scalp" series, the Sweet Sue dolls. The difference between the Sweet Sue and the Marion, is not only in "looks" but also in method of rooting. The Sweet Sue (and others) had the hair rooted in a vinyl scalp that was placed in a cut out, in the hard plastic head. The Marion has rooted "plugs" of hair embedded in drilled out holes in the hard plastic itself.

Monica--17" "Monica" Composition head and hard plastic body. Cream colored gown and cap of satin/net. Original. $60.00. (Courtesy Margaret Gronninger)

Monica--17" "Monica" Composition head with dark blonde inset human hair. Painted blue eyes. Hard plastic body. (Courtesy Margaret Gronninger)

Monica--21" "Monica" All composition with inset auburn human hair. Scarlett O'Hara type gown is off white with red ribbon trim and red berries. Hat is straw. Also has pantaloons. $75.00. (Courtesy Margaret Gronninger)

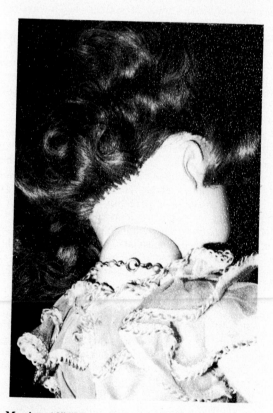

Monica--18" "Marion" All hard plastic with rooted hair into scalp. Blue sleep eyes and eye-shadow. Marks: none. Tag: Human Hair/Rooted in Scalp/Can Be Washed/Combed & Curled. Monica/Doll/Hollywood. Original clothes. $75.00

Monica--18" "Marion" Shows how hair was set in the hard plastic.

Nancy Ann--5" "One Two Button My Shoe" All bisque. One piece body and head. Glued on brown wig. Painted blue eyes. Painted on high boots with three painted buttons. Original clothes. Marks: Story/Book/Doll/USA, on back. Wrist tag: One-Two/Story Book Dolls/By Nancy Ann. 1941. $12.00.

Nancy Ann--5" "Polly Put The Kettle On" All bisque with glued on brown wig. Painted blue eyes. One piece body and head. Painted on shoes. Marks: Storybook/Doll/USA, on back. Original clothes. 1941. $12.00.

Nancy Ann--5" Painted bisque. All have blonde mohair wigs. All 1941-47 and all marked Story Book Dolls USA on back. Mint and original. $12.00 each. (Courtesy Maish Collection)

Nancy Ann--5" Painted over bisque. One piece body and head. Jointed shoulders. Painted features. Marks: Story Book Dolls USA. From the Storybook Series. Red taffeta dress. Black felt jacket and hat. High button shoes. 1941-1947. All original. $12.00. (Courtesy Maish Collection)

275

Nancy Ann--5" Painted over bisque. One piece body and head. Jointed shoulders. Painted features. Marks: Story Book Dolls USA. From Storybook Series. Dark blonde mohair wig. Red taffeta bodice, striped skirt. Net collar. Poppy hat. Boy is #136 "Jack." 1941-1947. All original. $12.00. (Maish Collection)

Nancy Ann--5" Painted over bisque. One piece body and head. Jointed shoulders. Painted features. Marks: Story Book Dolls USA. Wrist tag: 170 Rain Rain. Red mohair wig. Flowered taffeta dress, blue bodice, cape and umbrella. 1941-1947. All original. $12.00. (Maish Collection)

Nancy Ann--5" Painted over bisque. One piece body and head. Jointed shoulders. Painted features. Marks: Story Book Dolls USA. Wrist tag: 120 To Market. Brown mohair wig. Red taffeta dress. Poppy hat. 1941-1947. All original. $12.00. (Maish Collection)

Nancy Ann--5" Painted over bisque. One piece body and head. Jointed shoulders. Painted features. Marks: Story Book Dolls USA. Wrist tag: 183 Thursday's Child. Blonde mohair wig. Deep rose dotted taffeta dress. 1941-1947. All original. $12.00. (Maish Collection)

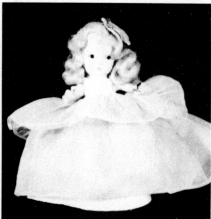

Nancy Ann--All Bisque: Clockwise: #194 "Curly Locks;" #92 "Autumn, One of the Nursery Rhyme Series. #56, "Colonial Dame;" #55 "Quaker Maid." All from 1941-1947. $12.00 each. (Maish Collection)

Nancy Ann--All Bisque: Left to right, red and white dotted Swiss dress. Whiskbroom tied to waist. Pink cotton dress/flowered apron. Deep pink taffeta with lace trim. $12.00.

Nancy Ann--5½" All hard plastic. Painted features. Glued on red mohair wig. Swivel neck. Jointed shoulders and hips. Red and white check gingham dress. 1952. $10.00. (Maish Collection)

Nancy Ann--7" "Muffie" All hard plastic, turning head walker. Glued on blonde mohair wig. Marks: Story Book Dolls California. Muffie on back. 1952. $8.00. (Maish Collection)

Nancy Ann--7" "Muffie" All hard plastic with glued on reddish blonde hair. Blue sleep eyes. Unjointed knees. An original dress. Marks: Story Book/Dolls/California, on back. $8.00. (Courtesy Kathy Walters)

Nancy Ann Storybook--10" "Lori Ann Walker" All hard plastic with glued on brown hair. Blue sleep eyes/molded lashes. Walker, head turns. Original dress. Marks: Nancy Ann, on head. Dress tag: Styled by Nancy Ann/Nancy Ann Storybook Dolls, Inc/San Francisco, Calif. Wrist tag: Lori Ann/Nancy Ann Storybook/Dolls/Inc. 1953. $10.00.

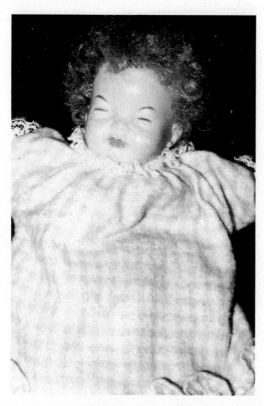

Nasco--10" "Nappy" Cloth and vinyl with rooted hair. Closed painted eyes. Original. Marks: 1963/Nasco, on head. $3.00.

Nasco--16" "Baby Sue" Cloth body. Vinyl arms, legs and head. Rooted white hair. Blue sleep eyes/lashes. Smiling closed mouth. Dimples. Marks: 1962/Nasco. $3.00.

279

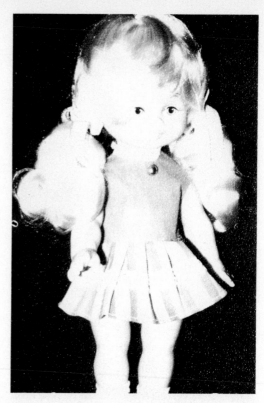

Playmate--12" "Tracy" Plastic and vinyl with rooted brown hair. Painted blue eyes. Original. Marks: Hong Kong, on lower back. Box: Playmate. 1972. $3.00.

Playmate--11" "Theresa" Plastic and vinyl with rooted white hair. Painted blue eyes. Original. Marks: Hong Kong, on head. By Playmate, in circle of world/a star. 1973. $3.00.

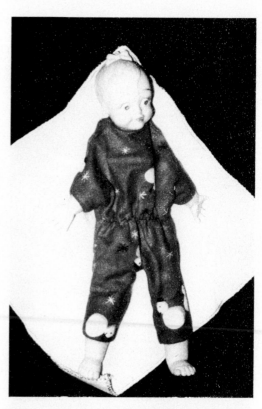

Puppet--13½" "Princess Summerfall, Winterspring" Wood body. Composition head, hands and feet (wooden dowel legs). Felt clothes. Yarn black hair. Painted features. Original. Marks: none. Instruction sheet: Peter Puppet Playthings. Inc./Long Island City NY. 1950. $22.00.

Puppet--12" "Joan Palooka" Cloth and vinyl. Hand fits under bunting to operate legs, body and hands. Marks: Box: Joan Palooka/National Mask & Puppet Corp. Birth Certificate: Sept. 25, 1952. Trademark Ham Fisher. $8.00.

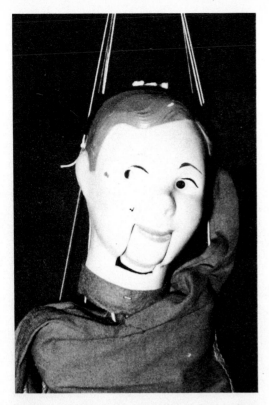

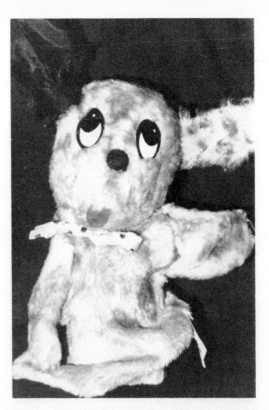

Puppet--14" "Mousekeeter" Wood body. Composition head, arms and legs. Molded red hair. Mouse ears of felt and large "M." Marks: PPP, on neck (Peter Puppet Playthings Inc) 1952. $22.00.

Puppet--11" "Klinker" Plush, with stuffed head. Paper eyes. Tag: Klinker/1960/Little Klinker Ventures Co. Other side: Gund Mfg. Co. This is Tennessee Ernie Ford's dog. $4.00.

Puppet--17" "Playboy Bunny" Stuffed plush head and hands. Felt and plastic features. Adult sized. Marks: Tag: Playboy TM Hand Puppet/ 1963 HMH Pub. Co. Inc. $5.00.

Puppet--5" "Pebbles Finger Puppet" Plastic and vinyl with molded red hair. Painted features. Original. Marks: 1969/Remco Inc. Inc./US & Foreign/Pat. Pending/Hong Kong. $1.00.

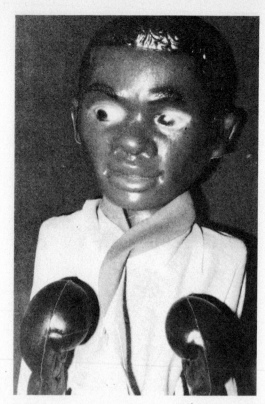

Puppet--5" "Adventure Boy and His Skymobile" Plastic and vinyl with molded hair. Painted features. Original. Marks: Remco Ind. Inc./1970, on head. $2.00.

Puppet--9" "World Champion Boxer" All plastic with painted features. Mechanism on back makes arms throw punches. Marks: SMC9 in circle/Made In/Hong Kong. 1972. $3.00.

Puppets--3" "Laurel & Hardy" All vinyl finger puppets. Marks: 1972/Larry Harmon/Pictures Corp. $1.00 pair.

Puppets--3" "Poppie Fresh," "Bun Bun" & "Biscuit." All vinyl finger puppets. Marks: Poppie Fresh/The Pillsbury Co 1974. $2.00 set.

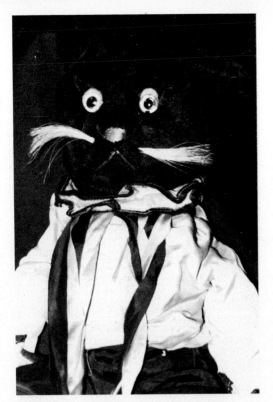

Rag--27" "Puss & Boots" Cloth body. Plush feet, arms and head. Glass eyes. Marks: none. 1936. $20.00.

Rag--30" "Drum Major" Plastic face mask/rest is stuffed plush. Marks: none. 1946. $16.00.

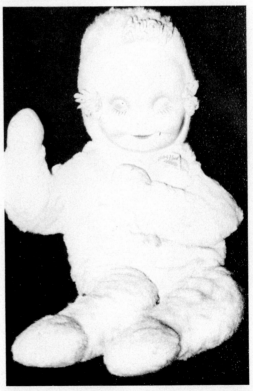

Rag--40" "Pin Up Girl" (1946) & "Sister Pat" (1949) All cloth with buckram face mask. Painted features. Original. Marks: none. Made by M&S Doll Co. $12.00.

Rag--18" "Sleepy Head" Cloth hands. Plush. Plastic face mask. Yellow yarn hair. Zipper back. Tag: Sleepy Head/Knickerbacher. 1947. $4.00.

Majestic Dolls--12" "Jack & Jill" Stuffed oil cloth with painted features. Marks: 1950 Majestic Doll, on back. Bag: Made by Feature Dolls. $1.00.

Rag--11" "Bebe Jetpartout" Cloth, stuffed so waist and hips are "jointed." Early vinyl masked face with painted side glancing blue eyes. Sewn on tuft of yellow yarn hair. Marks: Tag: Clodrey/Paris/Jetpartout/Deposee 1952. $8.00.

Rag--18" "Little Audrey" Cloth with vinyl head. Molded red hair. Painted features. Original. Tag: Little Audrey/Harvey Famous Cartoons. $25.00. (Courtesy Alice Capps)

Rag--27" "Lucy Arnez" All cloth. Plastic face mask. Orange yarn hair. Painted features. Marks: Apron: I Love Lucy/Desi. 1953. $18.00.

Rag--10" "Bunny" Stuffed corduroy. Plush hands and feet. Vinyl face mask. Yellow yarn hair. Plastic hat. Wire in ear holds hat on. Held something wired to left hand. Tag: Bunny Kuddles/CAL-T-5. Other Side: Cameo A-something I can't make out. 1954. $16.00.

Rag--23" "Eloise" Cloth with plastic face mask. Painted features. Yellow yarn hair. Tag: Eloise/ Eloise Ltd./Hollytoy Co. Ny. 1958. $22.00. (Courtesy Barbara Belding)

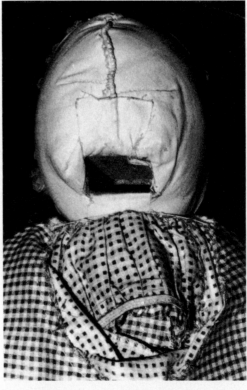

Rag--18" All cloth with pressed cloth face. Painted features. Blue side glancing eyes. Open mouth with slot that goes through head. Tailored slit in back of cap that gives access to mouth opening. Marks: none. Original clothes. $25.00.

Rag--Back view of rag doll with open mouth.

M&S Doll Co.--15" "Danny" Cloth with plastic mask face. Orange yarn hair. Marks: none. Box: M&S Doll Co. Mate to Daisy (Vol. 1) 1961. $5.00.

Rag--10" "Popeye" Plush and vinyl. Marks: 387, on head. 1961. Tag: Popeye/Copyright King Features Syn. Inc. Other Side: J. Swedlin Inc/ Gund Mfg. Co. Set Included: Little Audrey, Cinderella, Olive Oyl, Donald Duck, Mickey Mouse, Pinocchio, Casper, Dumbo, Pluto, Katnip, Merryweather, Goofy, Spooky Ghost and Jiminy Cricket. $4.00.

Rag--8" "Crib Angel" Stuffed body, arms and legs. Vinyl head. Blue inset eyes. 1963. Marks: Irwin, on head. $1.00.

Rag--10" "Tatters" All cloth with yellow yarn hair. Button eyes. Felt lids. Painted features. Original. Tag: Tatters/1964 Mattel Inc. $15.00. (Courtesy Connie Smith)

Rag--17" "McDonald's Hamburglar" All printed cloth. $2.00.

Rag--14" "Elsie, Borden's Cow" Plush body. Vinyl head. Moo voice. Tag: My Toy/Creation. Other side: Elsie Borden Co. Offered as a premium for $2.50 and flap from Borden's ice cream. 1958. $5.00.

Rag--21" "Gas Genie" Vinyl face mask. Rest all plush. Felt hands. Marks: Gas Genie/Gene Hazelton. 1969. $2.00.

Rag--20" "Dressy Bessy Teaching Doll" All cloth. Plastic eyes. Orange yarn hair. Original. Teaches child to buckle, button, tie, etc. Tag: Dressy Bessy/Teaching Doll/Playskool Inc/ Made in Hong Kong. Other side: Playskool/Div. of Milton Bradley Co. 1970. $2.00.

Rag--7" "Little Lulu Miniature Doll" All cloth. Removable clothes. Yarn hair. Marks: Lulu TM/ By Gund. Copyright Western/Publishing Co. Inc/MCMLXX11. $1.00.

Rag--12" "Mary, Many Face" A Uniworld of Unicef Doll. All polyester fiber stuffed. Dress flips up to make next face. Tag: Mary Many Face. Made by Aurora Products. This "face" is Israel. 1973. $7.00.

Rag--12" "Mary, Many Face" as Chili.

Rag--12" "Mary, Many Face" as Thailand.

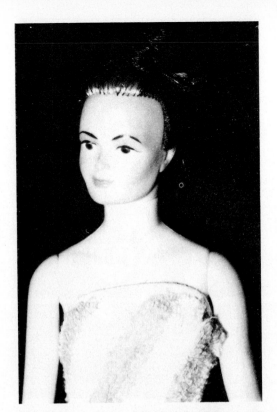

Remco--14½" "Dr. John Littlechap" Plastic and vinyl with molded hair. Painted features. Marks: none. Tag: Dr. John/Remco/Littlechap/ Hong Kong. 1963. $12.00. (Courtesy Sharon Hazel)

Remco--13¾" "Liza Littlechap" Plastic and vinyl. White streak in hair. No dimples. Blue eyeshadow. Original clothes. Marks: Lisa/Little- chap/Remco Industries/1963. Dress Tag: Lisa/ Remco/Littlechap/Hong Kong. B92, left leg. B95 right leg. $10.00.

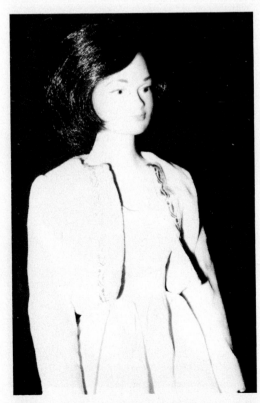

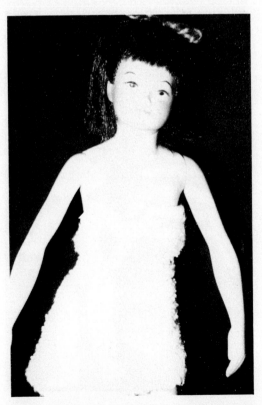

Remco--13" "Judy Littlechap" Plastic and vinyl. Rooted brown hair. Painted brown eyes. Dimples far out on cheeks. Original clothes. Marks: Judy Littlechap/Remco Industries/1963, on left leg. Dress tag: Judy/Remco/Little Chap/Japan. $10.00.

Remco--10½" "Libby Littlechap" Plastic and vinyl. Painted features. Dimples far out on cheeks. Wide spread legs. Original. Marks: Libby/Littlechap/Remco Ind. Tag: Libby Remco/Littlechap/Hong Kong. 1963. $10.00.

289

Remco--5½" "L.B.J." All vinyl with molded on clothes. Painted features. Removable hat. Marks: 74/Remco Ind. Inc/1964, on head. $18.00. (Courtesy Ronald L. Haines)

Remco--4¾" "Hildy & Herby" (Billy 1966) Both original. Marks: Hildy: Remco Ind. Inc./1966/F 16. Herby: Remco Ind. Inc./1966/F 105. $4.00 each.

Remco--5½" "Spunky" & "Pip" Spunky all original, including glasses. Stomach button makes arm raise. Marks: Spunky: F35/2/Remco Ind. Inc./1966. Pip: 2504/F3/Remco Ind. Inc./1966. $4.00 each.

Remco--6" "TV Jones" Plastic body and legs. Vinyl tail and head. Glued on fur. Painted features. Button in chest makes head shake "no." Marks: Remco/Inc. Inc./1966/K-41. Original clothes. $3.00.

Remco--15" "Orphan Annie" Plastic and vinyl. Rooted orange-red hair. No ears. Plastic disc movable eyes. Marks: Remco Ind. Inc./Copyright 1967. $12.00.

Remco--6" "Winking Heidi" Plastic and vinyl. Blue sleep eyes. Button in chest. Original. Marks: Remco Ind. Inc./1968. $4.00.

Remco--18" "Gingersnap" & 7" "Kewpie Doll" Plastic and vinyl. Original. Marks: Doll: E4/Remco Ind. Inc/1968, on head. Kewpie: 7A JLK/2/Cameo, on head. Kewpie, on foot. Cameo, on back. For a short two years, Remco had the "rights" to make Kewpies. 18.00.

Remco--19" Plastic and vinyl with rooted white hair. Painted blue eyes. Flat in back of head with very heavy rooted hair. Marks: 21/Remco Ind. Inc/1969, on head. $9.00.

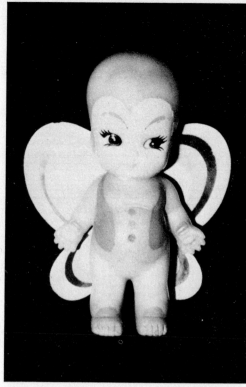

Remco--3½" "Hug A Bug" All green vinyl with painted clothes and features. Plastic clip on back to wear on clothes. Marks: 1971/Hong Kong/ Remco Ind. Inc., on wings. The Legend of the Hug A Bug: From the Magical Kingdom: Of Hug A Bug Land: Livid Gossamer People: As Small as your hand: They dressed in bright kisses: And of all things: They transfer their magic: When you touch their wings. $2.00.

Remco--19" "Laurie Partridge" Plastic and vinyl. Painted blue eyes. From TV series "The Partridge Family," played by Susan Day. Original. Marks: 1973/Remco Ind. Inc/Harrison NJ/ Item No. 3461, on back. Hong Kong/Remco Ind. Inc./1973, on head. $18.00.

Remco--19" "Mimi" Sings "I'd Like To Teach The World To Sing In Perfect Harmony." Plastic and vinyl. Painted blue eyes. Record insert on side. Marks: Hong Kong/Remco Inc/ 1972, on head. 1973/Remco Ind. Inc./Harrison NJ, on lower back. Sound device: Made In Japan. Battery operated. Doll: $20.00. Outfits: $4.00 each. Left to right: German #3507, Polish #3506, Scot. & English #3504.

Remco--19" "Mimi" 1973. Sings in 8 different languages. Uses records and batteries. Left to right: Spanish #3502, French #3501, Israeli #3503 and Italian #3505. Doll: $20.00. Outfits: $4.00 each.

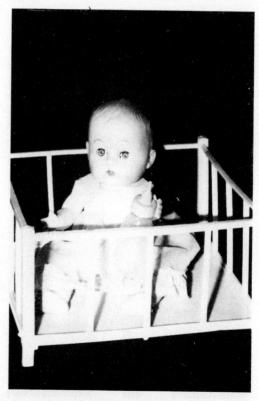

Rite-Lee--7" "Baby Lynne" All vinyl. Blue sleep eyes. Nurser. Separate toes. Marks: none. The mold marks have been scraped out, this mold was sold to Rite-Lee Mfg. Co. by Vogue Doll Co. Box: Baby Lynne/Rite-Lee Mfg. Co. $3.00.

293

Roberta--15" "Roberta Ann" All hard plastic with brown glued on wig. Blue sleep eyes. Open mouth/four teeth. Original. Marks: Series of unreadable letters, on head. Tag: Your/Roberta Ann, etc. 1952. $22.00. (Courtesy Virginia Jones)

Roberta--25" "Debutante Bride" Plastic and vinyl. Blue sleep eyes. High heel feet. Pierced ears. Original. Marks: 3, on head. Box: Roberta Dolls. 1959. $16.00.

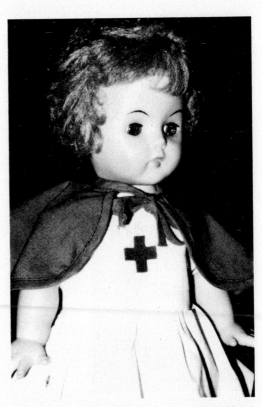

Roberta--17" "Dr. Ben Casey's Nurse, 1963" Was Dr. Kildare's nurse in 1967. Plastic and vinyl. Rooted dark brown hair. Blue sleep eyes. Marks: none. Dress tag: Dr. Ben Casey/Roberta $5.00.

Roberta--13" "Dr. Kildare's Nurse. 1964" Plastic and vinyl. Rooted blonde. Blue sleep eyes. Original. Marks: AE 153/14, on head. $5.00.

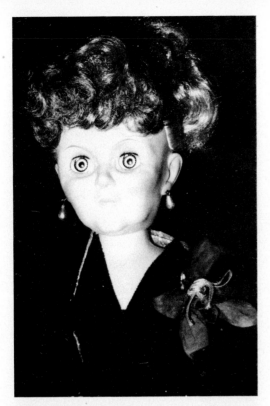

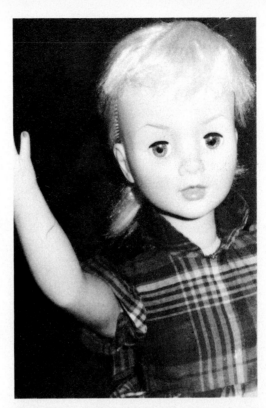

Royal--19" "Granny" All vinyl with rooted black/gray hair. Blue sleep eyes. Pierced ears. Original clothes. Marks: 40-B-SG, on back. One is marked: A Royal Doll, on head. $22.00. (Courtesy Terry)

Royal--21½" "Polly" Plastic and vinyl with ball jointed waist. Long neck that is posable. Blue sleep eyes. Marks: A Royal Doll, high on head. 1960/Royal Doll, lower on head. Royal Doll/1960, on back. $5.00.

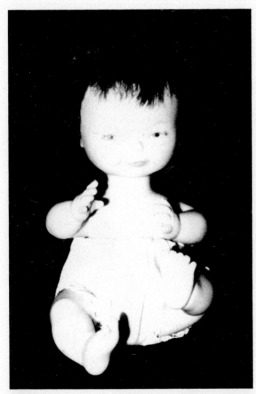

Royal--9½" "Raggy Muffin Baby" All vinyl with rooted brown hair. Painted blue eyes. Sold in 1960 F.O.A. Swartz along with boy: Shabby O'Hair and Girl: Jette. Marks: Royal Doll, on head. $2.00.

Royal--23" "Lisa Toddler" Plastic and vinyl with rooted white hair. Blue sleep eyes. Posable head. Marks: 1962/Royal Doll/3, on head. $6.00.

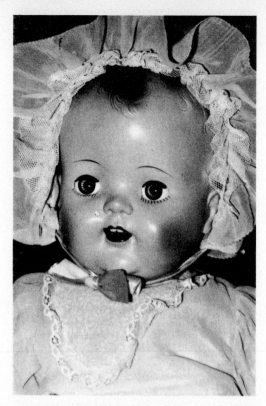

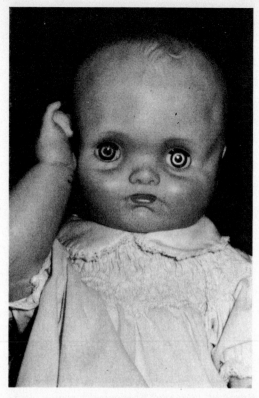

Sayco--26" "Playgirl" Cloth body, layex arms and legs. Hard plastic head. Blue sleep eyes. Two teeth. Original. Marks: Made in USA/750, on head. Box: Sayco. 1950.

Sayco--22" All stuffed vinyl. One piece body and legs. Disc jointed narrow shoulders. Molded hair. Blue sleep eyes/lashes. Pouty mouth. Left 2nd and 3rd finger molded together. Right 2nd and 3rd fingers curled and molded into palm. Marks:. Sayco/Doll Corp NYC/6U, on head. $12.00.

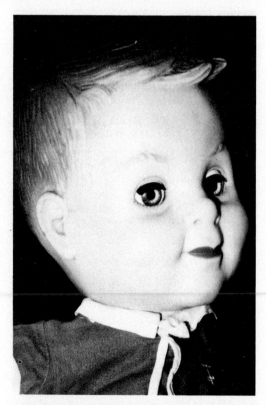

Sayco--27" "Peter Pan" Latex with stuffed early vinyl head. Molded red hair. Blue sleep eyes. Turned up nose. Light cheek dimples. Marks: Sayco/18-1, on head. 1953-56. $18.00.

Sayco--19" "Mother" All vinyl with glued on wig. Blue sleep eyes. Marks: Sayco Doll/NYC, on head. 1957. $12.00. (Courtesy Marie Gordon)

Sayco--19" "Carrie Cries" Plastic and vinyl with rooted dark brown hair. Blue sleep eyes. Open mouth with plunger. Doll cries, and when her thumb or dry nursing bottle is in mouth she stops crying. Plunger acts as stop. Start button in center of back. Battery operated. Marks: Sayco Doll, on head. 1963. $6.00.

Shillman--11½" "Maxi-Mod" Plastic body. Jointed waist. Vinyl arms, legs and head. Rooted blonde hair. Painted blue eyes. Marks: M&S/Shillman, on head. Made in Hong Kong, on back. 1973. $4.00.

Sayco--16" "Brother & Sister" All rigid vinyl with rooted dark blonde hair. Marks: Sayco Doll Inc/NYC, on head and back. 1957. $12.00 each.

Shindana--13" "Black Nancy & White Kim"
Plastic and vinyl. Painted features. Nursers.
Original. Marks: Div. of/Operation Bootstrap
Inc USA/1968 Shindana. $17.00 set.

Shindana--15" "Malaika" (in Swahili: Angel)
Plastic and vinyl with rooted black hair. Painted
brown eyes. Original. Marks: 1969/Shindana
Toys/Div. of Operation/Bootstraps Inc USA.
$10.00.

Shindana--9" "Wanda, Career Girl Nurse" All
vinyl with rooted black hair. Painted brown
eyes/lashes. Snapping knees. Original. Marks:
1972/Shindana Toys/Hong Kong. Also came as
Ballerina and TWA Hostess, plus different outfits. $6.00.

Shindana--9" "Wanda" in extra outfit.

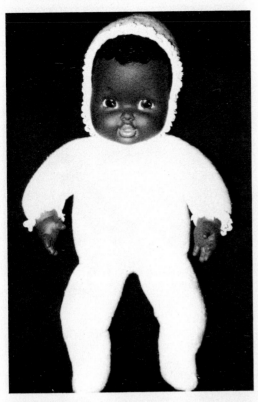

Shindana--11" "Lea" Cloth with vinyl face mask. Molded hair and painted features. Gauntlet vinyl hands. Tag: 1973/Shindana Toys/Div. of Operation/Bootstraps, Inc. $6.00.

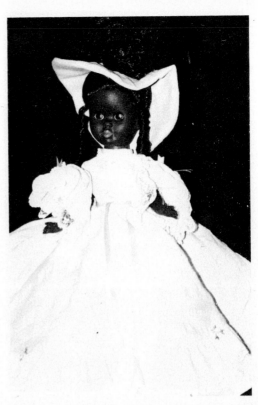

Shindana--16" "Kim" Plastic and vinyl with rooted black hair. Painted brown/black eyes. Original. Marks: 39/1969/Shindana Toy/Div. of Operation/Bootstrap Inc. USA. Sold in 1973. $20.00.

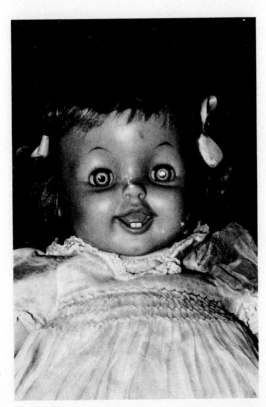

Skippy Doll--21" "Baby Ellen" Cloth and vinyl with rooted blonde hair. Blue sleep eyes. Two molded, painted lower teeth. Marks: S/1968/Skippy Doll. Colored version called "Baby Sue." $6.00.

Starr--7½" "Cowgirl Annie" All hard plastic. Glued on black wig. Blue sleep eyes. Removable shoes. Marks: Tag: A Starr Doll/1953/Annie. $2.00.

Starr Doll Co.--7½" "Miss Christmas" All hard plastic. Glued on brown hair. Blue sleep eyes. Marks: 7/3, on head. Tag: A Starr Doll. 1954. $2.00.

Star Doll Co.--14" "Dorothy Collins" All hard plastic with glued on yellow hair. Blue sleep eyes. Walker, head turns. Marks: 14, on head. Made In USA, on back. 1954. $25.00. (Courtesy Virginia Jones)

Sunland--20" "Baby Skin Doll" One piece stuffed vinyl arms, legs and body. Vinyl head. Blue sleep eyes. Original. Marks: none. Box: Baby Skin Doll of Quality/Sunland Dolls of California. $12.00.

300

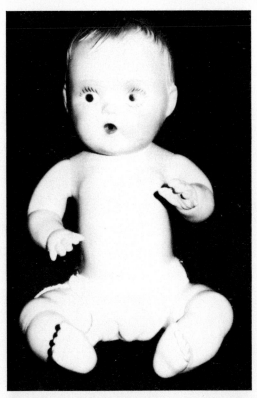

Sun--11" "Sunbabe" All rubber with molded hair. Painted blue eyes. Open mouth/nurser. Marks: Mfg. by/The Sun Rubber Co/Barberton O USA/Pat 2118682/Pat 2160739. 1950. $10.00.

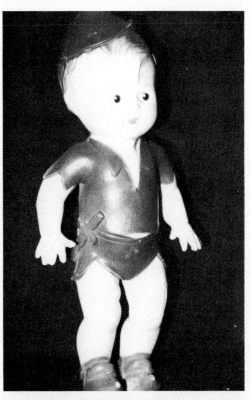

Sun Rubber--10" "Peter Pan" All one piece. Molded on clothes. Marks: Peter Pan/W. Disney Prod./The Sun Rubber Co/Barberton, O. USA, on back. 1953. $3.00.

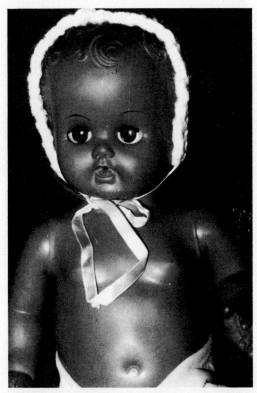

Sun Rubber--17" "Colored Sun-Dee" All lasiloid vinyl Sleep brown eyes. Nurser. Marks: Sun-Dee/Sun Rubber 1956, on head. Mfg. By/ The Sun Rubber Co/Barberton, Ohio USA/Under one or more US Pat./2118682, 2160 739, 2552216/2629131, 2629134 Other/Pat. Pend., on back. $15.00.

Super Doll--9½" "Carrie" Plastic and vinyl with rooted ash blonde hair. Blue painted eyes. Marks: S.D., on head. $4.00. (Courtesy Yvonne Baird)

301

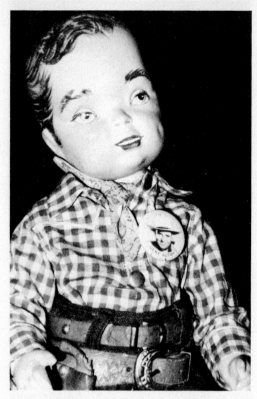

Terry Lee--16" "Gene Autry" in Round Up outfit. All rigid plastic. Hand brush painted brown hair and eyebrows. Decal blue eyes. Painted teeth. Original. Gene Autry button. Marks:Terri Lee/Pat. Pending, on back. Shirt tag: Gene Autry. Was issued in two outfits, the other was : Rodeo (light pants and silk shirt). 1950. $165.00.

Terri Lee--19" "Connie Lynn" All hard plastic with glued on red/brown fur hair. Blue sleep eyes. Open/closed mouth. Curled toes. Marks: none. 1955. $45.00.

Gene Autry shown in a pose from "Apache Country"

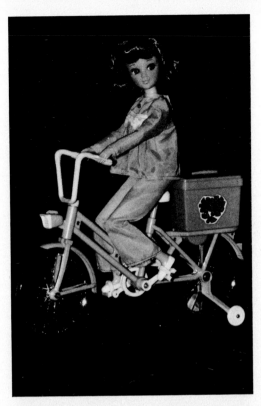

Tomy--14½" "Cindy" Plastic and vinyl with rooted brown hair. Brown sleep eyes. Pull string talker. She laughs. Says "Tell me a story, Mommy," etc. Original. Marks: M/Zape, in a diamond, on head. Figure of boy and girl/Tomy/ Pat. P. 7910,8535,24065/25767,32629/U.K. Pat. P. 50385/Made in Hong Kong, on back. $8.00.

Tomy--10" "Cycling Cheri" Plastic and vinyl with rooted red hair. Painted blue eyes. Jointed knees. Legs molded so doll will not stand up straight. Battery operated. Marks: 54, on head. Made in Hong Kong/picture of boy and girl/Tomy Corp, on back. Box: Tomy Corp/Long Beach, Calif. Also known as Peddling Polly. $12.00.

UFS--11" "Honest Abe Yokum" Latex with vinyl head. Molded orange hair. Painted features. Original clothes. 1953. Son of Li'l Abner Yokum of Dogpatch Comic Strip. (Mother: Daisy Mae) Marks: U.F.S. Inc/1953, on head. $18.00. (Courtesy Kathy Walters)

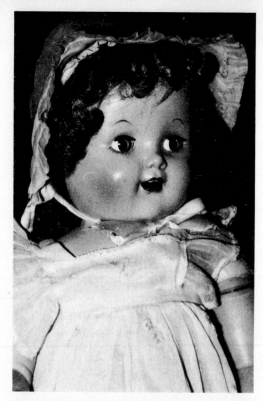

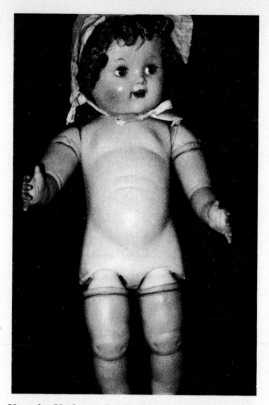

Uneeda--22" "Needa Toddles" This is the first issue of this line of dolls. Composition upper arms and legs. Wired on arms and legs of vinyl. Screw in center of stomach to attach weights that move legs. Hard plastic head. Glued on dark blonde hair. Blue sleep eyes. Two teeth. Dimpled cheeks. Marks: 20, on head. 1950. Original. $15.00.

Uneeda--Undressed 22" "Needa Toddles"

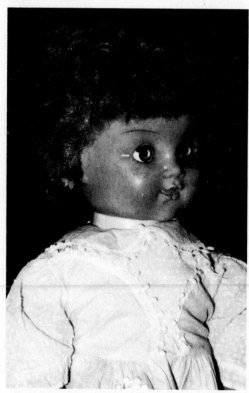

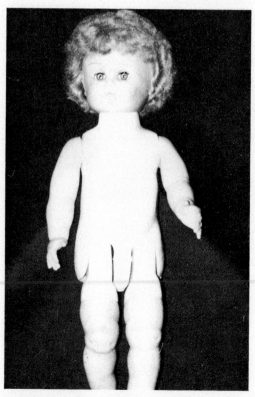

Uneeda--22" "Toddles" Hard plastic body and upper legs. Early vinyl head, arms and ¾ of legs. Rooted ash blonde hair. Blue sleep eyes. Open/closed mouth. Legs hinged to swing and sit. Will lay on tummy and legs lock in kick position. Original dress. Marks: A, on neck. 1952. $12.00.

Uneeda--22" "Needa Toddles"

304

Uneeda--11½" "Suzette" Plastic and vinyl with rooted red hair. Painted black eyes. Tiny high heel feet. Molded lashes. Posable head. Marks: N.F., on head. Uneeda Doll Co Inc./1962., on back. Also known as Judy and Lynn. $5.00.

Uneeda--10½" "Bride Sue" All vinyl with rooted ash blonde hair. Sleep blue eyes. High heel feet. Original. Marks: Uneeda, on head. $4.00. (Courtesy Yvonne Baird)

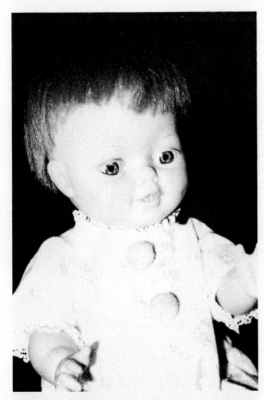

Uneeda--15" "Sunny Face" All vinyl with rooted dark blonde hair. Stationary blue eyes. Two molded lower teeth. Dimples. Squeeze stomach to make a grin. Called the "doll with the sunny disposition." Marks: Uneeda/Doll Co/Inc, in a circle. 516.32/Uneeda, on back. 1963. $10.00. (Courtesy Margaret Weeks)

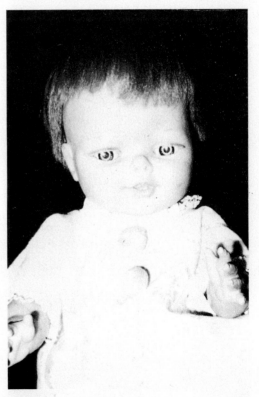

Uneeda--15" "Sunny Face"

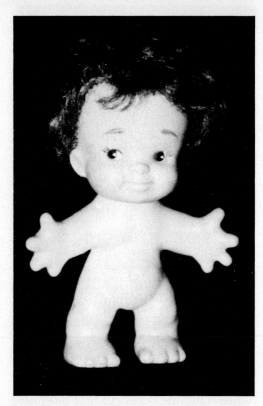

Uneeda--7" "Wish-Nik" All vinyl. Jointed only at neck. Rooted brown hair. Painted brown eyes. Marks: Uneeda/Wish-Nik/Patented, on back. Uneeda/1964, on head.

Uneeda--7" "Impish Elfy" Rigid vinyl, one piece body, arms and legs. Vinyl head with molded purple hair. Slanted eyes. Marks: Uneeda Doll Co, in a circle/1964/22, on head. Original clothes. $1.00.

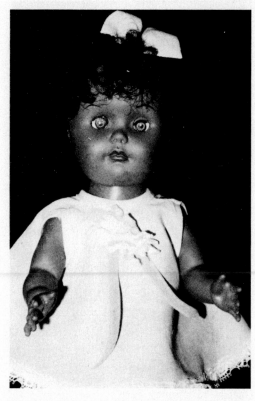

Uneeda--12" "Teenie Toddles" Plastic and vinyl. Brown sleep eyes. Pouty expression. 1965. Marks: Uneeda, on head. $1.00.

Uneeda--3½" "Hee Wee" Marks: U.D. Co Inc/ 1965, on right foot. Pee Wee/TM, on left. $2.00.

Uneeda--3½" "Dance Time Pee Wee" Marks: Pee Wee/TM/U.D. Co.Inc/1965/Hong Kong, on back. Hong Kong on head. $1.00.

Uneeda--3½" "Bride Time Pee Wee" Original. Marks: U.D.Co/1965 Inc, on one foot. Pee Wees T.M., on other. $1.00.

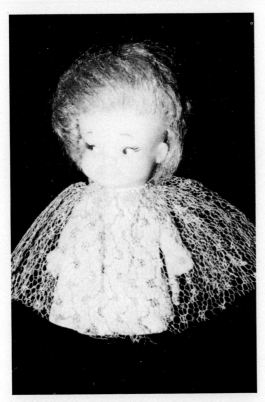

Uneeda--3½" "Angeltime" Original. Marks: U.D.Co/Inc/1965, on right foot. Pee Wee/TM, on left foot. $1.00.

Uneeda--3½" "PeeWee: Springtime & Shoppingtime" Marks: U.D. Co./1965 Inc, right feet. PeeWees/TM, left feet. Both original. $1.00 each.

307

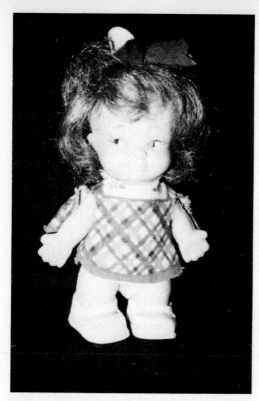

Uneeda--3½" "Schooltime" minus glasses. Original. Marks: U.D.Co. Inc./1965/Pee Wee, on back. $1.00.

Uneeda--11½" "Moonmaid" Plastic and vinyl with rooted dark blonde hair. Painted brown eyes. Original. Marks: Uneeda/Doll Co/Inc, in a circle/1966, on head. $12.00. (Courtesy Mary Partridge)

Uneeda--4" "Baby Pee Wees" Original. Marks: Uneeda Doll Co Inc., in a circle/1966, on back. $2.00 each.

Uneeda--3" "Batman Troll" All vinyl with inset, stationary blue eyes. Clothes stapled on. Marks: none. Original clothes. 1966. $2.00.

Uneeda--11" "Pretty Portrait" Plastic and vinyl with rooted blonde hair. Painted eyes. Original. Marks: Uneeda Doll Co Inc, in a circle/1966. $4.00. (Courtesy Kathy Walters)

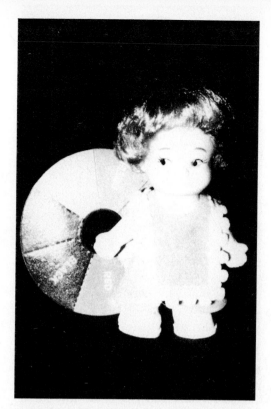

Uneeda--4" "Educational Pee Wee" Plastic and vinyl with rooted orange hair. Painted features. Original. Tells colors. Marks: U.D. Co. Inc./ MCMLXV1/Hong Kong. Set of ten, others are: Tell Time, Comb & Brush, Spell, Count To Ten, Piece A Puzzle, Build With Blocks, Save Money, Know Pets, Lace & Tie a Shoe. $1.00.

Uneeda--8" "Little Sophisticate Kristina" Plastic body and legs. Vinyl arms and head. Rooted dark brown hair. Posable head. Marks: Uneeda Doll Co Inc/1967/Made in Japan, on head. Tag: Little Sophisticate/Uneeda Doll Co Inc 1967/ Made in Japan. Uneeda Doll Co Inc/1967/Made in Japan, on back. Original clothes. One of a set of six. $3.00.

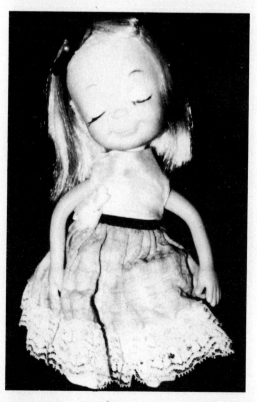

Uneeda--8½" "Marika, Little Sophisticate" Plastic and vinyl with rooted yellow hair. Blue eyeshadow. Pierced nostrils. Original. Marks: Uneeda Doll Co Inc./1967/Made in Japan, head and back. Others in set: Rosanna, Georgina, Penelope, Suzana and Kristina. $3.00.

309

Uneeda--5" "Fun Time" One of the Tiny Teens.
Brown hair and brown eyes. Original. Marks:
U.D.Co. Inc./1967/Hong Kong. $4.00.

Uneeda--5" "Beau Time" One of the Tiny Teens.
Blonde hair and brown eyes. Original. Marks:
U.D.Co.Inc./1967/Hong Kong. $4.00.

310

Uneeda--5" "Vacation Time" One of the Tiny
Teens. Plastic and vinyl with rooted black hair.
Painted blue/brown eyes/lashes. Posable head.
Came with doll stand. Others in series: Date
Time, Prom Time, Beau Time, Sport Time,
Winter Time, Bride Time, Shower Time, Tea
Time, Fun Time, Party Time, Mini Time.
Original. Marks: U.D.Co. Inc./1967/Made
in/Hong Kong. $4.00.

Uneeda--5" "Prom Time" One of the Tiny Teens.
Original. Marks: U.D.Co. Inc/1967/Hong Kong,
on head and back. $4.00.

Uneeda--5" "Bride Time" One of the Tiny Teens. Plastic and vinyl. Rooted blonde hair. Painted eyes. Original. Marks: U.D.Co. Inc./1967/Hong Kong, on back. Same on head. $4.00.

Uneeda--5" "Winter Time" One of the Tiny Teens. Red hair and brown eyes. Original. Marks: U.D.Co. Inc./1967/Hong Kong. $4.00.

Uneeda--5" "Date Time" One of the Tiny Teens. Red hair and brown eyes. Original. Marks: U.D. Co. Inc/1967/Hong Kong. $4.00.

Uneeda--5" "Party Time" One of the Tiny Teens. Brown hair and brown eyes. Original. Marks: U.D.Co. Inc./1967/Hong Kong. $4.00.

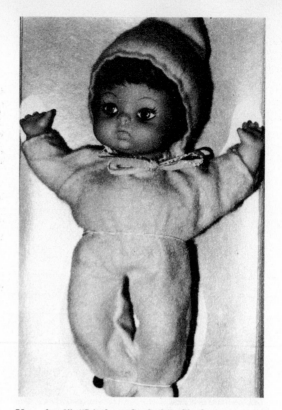

Uneeda--15" "Connie" One piece body, arms and legs. Rooted red hair. Blue sleep eyes. Nurser. Had brother "Ronnie" and was sold to teach pre-schoolers how to lace, zip, open buttons, wash and groom. Marks: Uneeda Doll Corp/ 1968/1969 DW. $5.00.
1969 DW. $5.00.

Uneeda--6" "Littlest So-Soft" Cloth and vinyl with rooted brown hair. Painted blue eyes. Original. 1970. Marks: U.D. Co. Inc/Hong Kong, on head. $3.00. (Courtesy Margaret Esler)

Uneeda--11" "Lovable Lynn" Plastic and vinyl with rooted reddish hair. Blue sleep eyes. Rosy complexion. Eyeshadow. Marks: Uneeda Doll Co Inc./MCMLXX/Hong Kong, on head and body. $3.00.

Uneeda--20" "Patti-Cake" Foam body with music box and key wind. Plastic arms and legs. Vinyl head with rooted white hair. Blue sleep eyes. Open mouth/dry nurser. Wiggles. Marks: Uneeda Doll Co. Inc/1970/2072 WW. $3.00.

Uneeda--5½" "Donna Fashion Doll" Plastic and vinyl with rooted dark blonde hair. Painted brown eyes/lashes. Original. Marks: U.D.Inc/MCMLXX/Made in/Hong Kong, on back. 3/U.D. Co. Inc/MCMLXX/Hong Kong, on head. $4.00.

Uneeda--16" "Magic Meg" Plastic and vinyl with rooted frosted blonde hair with grow feature. Blue sleep eyes. Original. Marks: Uneeda Doll Co Inc./MCMLXXI/616, on head. Uneeda Doll Co Inc/MCMLXXI/Made in Hong Kong/Pat. Pend., on back. $6.00.

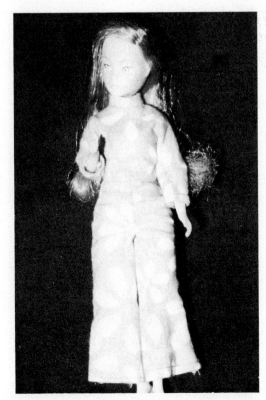

Uneeda--6½" "Little Miss Dollikin" Plastic and vinyl with rooted blonde hair. Painted blue eyes. Jointed (pin) elbows, knees. Jointed waist. Original. Marks: Uneeda 1971, on head. Little Miss/Dollikin/US Patent/No. 3010253/Other US and For. Patents Pending/Made in Hong Kong. $3.00. (Courtesy Leslie White)

Uneeda--4" "Lin" also "Sue" All vinyl with rooted black hair. Painted black eyes. Original. Marks: UD Co Inc/MCMLXXI/Hong Kong, on back. $2.00.

313

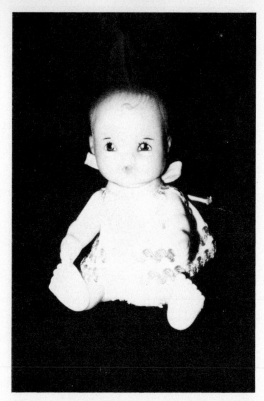

Uneeda--4" "Lin," also "Loo" All vinyl with black rooted hair. Painted black eyes. Open mouth/ nurser. Original. Marks: UD Co Inc/MCML XXI/Hong Kong. $2.00.

Uneeda--4" "Weepsy" Plastic and vinyl. Molded hair and painted features. Nurser. Cries tears by pressing tummy when full of water. Marks: U.D. Co Inc/MCMLXXII/US & For. Pats Pend/ Made in/Hong Kong. $1.00.

Uneeda--4" "Thum-Fun" (Thleepy, Thmart, Thilly) Plastic and vinyl with molded brown hair. Only jointed at neck. Face revolves. An original dress but sold in several styles. Marks: UD Co/INC. MCMLXXIII/Hong Kong. $2.00.

Uneeda--4" "Thmart"

Uneeda--4" "Thilly"

Uneeda--7¾" "Janie" Hard plastic with vinyl head. Rooted white hair. Blue sleep eyes/molded lashes. 2nd and 3rd fingers molded together. Marks: none.

Unique--12" "Vickie" All plastic with a vinyl head. Rooted brown hair. Painted blue eyes. Marks: Unique, on head. $3.00. (Courtesy Sharon Hazel)

Unique--12" "Calico Lass" Plastic and vinyl with rooted blonde hair. Painted blue eyes. Small life like breasts. Same doll as used for Ellie Mae Clampett. Original, minus shoes. Marks: Unique, on head. Premium doll offered by Kelloggs. $4.00.

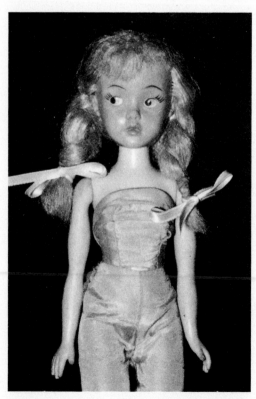

Unique--11½" "Ellie Mae Clampet" Plastic and vinyl. Rooted blonde hair. Painted blue eyes. Original clothes. Same doll used for Kelloggs Corn Flakes in 1964, called "Calico Lassie." Ideal made these dolls for Unique. Marks: Unique, on head. $4.00.

Vale--14" "Rusty" All excellent quality early vinyl. Beautifully molded reddish/brown hair. Blue sleep eyes. Not original clothes. Marks: Vale/D.C., on head. From Danny Thomas Show "Make Room For Daddy." 1954. Sold as "Alden's Cuddliest" in 1952. $12.00.

Valentine--17½" "Happi-Time Walker" All hard plastic with glued on blonde hair. Blue sleep eyes. Open mouth/four teeth. Marks: A Product of/Doll/Bodies/Inc/New York, on back. Walker. Head turns. 1953. $25.00.

Valentine--15" "Dondi" One piece stuffed vinyl body, arms and legs. Vinyl head. Painted features. Almost black sleep eyes. Painted teeth. Original. Marks: 14 VS/100. $35.00. (Courtesy Viriginia Jones)

Valentine--14" "Roxanne" All hard plastic walker, head turns. Glued on saran hair. Blue sleep eyes. Open mouth, 4 upper teeth. Original. Marks: Made in USA/Pat. Pending, on back. Tag: Fashioned after the glamorous hostess of TV "Beat The Clock" program. 1953. $25.00.

Valentine--14" "Luann Simms" All hard plastic with knee length dark hair. Blue sleep eyes. Walker. From Arthur Godfrey's TV Show. Original dress. Marks: Made in USA/Pat. Pend., on back. $30.00.

317

Virga--8" "Lucy" Hard plastic with vinyl head. Rooted ash blonde hair. Blue sleep eyes/molded lashes. Molded on shoes (with T straps). Walker, head turns. Marks: Virga, on head. By Beehler Arts. 1956. $5.00.

Virga--7" "Lucy" All hard plastic with glued on black hair. Brown sleep eyes. Original. Same doll as "Walking Joan" Marks: none. $8.00. (Courtesy Dorothy Westbrook)

"Lucy" is a Virga Doll of the 1950's. A hard plastic, straight leg walker and unmarked or with "Virga" incised. She looks more like the Ginny than others, except her legs are slightly curved and she has molded on T strapped shoes, painted or left natural. Her belly is quite rounded and has a small dot for a navel. The Virga trademark is by the Beehler Arts Co. In April of 1950 Lucy was marketed under several names: Olympic Princess, Cuddlee Bride, Joanie Pigtails and was the starlet doll promoted by Lustre-Creme Shampoo. She was issued as Colored, Hawaiian, and Indian also. The above information on Lucy, comes from Jeannie Niswonger, President of the Ginny Doll Club.

VOGUE DOLLS INC.

Edited by
Jeanne Niswonger, President
Ginny Doll Club
305 West Beacon Rd.
Lakeland, Florida 33803

Editor's Note: The following is from a release from Ted Nelson, president of Vogue Dolls Inc., a subsidiary of Tonka Corporation.

In January, 1973, the "new" Tonka Corporation took its first step toward further diversification and acquired Vogue Dolls, Inc., a long established (more than 50 years) producer of quality traditional dolls that are "made to be loved," dressed in exquisitely designed clothing and particularly noted for their lovely faces.

Vogue Dolls had their beginnings in the early 1920's in Somerville, Mass., where Mrs. Jennie H. Graves opened a small "home industry" making clothing for dolls that were being sold in a department store in nearby Boston. As the demand grew, she hired her neighbors to, at first, come into her home to assist her in cutting and sewing the doll dress that she created.

The business grew through the normal peaks and valleys and in the early 1930's Mrs. Graves began buying undressed dolls made by the finest craftsmen in Germany, creating clothes for them and selling them at shops across the country. Some of these dolls retailed as high as $50 to $75, a "dear" price at that time, which will testify to the quality of the dolls and the delicacy of their clothing. The political situation in Europe in the late 1930's forced Mrs. Graves to purchase her dolls from U.S. manufacturers, and she was recognized nationally for upgrading the quality of U.S. made dolls through her insistence on perfection.

It is she who conceived the idea of a "miniature" doll--one that the child could not only love but one that a little girl could more easily relate to in her own tiny world. Despite the negative attitude of her suppliers and her customers, Jennie Graves persisted and commissioned a sculptor to create an 8-inch little girl figure and thus, Ginny, the "original" miniature doll came into being. Ginny was an instant success and the demand for more and varied clothing for her caused Mrs. Graves to enlist the aid of her first-born daughter, Virginia, to take over the responsibility for creating the original fashions while Mrs. Graves attended to the growing manufacturing needs (more women working in their homes) and to the selling function. Virginia Graves Carlson was to remain as the clothing designer for more than 20 years.

In 1950-51, Mrs. Graves came up with the idea of selling 8" Ginny also as an undressed basic doll and marketing her fifty or more clothing sets separately. This plan was an instant success and sales quadrupled through the million dollar mark. Thus encouraged, Jennie Graves' fertile mind brought forth further accessorization for Ginny (not only separate clothes, but shoes, socks, jewelry, handbags, etc. and even custom-made wooden doll furniture and a little dog) all scaled to her 8" miniature size. This was followed by the expansion of the "Ginny Doll Family" to include little baby sister, 8" Ginnette, teenage sisters, 10½" Jill and Jan, big brother, 11" Jeff, and baby brother, 8" Jimmy, all with their own wardrobes and accessories. Mrs. Graves' creations resulted in building Vogue Dolls to its peak in the mid 1950's when it was believed to be the largest doll manufacturer in the world employing nearly 800 "home sewers" and 350 in-plant workers to make millions of little girls happy.

Mrs. Graves did not believe in TV advertising, and heavy competition brought on difficult times, complicated by advancing years and failing health. In 1961, the company was sold to Ted Nelson (the husband of Mrs. Graves' younger daughter, June) who had joined the family company several years earlier. The company continued the diversification program instituted by Mrs. Graves and Virginia Carlson in the late 1950's away from the "miniature" only image into larger, more varied dolls while maintaining the family devotion to quality, integrity of product, lovely faces and fine garments--dolls that are "made to be loved." Nelson remains as the general manager of Vogue Dolls in its new relationship as a member of the Tonka Family, as do many of the other "Guys and Dolls" who have contributed to so much of its success, some more than 25 years.

Vogue Dolls continues to be basically a creative, sewing, assembly and shipping facility. New doll creations are commissioned to independent sculptors and the basic manufacture of the dolls and much of the clothing is sub-contracted to quality resources.

The original 8" Ginny is now produced in the Far East (where the infinite detail is possible in the many home industries) in a series of "Far-Away Land" dolls dressed in a variety of "native" costumes.

Author's Note: It should be noted, in the above release, that the German dolls of the early 1930's were made of bisque and dressed by Vogue. To date I have not been able to find out if a "Vogue" label was used.

Pricing Your "Ginny" Doll

These prices are based on clean, good hair, and originally dressed in tagged clothes.
Composition Ginny: $16.00
Early Non-Walker: $14.00.
Early Walker: $12.00.
Molded lashes/Walker: $10.00.
Bending Knee/Walker: $8.00.
Add $2.00 for brown eyes.
Ginny outfits: $3.00 to $12.00 each.

The Family of Ginny

1953: Ginny dolls were given a different name with every outfit and were made up in groups of six. Kindergarten Afternoon Series: Linda (21), Donna (22), Kay (23), April (24), Connie (25), Carol (26). Kindergarten School Series: Hope (27), Margie (28), Tina (29), Dawn (30), Pat (31), Nan (32). Twin Series: Hansel (33), Gretel (34), Dutch Boy (35), Dutch Girl (36), Cowboy (37), Cowgirl (38). Tiny Miss Series: Lucy (39), Wanda (40), June (41), Glad (42), Beryl (43), Cheryl (44). Gadabout Series: Ballet (45), T.V. (46), Roller Skater (47), Beach (48), Ski (49), Ice Skater (50). Fable and Bride Series: Alice (51), Red Riding Hood (52), Bo Peep (53), Mistress Mary (54), Bride (55), Bridesmaid (56). Debutante Series: Pamela (60), Cathy (61), Becky (62), Karen (63), Ginger (64), Angela (65). Numbers are order number of outfits.

1954: Ginny is now a walker with straight legs. Clothes are grouped into sections, with six outfits to a group but lack the names given to them in 1953. My Kinder Crowd Dresses, My Tiny Miss Styles, For Fun Time, For Rain or Shine, My Twin Sets, The Whiz Kids Group, The Candy Dandy Series, My First Corsage Styles.

1955: Introduced: Ginnette (painted eyes), Ginny's little sister. Molded, painted hair only. Clothes are grouped, once again, with six outfits per group. Kinder Crowd, Ginny Gym Kids, Merry Moppets, Tiny Miss, Fun Time, Bridal Trousseau, And Away We Go, Bon Bons.

1956: Six outfits per group: Kinder Crowd, Gym Kids, Merry Moppets, Tiny Miss, Fun Time, Play Time, Formals, Debs.

1957: Introduced: Ginny's big sister teenage doll: Jill.

1958: Ginny dresses and Vogue patterns for children's dresses for look-a-like series:

Vogue Pattern #2748.......Ginny Outfit #1301.
Vogue Pattern #2771.......Ginny Outfit #1336
Vogue Pattern #2741.......Ginny Outfit #1341
Vogue Pattern #2765.......Ginny Outfit #1311
Vogue Pattern #2755.......Ginny Outfit #1332
Vogue Pattern #2766.......Ginny Outfit #1325
Vogue Pattern #2757.......Ginny Outfit #1358
Vogue Pattern #2786.......Ginny Outfit #1335

1958 also introduces 8" "Jimmy," Ginny's brand new brother with painted eyes and molded hair. (Ginnette dressed as a boy). The new Ginnette now has sleep eyes. Introduces 10½" "Jan," all vinyl with straight legs (another sister for Ginny) and wears Jill's clothes. Also introduces Ginny's big brother, all vinyl 11" "Jeff."

"Jimmy" Outfits: 4331: Blue cotton overalls with suspender straps and checkered blue/white shirt.

4330: Denim shorts, red checkered shirt and visor cap of blue denim.

4332: Suspender pants of blue and red plaid. White jersey T-shirt.

4350: White cotton shirt. Brass buttoned red felt vest and matching shorts. Visor cap in tartan plaid.

4351: Two-tone taffeta clown suit. Tulle ruffle and matching hat.

4352: Denim overalls (clipped side seam), red jersey shirt. Black felt cowboy hat. Gun.

1959: Ginny costumes from Far Away Lands: #1459, Hawaiian; #1457, Hollander; #1455, Israelian; #1454, Oriental; #1458, Alaskan; #1453, Scandinavian; #1456, British Isles. 1959 also introduces tomboy "Li'l Imp." Red hair/freckles. Also "Brikette," in her own words: I'm a sassy freckled-faced rascally emerald-eyed Pixie! I'm a flirty show off and a winsome charmer. I have straightest orange-taffy hair you've ever seen and the greenest eyes! Personality... that's me" quote from 1960 Ginny Club News funny book. This same booklet carries an ad for Arranbee dolls: My Angel, Angel Face and Littlest Angel.

1961: Jill was not issued in 1961. Introduces Baby Dear, 12" and 18" painted eye version.

1962: Introduces through Vogue: 11" Littlest Angel, in 10 different outfits. Also the new Ginny Baby, 8", 12", 16", 18" and 20". With molded and rooted hair. New also is the E. Wilkin's Baby Dear One. 25", sits up and has 2 lower teeth. An all new Jill. 10½" all vinyl with soft vinyl head.

1963: New this year is the 16" Miss Ginny (jointed waist). Ginnette is now called Ginny Baby and comes in 8", 12", 16" and 18" sizes and with rooted hair. Also new is the 8" Li'l Dear with molded or rooted hair.

1964: Introduces 8" cloth bodied Li'l Cuddly Dear and 10" all fleece with vinyl head Bunny Hug. 12" and 18" New Baby Dear with sleep eyes. (E. Wilkin) and 17" Too Dear (E. Wilkin) all vinyl with sleep eyes. Came as boy or girl and is a two year old likeness of Baby Dear. New also is 'Jama Baby, a pajama bag with a vinyl head. Negro dolls: 8" Ginnette (molded hair), 11" Li'l Imp, Ginny Baby in the 8", 12", 16" and 18" sizes.

1965: Ginny Baby came in 12" and 16" only.

1966: The only 8" baby was Li'l Dear (cloth body) and during 1966 the original mold for Ginnette was destroyed and 1967 Vogue introduced a new Ginnette with painted and rooted hair and is marked Vogue Dolls, Inc/1967.

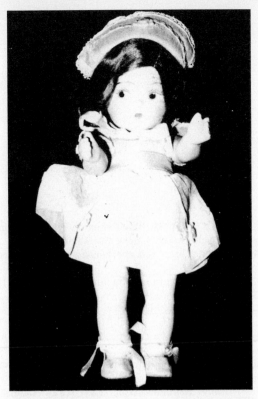

Vogue--8" "Ginny" All composition with painted blue eyes. Original. Marks: Vogue, head and back. $16.00. (Courtesy Edith Goldsworthy)

Vogue--Outfit called "Bo Peep" #53. 1953. (Courtesy Dorothy Westbrook)

Vogue--"Ginny" (left) in the 1953 outfit named "June" #41. The necklace, purse and bracelet are from an accessory pack of 1958. The shoes are not original. (right) Called "My First Corsage" styles.

Vogue--#355 "Candy Dandy" series. 1954. (Courtesy Margaret Weeks)

Vogue--7" "Ginny" All hard plastic. Glued on wig. Blue sleep eyes. Dressed in #24 "April," 1953. Marks: Vogue Doll on back. Vogue Doll Inc dress label. Ginny made in USA on shoes. All original. (Maish Collection)

Vogue--"Ginny" in #123. 1954. Shoes not original. (Courtesy Margaret Weeks)

Vogue--Hat from #240 outfit. 1954. Dress from #1750 Weekender package.

Vogue--7" "Ginny" All hard plastic. Glued on blonde wig. Blue sleep eyes. Original Nurse's outfit, #131. Marks: Vogue Doll, on back. Vogue Dolls Inc/dress label. Ginny, made in USA, on shoes. 1954. (Maish Collection)

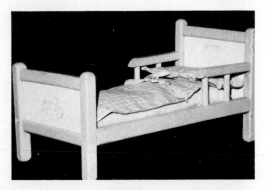

Vogue--"Ginny's Bed" 1955. Cover not original.
$18.00. (Courtesy Kathy Walters)

Vogue--#180 "Sunday Best" 1955. (Courtesy
Margaret Esler)

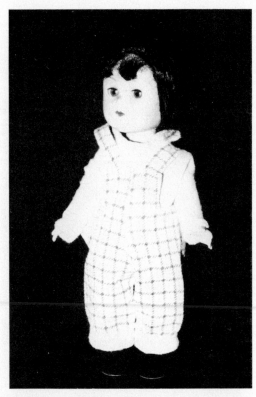

Vogue--"Ginny Gym Kids" series. #129. 1955.
(Courtesy Margaret Esler)

Vogue--"Ginny" in "Merry Moppets" series #236.
1955.

Vogue--"Ginny" in #6180. Shoes not original. 1956. (Courtesy Margaret Esler)

Vogue--Camping dress #6032. 1956. Listed under "Ginny Gym Kids" series.

Vogue--#1451 Rodeo outfit. Had boots, hat and gun. 1956. (Courtesy Kathy Walters)

Vogue--"Ginny" on the left has a tagged Vogue dress that seems too large for Ginny and is too small for Jill. Right: outfit #6143. 1956. Also had satin ribbon sash tying in back and a straw bonnet. (Courtesy Kathy Walter)

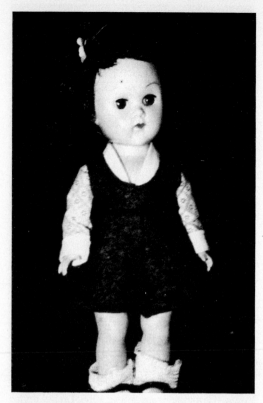

Vogue--#6155 minus hat. 1956. (Courtesy Margaret Weeks)

Vogue--Ginny in #6126 "Kinder Crowd" series. 1956. (Courtesy Dorothy Westbrook)

Vogue--Coat, hat and muff #6184. 1956. (Courtesy Margaret Esler)

Vogue--Jill's Bridal Outfit. 1957. #7415. $15.00.

Vogue--1957 "Ginny" bed. $15.00. (Courtesy Margaret Weeks)

Vogue--10" "Jan" Rigid vinyl body, arms and legs. Vinyl head with rooted yellow blonde hair. Blue sleep eyes/molded lashes. Smiling mouth. Swivel jointed waist. High heel feet. Marks: Vogue, on head. 1957. Not original clothes. $15.00.

Vogue--#7134 had a long sleeve blouse. 1957. (Courtesy Dorothy Westbrook)

Vogue--This is "Wee Imp" with a changed wig! And in an original "Ginny" outfit. 1957. Outfit #7150.

Vogue--"Ginny" in dress #243 of the "My Tiny Miss" styles (had hat with matching trim) 1957.

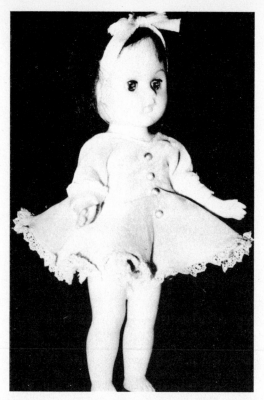

Vogue--A vinyl "Ginny" wears #7160 dress. 1957. Doll ca. 1960's.

Vogue--1957 Outfit #6131. Came with long sleeve blouse. (Courtesy Kathy Walters)

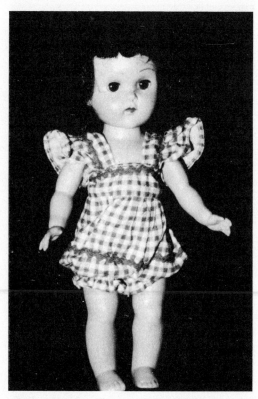

Vogue--"Ginny" in dress #7026. 1957. (Courtesy Kathy Walters)

Vogue--"Ginny" wardrobe case #1710. 1957. $12.00.

Vogue--Outfit #7138. 1957. Missing is small organdy apron that ties on with a velvet ribbon and matching panties.

Vogue--1958 outfit #1314. (Courtesy Kathy Walters)

Vogue--#1334. 1958. Had straw hat. (Courtesy Margaret Weeks)

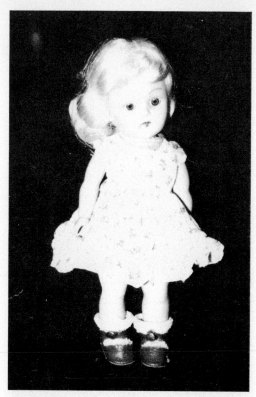

Vogue--1958. #1360. Had navy coat and flower pot white straw hat. (Courtesy Margaret Esler)

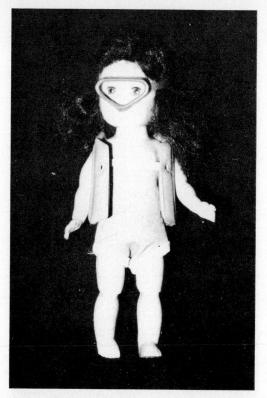

Vogue--#1353 outfit. Had pail and beach towel. 1958. (Courtesy Dorothy Westbrook)

Vogue--#1230. 1958. Had jacket and tam. Shoes not original. (Courtesy Dorothy Westbrook)

Vogue--"Ginny" in dress #1403. 1958. Hat is not part of the outfit. Ginny's pup is #1591. (Courtesy Margaret Weeks)

Vogue--(left) Ginny in outfit #1430 (Vogue pattern dress alike) 1959. (right) Outfit #460. 1954. The yellow beret marked "Ginny" is from accessory pack of 1958 (left)

Vogue--"Hawaiian" #1459. 1959.

Vogue--"Hollander" #1458. 1959.

Vogue--"Oriental" #1254. 1959.

Vogue--"Israelian" #1455. 1959.

Vogue--"Alaskan" #1258. 1959.

Vogue--7" "Ginny" All hard plastic. Glued on red wig. Turning head walker. Outfit is #1413. 1959. Marks: Ginny/Vogue Dolls In, on back. Vogue Dolls Inc. on pink and white cotton dress. Ginny on shoes. (Maish Collection)

Vogue--9" "Pinky Toe" 1962. All vinyl with rooted white hair. Blue sleep eyes/long molded lashes. Nurser. Baby legs. Marks: Vogue Dolls, on lower back. $8.00.

Vogue--13" "Littlest Angel" in original clothes. Marks: Vogue Doll/1963, on head and body. $6.00.

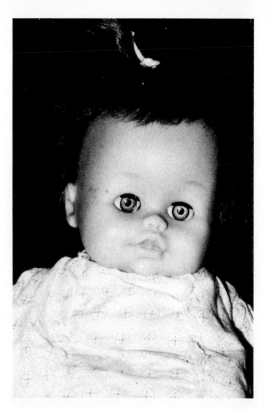

Vogue--17" "New Baby Dear" Cloth with vinyl arms, legs and head. Rooted blonde hair. Blue sleep eyes. Dimples in chin and cheeks. Marks: Vogue Doll/1964, head. Body tag: Vogue Dolls Inc. 1960/E. Wilkin, back of left leg. $20.00.

Vogue--14" "Angel Baby" All vinyl with rooted reddish blonde hair. Blue sleep eyes. Original. Marks: Vogue Doll/1965, on head. $6.00. (Courtesy Patricia Allin)

Vogue--15" "Miss Ginny" shown in an original outfit. Dress tag: Vogue Dolls Inc. Paper tag: Hi! I'm 15" Miss Ginny. Created by Vogue Dolls Inc. 1970. $7.00.

Vogue--9" "Jeff" Wearing an original blue suit, white shirt, red tie, loafers. $15.00. (Courtesy Ruth Lane) Photo by Bud Lane.

Vogue--8" "Ginny" #201 The American Indian. Marks: Ginny, on head. Vogue Dolls Inc, on back. Tag: "Ginny From Far Away Land" The headband is missing and has on the wrong shoes, rest is original. $8.00. (Courtesy Edith Goldsworthy)

Vogue--8" "Ginny" All vinyl with yellow rooted hair. Blue sleep eyes. Original. 1966. Marks: Ginny, on head. Vogue Dolls Inc, on back. Dress tag: Vogue Dolls Inc. Paper tag states "Ginny Dolls From Far Away Land." "#520-Ginny Cowgirl" $8.00. (Courtesy Edith Goldsworthy)

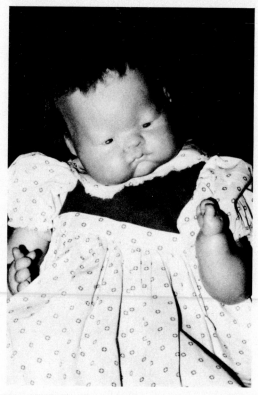

Vogue--"Baby Dear" 1961. Shown in original outfit. Sold through home toy party. Childhood doll of Lana Hill Butler. $22.00.

Vogue--"Ginny" I can not find this outfit. It is tagged and from between 1952-56.

Reference and Bibliography

Ellenburg, "Effanbee. The Dolls With Golden Hearts"

Schoonmaker, Patricia. "The Effanbee Patsy Family and Related Delights."

Desmonde, Kay. "All Color Book Of Dolls"

Burdick, Loraine. "A Doll For Christmas." "Child Star Dolls & Toys." "Shirley Temple And Related Delights."

Celebrity Doll Club: Feb, May, Aug, Nov. 1967; Feb, May, Aug, Nov, 1968; Feb, May, Aug. 1969.

Fawcett, Clara Hallard. "Dolls, A New Guide For Collectors," Hobbies Magazine (May, July, September, December 1967)

St. George, Eleanor. "Dolls Of Three Centuries," "The Dolls Of Yesterday."

Hart, Luella. Spinning Wheel (July/August 1963). "Part IV Directory of United States Doll Trademarks" (2nd Revised Edition)

South, Brenda. "Heirloom Dolls"

Coleman, Dorothy, Elizabeth, Evelyn. "The Collector's Encyclopedia Of Dolls." "Doll Makers & Marks"

Bullard, Helen. "The American Doll Artist"

Cooper, Marlowe. "Dimples & Sawdust, Vol. 1 & 2." "Doll Home Library Series" Vol. 12, 13, 14.

Johl, Janet Pagter. "Your Dolls and Mine"

Anderton, Johana Gast. "Twentieth Century Dolls"

Shoemaker, Rhoda. "Composition Dolls Cute And Collectable" Vol. 1 & 2.

Tavores, Olinda. "The Armchair Museum Of Dolls"

Jacobsen, Carol. "Portrait Of Dolls" Vol. 1 & 2.

Doll Collector's Manuals by the Doll Collectors of America. 1956, 57, 1964, 1973.

"Louisville, 1973." N.F.D.C.

Western Auto Supply Catalogs: 1949, 1950, 1951, 1954, 1956, 1957, 1960, 1961, 1963, 1964, 1966.

Macy Catalog: 1960, 1961, 1964, 1967.

Holiday Gifts Catalog: 1942, 1946.

Rohde-Spencer Catalogs: 1934, 1935, 1936, 1937, 1938, 1939, 1940.

Walt Disney Archives Report For: 1938, 1939, 1940, 1944, 1947.

Slack Mfg. Co. Catalog: 1940, 1942, 1946.

Sears & Roebuck: 1935 through 1973.

Montgomery Wards Catalogs: 1935 through 1973.

Continental Products Inc.: 1940, 1941, 1942.

John Plain Catalogs: 1941, 1942, 1945, 1946, 1949, 1968, 1970, 1972, 1973.

Hagns Catalogs: 1938, 1943, 1946, 1949, 1954.

Brecks Catalogs: 1948, 1950, 1956.

Effanbee Doll Co. Catalogs: 1952, 1954, 1955, 1958, 1959, 1966, 1968, 1969, 1971.

Womens Home Companion Magazine: December 1946, December 1951, December 1953.

World Wide Doll News: August 1969.

Toy Yearbook: 1953, 1954, 1958.

Alexander Co. Catalogs: 1942/43, 1952 through 1972.

John Wanamaker: 1956, 1959, 1960, 1961.

Woolworths Catalog: 1952, 1954, 1955, 1956, 1957, 1961.

Nirisk Catalog: 1955, 1957, 1958, 1959, 1961.

Strawbridge & Clothier: 1957.

Coast To Coast Stores Catalogs: 1948, 1949, 1955, 1957, 1959, 1960.

Toy Fair Catalogs: 1957, 1961, 1963, 1964, 1965, 1966.

F.A.O. Swartz: 1944, 1945, 1947, 1949, 1950, 1952, 1956, 1957, 1958, 1965, 1967, 1969, 1970, 1971, 1972, 1973, 1974.

Frank's Children Center: 1955, 1957.

Time & Toys: 1957.

Toyland Catalogs: 1960, 1961, 1962, 1963.

Uncle Harry's Corner: 1959, 1960.

Midwestern Catalog: 1961.

Toy Partners Inc.: 1954, 1955, 1960, 1961, 1963.

Dolls & Toys Catalog: 1962.

S & H Green Stamp: 1961, 1964, 1965, 1967, 1969, 1970, 1972, 1973.

National Bella Hess: 1947, 1964, 1967, 1968.

Topper Toy Co. Catalogs: 1961, 1963, 1964, 1965, 1967, 1970.

Top Value Catalog: 1965.

Remco Co. Catalog: 1966, 1967.

Uneeda Co. Catalog: 1946, 1948, 1950, 1951, 1966, 1967, 1968, 1969, 1970, 1971.

Bennett Bros. Catalog: 1967, 1969.

Altmans Catalog: 1967, 1970, 1972.

Buchsbaum Co. Catalog: 1957, 1958.

Peg O' My Heart Co. Ad: 1940.

Saroff Studios: 1941.

Jim Brown: 1941, 1942, 1946, 1947.
Noahs Ark Catalog: 1951, 1953, 1954.
Joy Bring Catalog: 1957.
Hill's Toy Yearbook: 1954.
Young Playways: 1960.
Dolgins: 1960.
Ronnie's Dept. Store: 1957, 1958, 1959.
Billy & Ruth: 1957, 1963.
Brantz Kiddie Korner: 1958.
Helen Gallagher: 1959.
Aldens Catalogs: 1945, 1946, 1949, 1952, 1957, 1958, 1961, 1966, 1967, 1968, 1969, 1970, 1971, 1972, 1973.
Speigels: 1951, 1957, 1961, 1962, 1964, 1967, 1968, 1969, 1970, 1971, 1972.
Monroe: 1961.
Peoples: 1964.
Goodyear: 1949, 1952.
Marshall Fields: 1947, 1970, 1972, 1973.
Enchanted Doll House: 1972, 1973.
Mattel Toy Catalogs: 1961, 1962, 1963, 1964, 1965, 1966, 1967, 1969, 1970.
Vogue Co. Catalogs: 1965, 1972. Booklets: 1953 to date.
Creative Playthings: 1965, 1966, 1973.
Holiday Whirls: 1965.
Toys & Novelties: 1966.
Block Catalog: 1968.
Continental-Harrison: 1968.
Mark Farmer: 1969. J.C. Pennys: 1968, 1969, 1971, 1972, 1973.
Zebra Stamp Book: 1970.
Jolly Toy Catalog: 1963, 1966, 1970.
Kruse Catalog: 1969, 1970, 1971, 1972, 1973.
Tru Value: 1972.
Draytons: 1972.
Downs: 1972.
Bon Marche: 1972.
Child Craft: 1973. International: 1973.
Doll Castle News: 6 issues 1970, 3 issues 1971, 1 issue 1972.
Mary Hoyer's "Mary's Dollies" #1 through #8.
Spinning Wheel: May, Sept. 1972.

Doll News: Feb. 1970.
Life Magazine: April 1939, Oct. 1953.
Toy Trader Magazine: May 1955.
McCall Needlecraft: Fall/Winter 1952/1953.
Look Magazine: Dec. 1969.
Fortune: Dec. 1936, Oct. Dec. 1940.
Playthings Magazine: Feb.1963, Mar., Apr., May, Aug., Sept., 1964, Mar., Aug. 1965, Mar., Apr., June, Sept, Nov. 1966, Jan. Feb., Apr., Sept., 1967. Mar., Apr., June, Aug. 1968. Mar., Apr., June, Aug., Dec., 1969. Mar., July, Aug., Sept., 1971.
Toy & Novelties Magazine: Apr., May, July, Nov., Dec., 1966. Feb., Mar., June, July, Aug., Dec., 1967. Mar., Apr., Aug. 1968. Apr., May, 1969, Jan., Mar., May 1970
Philadelphia Inquirer: Dec. 1967, Aug., Oct., Nov. 1969.
Sunday Bulletin: Philadelphia: Nov. 1964.
New York Times: Nov. 1964, Nov.1965.
McCalls: Nov. 1961.
Capers Weekly: Nov. 1947.
News Ad for "Sue" 1949.
News Ad for Lenci dolls: 1949.
News Ad for Terri Lee, Gene Autry Doll 1950.
Life Article: "Toys For Christmas" 1951.
Life Article on Negro dolls by Ideal. 1951.
Mag. Ad on Procter-Gamble doll 1952.
Needlecraft ads for 1952, 1953.
A&H Co. Ad on "Dolls Of Destiny" 1953.
Life Article on Comic dolls: 1953.
News Ad on "Talking Tot" 1954.
News Ad on Uneedas "Needa Toddles" 1954.
Needlecraft Ad on "Cindy Lou" 1955.
News Ad on Borden's Elsie. 1957.
McCall Rag Doll Ad: 1958.
Diners Club Ad: Walking doll. 1960.
Life Article: Adams Family 1962.
News Ad on "Serenade" 1963.
P&M Doll Co. Ad: 1963.
Grants Ad: 1963.
New York Times: Royal Dolls 1964.
Philadelphia Inquirer: Jolly Toy dolls: 1964.
New York Times: Nov. 1966, Nov. 1968, Dec. 1970.

Prices

The following is the REVISED PRICES for Volume 1 of Modern Collector's Dolls and once again I must repeat myself by saying that these prices are for Completely Original And In Mint Condition Dolls. If your doll is any less than perfect, then deduct accordingly.

Now a word about the actual prices. Because of the stimulated interest in modern dolls brought about, due to the pioneer work of Johanna Gast Anderton, the prices on all and every modern doll shot up to a level that was hard to keep up with and now, three years later, the market is beginning to level out and many prices are dropping. This is good and healthy and the only areas where prices have increased is in the "Alexander" area, where the collector's desires are as great as the money they seem to have to spend. Some compositions have increased in price and will

continue to rise. The "Barbie" dolls by Mattel have "come into their own," as well as Mattel's "Kiddles." The entire "Dawn" series by Topper have become extremely collectible as well as the "Flatsy" by Ideal. The above areas of collecting have increased in prices. The Vogue, "Ginny," has always been a highly desirable doll and now all her clothes and items sold with her are of collector interest. As always the trends change but the look of the collecting field is now toward smaller dolls, perhaps to conserve space, and to trying to build accessory and clothes for dolls.

Of the 1056 pictured dolls of Volume 1, 391 have come DOWN in prices and 142 have gone UP in price, and 523 have remained the same. Prices are gathered from dealers, Mail Order price sheets, Trends, by Collector's United, ads in Trade Papers and other price guides.

Volume I Revised Price Index

337

Picture Index

Numbers, Letters and Symbol Index